A Likely Story

Sharon Mehesy
and
Eberly Mehesy

A Likely Story

Printed by CreateSpace, an Amazon.com company

Available from Amazon.com, CreateSpace.com, and other retail outlets

ISBN-13: 978-1530730896
ISBN-10: 1530730899

Authors' Notes

Because this is a co-authored book, we have used different styles of type to differentiate between each voice. When Eberly is "speaking," her narrative will be displayed in regular type, but in order to set Sharon's comments apart, they will appear in *italics*.

Some names have been changed to protect the privacy of the individuals involved.

Table of Contents

About the Authors

Sharon was raised in Colorado where she has resided most of her life and is proud to call herself a "native." At the age of 20 Sharon was involved in a major car accident in which she sustained a severe traumatic brain injury (TBI). She was hospitalized for three months during which time she had to relearn how to do everything again from swallowing to walking. After intense rehabilitation, she returned to college where she earned her Bachelor's degree in Therapeutic Recreation. She has worked in the field for nearly ten years, but now devotes much of her time to writing. She has recently published a book of poetry titled <u>Seasons: A book of poetry reflecting on the Seasons of life</u>.

In her free time Sharon enjoys downhill skiing, working on arts & crafts projects, making macramé jewelry, spending time with friends and family and playing with her cat. She can be found most days taking her daily walk where she continues to improve the mechanics of her walking as well as working to improve other aspects of her life.

Eberly was born in Chicago, Illinois and was raised in the United States, but she is now proud to call herself a native of Colorado, since she has lived there for the past 36 years. Eberly and her husband Joe have been missionaries to the Native American people for the past 44 years. They have 4 children and 5 grandchildren. Eberly began writing stories as a young child, as soon as she was able to read and write. As a young woman, she had a story published in the magazine "Young Ambassador".

In her spare time, Eberly enjoys reading, writing stories, poems, and songs, singing and playing music, swimming, and spending time with her children and grandchildren. She can be found most days either spending time with her grandchildren or curled up somewhere with a good book.

DEDICATION

This book is dedicated to our Lord and Savior Jesus Christ without whose miraculous intervention this story would not be possible!

Prologue

May 1997

It began like the previous two summers – with a tearful parting, although this time possibly more tears than in years past, with my fiancé. He had just proposed to me a week earlier and I had accepted. I never thought I would find anyone that I could picture myself spending the rest of my life with, but here I was, after a little more than two years of dating, agreeing to spend the rest of my life with Ernie. I had always been quite skeptical of marriage and the changes that transpired after making a lifelong commitment. Even though I was apprehensive, I truly felt that I had discovered something new and different, thus inspiring the poem I wrote for him in October 1996 ...

TRUE LOVE

In times past, each day was a landmark, a milestone
No longer
Time now has no boundaries—except when we are apart—
How the months have slipped by,
Not unnoticed, but unhindered.
Allowed now to flow freely as the unmasked feelings flow
The pent up emotions now rushing forth
As the walls begin to crumble
Unveiling the inner being
No longer timid and shy, discovering a new found courage
To love and be loved without fear
All of this I bring to you
My masterpieces
My mistakes
My hopes
My shattered dreams
All that I am
I step forth from the shadows of my heart
Face to face to embrace all that you are

I had attended a boarding school in Oklahoma for all four years of high school and in November of my senior year, I met and began dating Ernie. Each year during the school year, I would live in Oklahoma and every summer I would return to Colorado to stay with my parents. After I graduated in May 1995, I went home to Colorado for the summer to work and save money for college.

In the fall of 1995 I began attending Northeastern State University (NSU) in Tahlequah, OK. I declared my major to be English Education shortly after beginning my studies there. I had a clear vision of what I wanted to be "when I grew up." After I completed my freshman year at NSU, I again returned to Colorado for the summer of 1996.

Each year it was the same story, getting harder with each separation. Ernie and I missed each other terribly and lived for our excessive letters and phone calls. We wrote each other almost every day and talked on the phone every other day. We were crazy in love! We each anxiously counted down the days until we would see each other again. As we approached our third summer apart in May 1997, I was utterly inconsolable. Ernie and I had talked about marriage and tentatively planned for a summer wedding in 1998 so that we would no longer have to endure these long separations. All of our friends would try to encourage us with the glib, trite saying, "Absence makes the heart grow fonder." But we had our own little saying we would internally recite to ourselves every time we heard these empty words intended to console us. We would say to ourselves, "Blah, blah, blah! Three times stupid!"

The summer of 1997 was different in the fact that I did not live with my parents, but instead I lived in Durango with my sister Carol and her husband Robert. I got a job at Christina's Grill & Bar waiting tables. I soon became friends with Shoni, another waitress who worked there. She and I started hanging out much of the time when we were not at work. Shoni asked me to accompany her on a drive down to Lake Abiquiu, NM the weekend of July 4, 1997. We had driven down there after working all day, about a four hour drive one way from Durango, but her friends were not there, so we came back early.

Because my parents lived near Dolores, only an hour's drive from Durango, I occasionally would go and visit them. My younger sister, Janet, still lived at home and she had asked me to come over to her friend's house to go swimming. On July 10th I was off work, so I drove over to Cortez to spend time with her. I went swimming with her and her friends and then drove back to Durango that night so that I could work the next morning. I went to sleep on July 10th...

Sharon Mehesy and Eberly Mehesy

Part 1—The Crisis

Chapter 1

...6:20 a. m., July 12, 1997, the day after our 27th wedding anniversary—the insistent ringing of the phone jarred me out of a sound sleep. "Who on earth could be calling at this hour of the morning?" I muttered, irritated that our traditional Saturday morning ritual of "sleeping in" had been so rudely interrupted. "Hello," I mumbled sleepily.

Instantly, I was shocked awake by the serious business-like voice on the other end of the line. "Mrs. Mehesy, this is Officer Chad Martin of the Colorado State Patrol. I'm sorry to inform you that your daughter Sharon was involved in a serious car accident early this morning. She has a severe head injury and is in the intensive care unit of the Mercy Medical Center in Durango. She is presently in a drug-induced coma."

In response to this mind-numbing news, I could only moan into the phone. A moment later, however, I began to protest. "Are you sure it's Sharon?" I asked. "My youngest daughter Janet left a couple of hours ago for her job at the grocery store. Are you sure it's not Janet?"

"No, ma'am," he assured me. "It's Sharon. She was involved in a multiple rollover accident sometime between 3:30 and 4:00 this morning on Highway 160 about 10 miles east of Durango."

My head whirled in confusion. I had heard Janet's car pull out of the driveway when she had left for work earlier. I also knew that Sharon didn't have to be at work until 6:30 or 7:00 in the morning. I couldn't imagine why she would have been out on the road at that hour. Also, Sharon had just been home for a visit, and she hadn't mentioned anything about making a trip out of town.

"Are you sure it's Sharon?" I repeated.

"Yes, ma'am. Her name was on her driver's license," Officer Martin patiently replied.

"What was she doing out on the road at that time in the morning?" I questioned.

"I don't know, ma'am, but there's someone here who might be able to tell you," he continued. "There was a passenger in the car, Shoni Witt. She only received minor injuries. Would you like to talk to her?"

"Yes," I replied eagerly.

"Shoni..." I thought. "That's the new friend from work that Sharon was telling me about."

A moment later, I heard a girl's soft voice sobbing into the phone. "Oh, Mrs. Mehesy, I'm so sorry! It's all my fault," she cried. "If only I hadn't asked Sharon to go on that trip with me, she'd be all right!"

Strangely, hearing Shoni's heart-broken sobs calmed me, and I found myself reassuring her. "Don't blame yourself, Shoni. It's not your fault. Please, just tell me what happened."

Shoni's story poured out, punctuated by sobs. "I invited Sharon to drive up to Lake Abiquiu, New Mexico with me last night to visit some friends of mine. We left right after work and got there about 8:00. We started home about midnight. When we were about an hour away from Durango, we stopped and asked each other if we were too tired to go on, but we felt fine. I'd been doing all of the driving, and not long after we stopped, I got really tired, and my contacts started bothering me. Sharon was asleep, so I woke her up and asked if she could drive the rest of the way home. She said, 'Sure,' so we traded places and I lay back and went to sleep. The next thing I remember is hearing Sharon scream, 'Oh no, Shoni!' and then we hit a mailbox and rolled. I guess I was knocked out for a minute. As soon as I woke up, I called, 'Sharon, are you all right?' but she didn't answer. All I could hear was her moaning in pain. Then, in just a few minutes the ambulance came. Someone here at the hospital told me that a girl driving by saw our car roll and called 911 on her cell phone as soon as it happened. If she hadn't seen us roll, I don't know when we would have gotten help."

"Were you hurt, Shoni?" I inquired.

"Just a little bit. I have a broken hand and a bump on my head. I guess they're going to let me go home pretty soon. They just put a cast on my hand. Oh, I feel terrible about Sharon! I hope that she's going to be all right."

I then asked to speak to Officer Martin again, and told him that we would be over as soon as possible. As I hung up the phone, I turned to my husband Joe, who had been listening in shocked silence to my side of the conversation. "It's Sharon," I explained. "She was in a serious car wreck. The patrolman says that she has a head injury and that she's in a drug-induced coma."

As we hurriedly dressed, we tried to reassure each other. "He said that she was in a drug-induced coma. Maybe it's not really as bad as it sounds," I remarked. In my mind, I hoped that Sharon would be awake within a few hours.

Quickly, we called our son Paul and his wife Nancy in Pennsylvania to give them the news and then called our pastor. We also called Carol and Robert's house and left a message on their answering machine. On the way to Durango, we stopped briefly at the supermarket where Janet worked and told her what had happened. She arranged to leave work and said that she and her boyfriend Jeremy would meet us in Durango. The hour's drive to Durango had never seemed so endless.

At last we arrived at the hospital and rushed to the intensive care unit. A nurse drew back a curtain and revealed Sharon lying motionless on a bed, her eyes closed. She was hooked up to a multitude of monitors, which displayed her pulse, blood pressure and the level of oxygen in her blood. Various intravenous medications were passing through tubes into her veins, and the blue plastic tube of a respirator was inserted into her mouth and down her throat to aid her in breathing.

Amazingly enough, there was no outward evidence of the severe trauma which Sharon had suffered. There was no swelling, cuts, or bruises on her face or head. She looked as if she were merely sleeping. "She has a closed head injury," Lisa, the nurse, explained. "Her brain has been severely battered against the inside of her skull, and even though she looks fine, she has sustained an extremely serious brain injury and she is in a coma. Dr. White will be in shortly to talk to you about the extent of her injuries."

A few minutes later, Dr. White arrived and asked us to join him in the intensive care waiting room. He looked grim. "Your daughter is in extremely critical condition," he informed us. "I have no good news for you, and I don't believe there is any hope for her. We have a scale which measures the severity of brain injury. The lower the number, the more serious the injury is. Fifteen is normal, and below eight is life-threatening. Right now, Sharon is a five on the brain injury scale. This is where we lose people."

Joe and I listened in stunned silence. Our hopes of Sharon soon waking up and being fine were shattered. He continued, "Sharon has a type of brain injury called shearing. That means that there are many tiny cuts and bruises all throughout her brain, and that nerve fibers are torn on the microscopic level. This was caused by her brain being battered against her skull and also by one part of the brain moving back and forth against the other. We have done a CT scan, and found that there are four major areas of shearing in her brain, as well as hemorrhaging inside her brain."

"She also has a bruised brain stem. That's extremely serious, because the brain stem controls many involuntary functions such as breathing and heartbeat. One of the most serious problems that may arise is brain swelling. If Sharon's brain swells too much, the pressure will cause her heart and breathing to stop, and she will die. If she makes it through the first four days, she has a chance to survive. However, I must warn you that there are three serious complications that may arise during this critical time. One is brain swelling, another is further hemorrhaging inside the brain, and the third is seizures. And I also must caution you that, given the severity of her injury, it is doubtful that she will ever wake up from her coma, even if she survives. If she should wake up, there is not much hope that she would ever be able to function as a normal adult again. Because of the great danger of brain swelling, I would like your permission to insert an intra-cranial pressure monitor into Sharon's brain. That will enable us to keep a constant watch on the pressure inside her head, and also to drain out a small amount of fluid if necessary."

Numbly, we signed the consent form for the surgery, and Dr. White left to perform it. Weeping, we fell into each other's arms, convinced that we were going to lose our precious daughter! A few minutes later, Lisa summoned us back to the ICU. A small area of hair had been shaved from the right side of Sharon's head, and a metal probe had been inserted into her brain through a small incision. Now there was a new number on the monitor— measuring the pressure inside Sharon's brain. Lisa informed us that if the pressure went above twenty, it would be dangerous and could cause further brain damage or even death. Thankfully, the number was fluctuating between five and eight, which was normal. The swelling had not yet begun. We stood beside Sharon's bed, holding her hand, telling her how much we loved her, and praying for her.

The rest of the day passed in a blur of tears. Carol, Robert, Janet, and Jeremy arrived, as well as our pastor, John Soden, and many dear friends from our church. Together, we shared tears, prayers, and hugs. Pastor John read Psalm 131, "O Lord, my heart is not proud, nor my eyes haughty; nor do I involve myself in great matters, or in things too difficult for me. Surely I have composed and quieted my soul; like a weaned child rests against his mother, my soul is like a weaned child within me. O Israel, hope in the Lord from this time forth and forever."

This may seem like a strange passage to read at Sharon's bedside, but it brought great comfort to my heart. I knew that Sharon's situation was totally out of our control. We were powerless to do anything to help her, and we couldn't begin to fathom the reasons that God had allowed the accident to happen. Our only means of enduring this crisis lay in resting in the Lord and hoping in Him. I realized that I couldn't afford to allow myself to even ask why. I needed to continually keep focusing on Jesus and how wonderful He is.

Calls were made to Paul and Nancy and to Ernie, Sharon's fiancé, and all three of them made arrangements to fly to Durango the following day. Joe and I committed Sharon into the Lord's Hands, but based on Dr. White's gloomy predictions, we feared that she probably would not live through the day. In our hearts, we were preparing to say goodbye to her.

"Mom," Carol scolded me, "You're crying as if Sharon were already dead! Don't give up hope. She's a fighter, and she's going to make it! I know she is." I felt that Carol was unwilling to face reality.

However, as I poured out my grief to the Lord later that afternoon, His still small Voice spoke to my heart. "She shall not die but live!" When this thought first occurred to me, I responded with, "Yeah, right. That is just the hopeless wishing of a heartbroken mother." However, the Lord assured me that it was indeed His gentle Voice speaking to me, and my despair was gradually replaced with a deep peace and assurance that Sharon would survive.

In addition to this, the Lord also led me to some other encouraging promises. I had been reading through the Psalms for my daily Bible reading. That day, July 12th, I had reached Psalm 68. Verses 19 and 20 seemed to be written especially to me, "Blessed be the Lord, Who daily bears our burden, the God Who is our Salvation. God is to us a God of deliverances; and to GOD the Lord belong escapes from death."

The following day brought little change in Sharon's condition, except for a rise in her intra-cranial pressure. We gathered around her bed, grateful that she was still alive. However, our eyes were fixed on the yellow numbers on the monitor, watching as the numbers fluctuated from the mid-teens to the upper teens. Thankfully, the pressure never climbed into the twenties. In the middle of the day, Ernie arrived from Oklahoma, and Paul and Nancy flew in from Pennsylvania. It was such a comfort to have all of our family together at last.

The next day, Dr. White ordered another CT scan of Sharon's brain to see if there had been any further hemorrhaging. When they moved her in preparation for this test, we were dismayed to see her intra-cranial pressure climb above 20 for the first time since the accident. However, we were relieved when the pressure dropped back into the teens again shortly after she returned to the ICU.

Later that day, Dr. White called us into the ICU waiting room once again to give us the results of the CT scan. "Sharon seems to be holding her own," he informed us. "She's made it through the first two of those four critical days, and there has been a very slight improvement, of perhaps 2 to 3 percent per day. Although she has had a few slight tremors, she hasn't had any seizure activity, and fortunately the CT scan shows no further hemorrhaging in her brain. However, she's not out of danger yet, and it's too early to make any prediction about her long-term prognosis if she should survive."

When we returned to the ICU again, Lisa remarked, "You know, Dr. White was really amazed when the CT scan showed that there was no further bleeding inside Sharon's brain. He had expected to see massive hemorrhaging."

The following day, we were overjoyed when Dr. White ordered the removal of Sharon's intra-cranial pressure monitor, since her brain pressure had returned to normal. How we praised God that she had made it through the critical four-day period without experiencing seizures, dangerously high pressure in her brain, or further hemorrhaging.

During the days following the removal of the intra-cranial pressure monitor, we felt as if we were riding on an emotional roller coaster. Sharon was no longer sedated, but she was still in a coma. However, she began responding to voice commands, such as "Squeeze my hand if you know I'm here."

Also, she even seemed to indicate that she was hearing and understanding some of the conversation that was taking place around her bedside. Ernie took her hand and said, "If you know that I love you, Babe, squeeze my hand twice," and he was ecstatic to feel Sharon respond with two definite hand-squeezes.

To our amazement, Sharon also seemed to respond to humor. Her friend Brandi said teasingly, "Ooh, Sharon, Ernie is so cute that if he weren't your boyfriend and I wasn't married, I'd go after him myself!" At this remark, Sharon squeezed Carol's hand in protest.

Later that day, I made a remark about Sharon to someone else, and Carol reprimanded me, "Mom, don't talk about Sharon. Talk to her."

Addressing Sharon, I said, "Oh, Honey, I'm sorry that I was talking about you behind your back in front of your face." And Sharon again responded by giving Carol's hand a hard squeeze. All of these things, combined with the fact that Lisa and Guy, two of the nurses, were able to get Sharon to move her right leg and foot on command, gave us hope that perhaps Sharon would wake up from her coma.

This is Sharon and I am going to interject my memories into my mother's narrative. My words will appear in italics to set them apart from the ongoing story.

Many times when a person is portrayed on TV as having sustained a head injury, or more accurately, a brain injury, there is much discussion and speculation about what, if anything, the person in a coma is hearing or understanding—or if they are even aware at all. Although I cannot speak for everyone who has sustained a brain injury, I can tell you what it was like for me.

During the first part of my hospitalization, my memories are very intermittent and have no continuity. It is like a dream with little memories here and there. Actually the only way I found out that some of my memories were real is because when my mom read me her journal, I would occasionally question, "Oh, that really happened? I remember that, but I didn't know it actually occurred." I will interject my memories into my mother's story whenever the fog lifts momentarily and I have a moment of clarity. I will make little comments throughout my mom's narrative, but once I begin having continuous memory, I will begin telling you my story.

However, although we were encouraged by Sharon's responsiveness, a new problem emerged. She suddenly developed a fever of 104 degrees, requiring ice packs to bring it down. Dr. White was unsure whether the fever was the result of an infection or whether it was caused by the brain injury. "Some brain injuries affect the body's ability to maintain a normal temperature and can cause high fevers even when there is no infection," he explained.

However, tests soon showed that Sharon had two infections-- pneumonia and a urinary tract infection. On the day of the accident, Dr. White had informed us that Sharon had a bruised left lung. This injury had seemed minor in comparison to her head injury, so we hadn't given it much thought. Now, however, we learned that her brain injury was not the only threat to her survival. Her injured lung had made her susceptible to life-threatening lung and chest infections. In addition to the pneumonia, Dr. White was very concerned about the fluid that was beginning to accumulate outside Sharon's left lung in her chest cavity.

"I'm calling in two specialists to deal with the infection – Dr. Brown, a pulmonologist, and Dr. Salka, an infectious disease specialist," he informed us. "Since there is nothing that I can do surgically to treat Sharon's brain injury, I'm turning her case over to them."

Immediately, the doctors began giving Sharon powerful antibiotics intravenously. Her fever decreased, but it didn't go away. Instead, it hovered between 101 and 102 degrees. Dr. Brown met with us in the waiting room. "We have decided that as soon as Sharon's infections are under control, she needs to be transferred to a low-tolerance rehabilitation hospital in Albuquerque, New Mexico," he said. "She's going to need long-term care and therapy, and we're not equipped to give her that here. Our ICU is an acute-care facility, designed for dealing with life-threatening injuries and illnesses, and we've done all that we can do for her here. A low-tolerance rehab hospital is a place where patients in comas can receive therapy that may help them to wake up, and where they can be given whatever amount of therapy they can tolerate until they are strong enough to be transferred to a regular rehabilitation hospital." With our permission, the doctors began making plans for Sharon to be airlifted from Durango to Albuquerque sometime within the next few days.

Dr. Brown spent a lot of time explaining Sharon's condition to us. "It is too early to tell whether Sharon will ever wake up from her coma or not," he warned us. "And if she does wake up, there is no way of knowing what her mental level will be. However, I have been able to get her to squeeze my hand on command, and I have been able to change the respirator setting so that she is initiating most breaths on her own. That shows that she is capable of breathing for herself. She does need the respirator to make sure that she is breathing deeply enough to get the level of oxygen that her brain needs. Because of her lung injury and the infections, she would tend to take very shallow breaths if she were taken off of the respirator. My main concern right now is getting her infections under control, but I am also concerned about the fluid that seems to be collecting in her chest cavity. There is a potential for a dangerous infection developing there."

Chapter 2

Since the antibiotics seemed to be bringing her infections under control, the doctors felt that the time had come to transfer Sharon to the Transitional Hospital Corporation (THC) facility in Albuquerque. On Friday, July 18th—6 days after the accident, she was airlifted to Albuquerque in a propeller plane, and I got to fly with her. I sat in the co-pilot's seat, since Sharon, a nurse, a respiratory therapist, and all the necessary medical equipment occupied the back of the plane. The medical records which accompanied her classified her as being in a deep coma. The rest of the family drove from Durango to Albuquerque, but two days later, Paul, Nancy, and Ernie had to fly back to their homes, and Carol and Robert had to drive back to Colorado. Only Joe, Janet, and I remained in Albuquerque with Sharon.

Although tests showed that Sharon's pneumonia and urinary tract infection were apparently gone, her fever soared to 104 degrees again the day after she was transferred to THC, and she acted lethargic and non-responsive. X-rays showed a large accumulation of fluid in her chest cavity outside her left lung. The pulmonologist felt that this was probably the source of the infection that was causing the fever, and decided to try to aspirate the fluid by inserting a needle into her chest to draw the fluid out.

Since I am not a squeamish person, I asked him if I could stay in the room with Sharon while they were doing this procedure. I held her hand and watched as he prepared to insert a long needle into her chest. Unlike the doctors in Durango, who had treated her as a person even though she was in a coma and explained to her everything they were going to do, this doctor seemed to see her as just "a body in a bed". Although there were five medical personnel in the room, not one of them said a word to Sharon. I began talking to her to try to prepare her for the pain of the needle. "Honey," I explained, "They're going to have to stick a needle into your chest to draw out the infection that is giving you this awful fever."

I watched as the doctor inserted the needle and pulled back on the syringe to try to suck out the infected fluid, and was dismayed to see only a very small amount of bloody fluid drip into the bottom of the tube. "It's not working," the doctor exclaimed in frustration. "The consistency of this fluid is like Jell-O instead of liquid. We'll never be able to get the fluid out this way, and if any more fluid accumulates, her lung will collapse. The only other way to clean out this fluid is by major surgery, and she'll have to be transferred to another hospital for that. We're not equipped to do it here."

For the next few days, while Sharon's fever raged and the infection worsened, the doctors debated among themselves concerning what would be the best treatment for her. The doctors who were responsible for her care belonged to a large pulmonology practice in Albuquerque, and each day a different doctor examined her, so there was no continuity in her care. Each doctor had to start at the beginning and familiarize himself with the details of her very complicated case. This disorganization gave us very little confidence in the quality of care she was receiving.

Several days after the failed attempt to draw out the infection with the needle, the doctor who was preparing to examine her that day told me he was going to try to do the same procedure. "But doctor," I protested, "they tried that several days ago, and it didn't work."

"No, that hasn't been tried yet," he contradicted me. "If it had been done, it would have been recorded on her chart, and there is no record of it here."

"Yes, they did," I assured him. "I was in the room when it was done."

After thumbing through Sharon's chart, which was already beginning to resemble a small book, he finally found the notation, and acknowledged that I was right. How thankful I was that I had been with Sharon when it was done, and was able to spare her the pain of another doctor trying to repeat a procedure that had already failed to solve the problem. I began to realize how crucially important it was for me to keep abreast of all the latest developments in Sharon's condition and to monitor the quality of the care she was receiving, especially since she was unaware of what was happening around her and unable to speak for herself.

The one bright spot in those dark and painful days was that on July 21st, nine days after the accident, Sharon's left eye began to open slightly. We were overjoyed when Dan, one of the nurses, reported that she opened her eye in response to his command, and that he believed that she had made eye contact with him briefly. The next day, her left eye opened wider and remained open whenever she was awake, and the following day, her right eye began to open. How thrilled and thankful we were to see Sharon beginning to awaken from her coma!

Since Sharon was still in the low-tolerance rehab hospital, there were therapists who were eager to begin doing passive therapy with her, in order to stimulate her brain and to keep her muscles from tightening up. However, they needed a doctor's order so that they could begin therapy. Unfortunately, the pulmonologists were so focused on Sharon's lung and chest problems that they seemed to be totally ignoring her brain injury. In spite of the fact that we repeatedly asked them to write an order for therapy, they refused to do so. We also felt that it was important for a neurologist to be brought in to examine her, but they also vetoed this request. "Your daughter has a life-threatening chest infection," one of them informed me soberly. "If we don't get that under control, there will be no need for her to see a neurologist or to have any therapy."

"I know that controlling the infection is of primary importance," I replied, "but why can't she be examined by a neurologist and receive therapy in addition to being treated for her infection?" However, my pleas fell on deaf ears.

Sharon's condition continued to worsen. Her fever fluctuated between 103 and 104 degrees, and this drained her strength so that she was unable to move any part of her body. She lay pale and motionless on her bed. A CT scan showed that her left lung had collapsed, just as the doctors had feared.

After much debate, the doctors finally decided that she should be transferred to another hospital for major chest surgery. They informed us that the only hope of saving her life would be to perform an operation called a thoracotomy to open her chest and clean out the infection. We learned that the incision would begin under her left breast and continue around to the middle of her back. On July 23rd, eleven days after the accident, Sharon was transferred to Presbyterian Hospital, and I rode with her in the ambulance.

As soon as Sharon was settled in the ICU at Presbyterian Hospital, a new doctor took charge of her case—Dr. Jacob, the surgeon who would be performing the thoracotomy. Unlike the pulmonologists, he seemed to see Sharon as a person, not just a lung. He explained what he was going to do and tried to get her to respond to him. He immediately called in a neurologist to consult with him, in order to learn all he could about her brain injury and how it might affect the surgery. We were so thankful that Sharon was once again under the care of a competent and caring doctor.

The day after Sharon was transferred to Presbyterian Hospital, Dr. Grigg-Damberger, the neurologist, came in to examine her. She informed us that the latest CT scan, which had been done several days before, showed only one small area of damage in the right hemisphere of her brain, rather than the four areas of damage which had shown up on the CT scans done in Durango. "The damage to the right side of Sharon's brain explains the weakness on her left side," she told us. "I also believe that she has some cranial nerve damage, which is keeping her eyes from working together properly. I think that her right eye has been affected by the injury, and that she probably has double vision, so I would recommend patching it. However, I am very encouraged because both of her eyes are wide open and she appears to be tracking objects with them, and also because she is responding to stimulation of her arms and legs. She's no longer in a coma, but she's not totally awake yet either." How we praised the Lord for this good report. There is no way of knowing whether the severity of Sharon's injury was misdiagnosed in Durango, or whether there actually <u>had</u> been four areas of damage to her brain and the Lord had healed three of them in answer to prayer. (I believe that the Lord healed her.)

Later that day, a physical therapist came in and began exercising Sharon's muscles to keep them from tightening up. She demonstrated the exercises to me, and I practiced them under her supervision so that I could learn how to do them for Sharon. That day, a routine began which lasted for many weeks. Two or three times each day, I would exercise her arms, hands, fingers, legs, feet and toes by moving them back and forth and up and down in every direction that they could move, in order to keep her joints from locking up and her muscles from getting tight. I began to realize how important family members are in the recovery of a patient who has sustained a brain injury. Though the therapists could spend only a short time with her each day, I was there, whenever she was awake, to stimulate her brain by talking to her, reading to her, singing to her, playing music for her, showing pictures to her, and exercising her muscles.

On July 25th, thirteen days after the accident, at 8:00 in the morning, Sharon was taken into surgery. Before she was taken to the operating room, Joe, Janet, and I stood by her bed and explained to her what was going to happen. Then we took her hands and prayed for her, once again committing her to the Lord. We were told that the surgery would take about 4 hours. As we waited and prayed together, the morning seemed endless. However, in spite of my concern, I felt a peace that I knew could only come from the Lord, because I am naturally a very fearful person. Halfway through the surgery, we received a phone call from a nurse in the operating room. "Dr. Jacob asked me to call you and let you know that the surgery is going well," she informed us. How thankful we were to receive that good news.

At last the operation was over, and Dr. Jacob asked us to join him in his office. "The procedure was successful," he informed us with a smile. "We removed a liter of bloody infected matter from

Sharon's chest cavity. It was the consistency of Jell-O. We also cleaned out an abscess, and scraped infected material off her chest wall and peeled it off the outside of her lung. Removing it from her lung and her chest wall was like trying to remove dried glue from a surface. I believe that we have eliminated the source of the infection though. Sharon should begin getting better now."

An hour later, we were able to join Sharon in her room. The expression in her eyes showed the intense pain that she was in, although she still was unable to make even the faintest sound. How my heart ached for her. As I had done each day since the accident, I explained what had happened and where she was, and then I sang to her and prayed with her.

Later that afternoon, Sharon experienced a sudden drop in blood pressure, and during the night she developed an irregular heartbeat. Two of the nurses said they feared that the infection might have spread to her heart and also throughout her entire body, and that she might even have blood poisoning. As we thought of the pulmonologists' incompetence, which had kept Sharon from having the surgery for six days after her infection was first discovered, we began to wonder if perhaps the operation had been performed too late to save her life. How we prayed and wept before the Lord during that long, terrifying night, wondering if, after all Sharon had been through, we were still going to lose her.

The following morning, however, we were encouraged by the wonderful news that Sharon's blood pressure and heart rhythm had returned to normal and that tests showed no sign of infection in her heart or bloodstream. Once again, we had no way of knowing whether the nurses had overreacted to her symptoms, or whether she actually had developed blood poisoning and the Lord had healed her. (I believe that the latter was true.) How thankful we were that she was still with us.

Later that same day, Ernie came from Oklahoma for another visit. This time, his mother, Coral, who is a nurse, was with him. When Sharon saw Ernie, there was no doubt in anyone's mind that she was very much aware of what was happening around her.

Although she still was unable to make a sound, the expression in her left eye, which was not patched, fluctuated between great joy at seeing him and extreme sadness, frustration, and discouragement at being unable to communicate with him. When Carol and Robert came to visit later that evening, the same conflicting emotions shone from Sharon's eye.

During the next several days, Ernie, Coral, and I visited several rehabilitation hospitals in Albuquerque to determine which one would be the best place for Sharon to go to whenever she was strong enough to begin intensive therapy. Coral's medical knowledge was invaluable in helping us to make this important decision. We finally settled on St. Joseph's Rehabilitation Hospital as our choice, since it was the largest and best-equipped rehab hospital in the area. However, they informed us that they could not accept Sharon until her respiratory problems were gone and she was strong enough to do 3 hours of rehab per day. As we looked at Sharon, lying pale and weak in her bed, with the respirator tube still in her throat, we wondered how long it would be before that wonderful day would come.

For more than three weeks following Sharon's surgery, we felt that the battle for her recovery was being fought on two different fronts. Although she was very gradually making progress in recovering from her brain injury, her body's battle against the life-threatening infections in her lung and chest raged on unabated. Much to the doctors' bewilderment, her fever continued to be consistently above 100 degrees, often soaring up to between 102 and 104 degrees. Also, her left lung was filled with thick congestion and was not inflating properly.

Another thing which concerned the doctors was that, because of Sharon's inability to be active, blood clots might form in her arms or in her legs, and cause life-threatening complications. To try to avert this possibility, her feet were kept continuously attached to a device called a PlexiPulse machine. Each foot was strapped into an inflatable plastic "bootie", which was connected by tubes to the machine. The machine simulated the effect of walking, by alternately inflating and deflating each "bootie", in order to put pressure on her feet and stimulate her blood flow. We also worked diligently at moving her arms and legs to keep her blood circulating properly. In spite of all this, though, there were several times during the next few weeks when Dr. Jacob suspected that Sharon might have a blood clot, and ordered ultrasound tests to be done. How thankful we were that all of these tests proved negative, and that she never did develop any blood clots.

However, at the same time that she was fighting for her life, Sharon was becoming more alert and responsive and was beginning to be able to move various parts of her body. Only a parent who has been through a similar ordeal can identify with our feelings as we observed our daughter's painfully slow progress. We had felt the impact of Sharon being transformed, in a split-second, from an independent, self-reliant, capable young woman into an individual who was more helpless than a newborn infant. Instantly, I felt as if I had been transported back 20 years in time, and I desired to help her and care for her as I had done when she was a baby. On the other hand, I believed that mentally, she was now aware of what was going on around her, and I wanted to treat her as an adult. It was extremely difficult to know how to relate to her properly in this unusual situation.

As the days went by, Sharon's smallest accomplishment became cause for tremendous rejoicing on our part. We would never have dreamed how thankful we would be to see our 20-year-old daughter make an almost imperceptible movement with her left leg or barely wiggle the toes on her left foot. We were overjoyed when Sharon was able to keep her legs from sliding back down after we had bent her knees and positioned her feet flat on the bed. We were thrilled when Sharon was able to turn her head ever so slightly toward the right, because ever since the accident, her head had remained stuck in an extremely unnatural position, turned all the way toward the left. And when she began making large movements with her right arm and leg, moving them up and down and back and forth, we were ecstatic.

July 30th was my birthday. How I thanked the Lord for the most wonderful birthday present He had ever given me—that Sharon was still alive! But He had still more gifts to shower on me that day. Dr. Grigg-Damberger, the neurologist, examined Sharon again that afternoon. She was greatly encouraged by the fact that Sharon was more alert, that she was able to move more and to respond to simple commands, and that her eyes were working together better. Before she left, she took Sharon by the hand, looked into her eyes and said, "Young lady, you're going to be fine! You're going to get well, and you're going to walk again!"

That same day Ann, one of the nurses, devised a way for Sharon to begin communicating with us. She instructed her to close and open her left eye slowly and deliberately if she wanted to say "Yes" to a question. How we rejoiced when she was able to do it. She communicated with the doctor, with the nurses, and with me this way. By the end of the day, everyone was convinced that Sharon was really "there" mentally and was able to understand and respond appropriately to what others said to her.

Sharon and I were actually able to carry on a short conversation using this method—the first definite communication that we had had since her accident. Just as I was about to leave for supper, a nurse came in and said that she was going to give Sharon a bath. I turned to Sharon and said, "Honey, do you want me to stay with you until after your bath?" She slowly closed and opened her left eye.

Then, seeing that Sharon looked uncomfortable, I asked, "Are you hurting, Honey? Do you want the nurse to give you some more pain medication?"

Once again she responded, "Yes."

I thought that it might relax Sharon to listen to some music, so I said, "Would you like me to turn on some music?" Very deliberately, she closed her left eye and opened it again.

"Christian music?" I inquired.

"Yes." she replied.

As I walked out of the hospital a few minutes later, I was greeted by a full double rainbow, a beautiful reminder of the fact that God always keeps His promises. I thanked my Heavenly Father, through tears of joy, for His very personal care for me, and for giving me such special love-gifts on my birthday.

On August 1st, Sharon reached another milestone. The physical therapists helped her to sit up on the side of the bed—for the first time since the accident. However, she was not able to reach a sitting position without their aid or to remain sitting without their support. Also, she was unable to hold her head up. It sagged down and to the left. Then on August 8th, the therapists assisted her to a standing position and helped her to a chair. When her feet touched the floor, she made a weak attempt to take a step with her right foot. How thankful we were to see her trying to walk.

However, at the same time that we rejoiced in the tiny steps that Sharon was taking in recovering from her brain injury, we feared that we still might lose her to the infections which continued to ravage her body and drain her strength. Her continuing fever mystified the doctors, who believed that the thoracotomy should have removed the source of infection that was causing her high temperature. They took numerous samples of her blood, sputum, and urine and of the fluid from her chest drainage tubes to try to identify where the infection was located and what organism was causing it. They also did CT scans and X-rays to determine whether Sharon had any more fluid in her chest cavity.

Also, in spite of the surgery, her left lung was still not inflating properly. It was filled with thick mucous, which made it extremely difficult for her to breathe. Many times a day, a nurse had to suction out the mucous by passing a smaller tube down through the respirator tube into Sharon's lung and pulling out the congestion. A large jar beside Sharon's bed, which was attached to the suctioning device rapidly filled up with thick varicolored phlegm. This miserable procedure was extremely uncomfortable, causing Sharon to gag, choke, and turn a brilliant shade of red. How our hearts ached to see her suffering so much.

The day after my birthday, when we returned from lunch, we were halted at the door of Sharon's room by one of the nurses. Ann was wearing a yellow paper gown over her uniform and also had on gloves and a facemask. "Stop right here." she warned us, pointing to a large sign that was hanging on the door of Sharon's room. "**Isolation**" it proclaimed in bold black letters.

"You'll have to 'gown up' before you can go in there." Ann continued. "One of the cultures of Sharon's sputum tested positive for MRSA—an antibiotic-resistant organism. Sharon is now in isolation, and no one can go into her room without wearing protective gear, which must be disposed of before leaving her room. That's to keep the germ from spreading to other patients."

Instantly, we were filled with fear. "Oh, no!" we gasped, tears streaming down our faces. We had heard about microbes which had developed a resistance to antibiotics, and now Sharon was infected with one of them. "She's been through so much already! How can she ever survive this?" we thought in despair.

Seeing our downcast faces, Ann tried to encourage us. "This 'bug' isn't resistant to all antibiotics—just to a certain type of penicillin," she explained. "There are other drugs that are quite effective against it." We breathed a sigh of relief as we donned our gowns, gloves, and masks and entered Sharon's room. A few minutes later, as we stood by Sharon's bedside, I couldn't help wondering what she was thinking. In our protective garb, we probably resembled aliens from outer space who, for some unknown reason, had voices that sounded just like her parents.

Two days later, a CT scan revealed that there was a new pocket of infected fluid in Sharon's chest cavity, located right on top of her diaphragm. It was pressing on her lung and keeping it from inflating properly. Dr. Jacob was disturbed and shocked. "I've done many thoracotomies, but this is the first time in my career that I've seen an infection return after that type of surgery," he exclaimed. "I'll have to drain out that fluid with another tube." Our hearts sank. The chest tubes from her previous surgery had been removed just the day before, and already Sharon was facing the insertion of another one.

The next morning, Dr. Jacob put a tube into the left side of Sharon's upper back to draw out the pocket of infected fluid. It was critical that the tube be placed in precisely the right spot. So, as he operated, another doctor manned a CT scan machine to determine the exact location where it needed to be positioned. How we prayed that this would solve the problem and that Sharon wouldn't need any more surgery.

However, for the next week Sharon's fever continued to rage, unabated. "How long is this going to continue, Lord?" our hearts cried out. "How much can one person's body take? Are we still going to lose Sharon?" In the midst of it all, though, God continued to encourage us with special promises from His Word. One of these was Romans 15:13, "Now may the God of hope fill you with all joy and peace in believing, that you may abound in hope by the power of the Holy Spirit." Not only did the Lord impress this verse on my heart in my personal Bible reading, but several friends mentioned it also when they called or wrote, confirming to me that this was a special message to us from the Lord. Another reassuring passage was Psalm 97:5, "The mountains melted like wax before the presence of the Lord—the presence of the Lord of the whole earth." As I read this, I was reminded that although Sharon's situation seemed like a huge, insurmountable mountain to me, God's almighty power was able to change it just as easily as fire melts wax.

About a week after the second tube was inserted, Debbie, one of the nurses, confronted me in the hall outside of Sharon's room. "I hope you realize that Sharon is not going to survive this infection," she said grimly. "There are no antibiotics that are effective against this organism, and it's going to kill her. But even if she should be lucky enough to live, her brain is so badly damaged that she will never be able to walk or talk again or to lead a normal life."

At this dismal pronouncement, tears began streaming down my cheeks. "I don't know if what you are saying is true or not,

Debbie," I sobbed, "but I do know one thing. Even if Sharon does die, I will see her again in heaven because we both know Jesus as our Savior!" Then I turned and hurried out of the hospital, looking for a place where I could weep in private.

One thing I had learned early in this ordeal was that, although I could never show my sorrow when I was with Sharon, it was impossible to keep my emotions bottled up inside. They were continually building up like lava in a volcano, and if I tried to repress them, I knew that I would "crack up". So at least once a day, I would go somewhere and have a "good cry". Often, my weeping would be done in Joe's arms, as we prayed and cried together.

That day, however, as we left the hospital, we noticed a young couple walking down the sidewalk ahead of us. To our amazement, we realized that they were Carl and Chris, dear friends of ours who lived in Gallup, New Mexico, several hours drive from Albuquerque. We called to them, and as soon as they turned around, I fell into Chris' arms and started bawling, as she held me close. When Carl, who is a dentist, heard what the nurse had told me, he was appalled at her lack of professionalism. "What right did she have to speak to you like that?" he demanded indignantly. "She doesn't know if what she said is true. And even if it is, only a doctor is qualified to give you that kind of information!" Before they left for home, they covenanted to be praying with us for Sharon to be healed of her infection.

Joe and I spent the next several hours praying fervently for Sharon. "Father," we prayed through tears, "once again we're putting Sharon into Your Hands. We'd love to keep her, if possible, but we want Your will to be done. Father, You made these germs that are causing her infection, and if You want her to live, please kill them!" When we returned to the hospital, we found that Sharon's fever was totally gone! Her temperature had been 102 degrees when we left the hospital, but now it was completely normal—98.6 degrees. How we praised the Lord for miraculously and instantly healing Sharon in answer to our prayers.

Through talking with other medical personnel, we soon found out that all the things that Debbie had told me were wrong. As Ann had assured us, although MRSA was resistant to penicillin, it was treatable with other antibiotics. Also, contrary to what Debbie had said, Sharon was gradually recovering from her brain injury, although it was still impossible to predict her long-term prognosis.

The day after my conversation with Debbie, she entered Sharon's room. As she was caring for Sharon, she turned to me and asked abruptly, "What kind of religion are you, anyway?" And I was able to share with her the hope that we have, even in the midst of sorrow, because we know Jesus. From that time on, she had only encouraging words to say about Sharon's condition. Evidently, she was either conscience-stricken about her outburst, or someone had reprimanded her for her inappropriate behavior. I will never be able to understand what motivated her to tell me such awful lies, but the Lord used this situation to give me an opportunity to tell her about Jesus.

For the next four days after we asked the Lord to kill the germs which were causing Sharon's infection, she remained fever-free, except for a brief period of time when she experienced an allergic reaction to one of the antibiotics she was being given. For a few hours, her fever soared to 102 degrees, her pulse skyrocketed to 150, and she appeared to be in great discomfort. Shortly after the medication was discontinued, her temperature and heart rate returned to normal.

However, several days later, a CT scan showed that five more pockets of fluid had collected in Sharon's chest, one of which was the size of an egg. "During my entire career as a surgeon, I've never had to redo a thoracotomy, but I'm afraid that this time I will have to," Dr. Jacob said gravely. "Even though Sharon doesn't have any symptoms of infection now, I'm certain that within the next few days, her fever will return and her white blood count will go back up again. I'm going to schedule the surgery for Sunday."

In spite of this discouraging news, we felt confident that God had indeed healed Sharon in answer to our prayers. We continued praying, and as the days went by, both Sharon's temperature and white blood count remained normal. At last Dr. Jacob conceded that the infection seemed to be gone, and that a second thoracotomy would not be necessary after all. "No symptoms—no surgery!" he announced happily, as he canceled the operation that he had scheduled. And when Sharon's chest was X-rayed again, all five pockets of fluid had disappeared! Once again, God had miraculously healed her in answer to prayer.

During the same time that Sharon was battling the chest infection, she also continued to struggle with the thick congestion in her left lung. The doctors felt that irritation from the respirator was aggravating this condition, so they decided to try to gradually wean her off of it. It was an agonizingly slow process. Before they could remove the tube from her throat, they had to be certain that she would be able to breathe adequately without the respirator. When they first disconnected the tube from the respirator and connected it to another tube that provided a source of oxygen for Sharon to breathe, she breathed too rapidly, and had to be reconnected to the respirator immediately.

However, as the days went by, they were able to disconnect her from the respirator for longer periods of time. Each day, the doctors decreased the amount of time that she was on the respirator by one more hour. The first day, she was taken off the respirator for one hour and then put back on it for four hours. Then the next day, she was off of it for one hour and on it for three hours. The following day, she was off of it for one hour and on it for two hours. The doctors' goal was to very gradually increase the time that Sharon was off of the respirator until she was totally free of it.

By this time, Sharon had been on the respirator for more than three weeks. The pulmonologists felt that she had already been on the respirator for too long a time, so they began urging Dr. Jacob to perform a tracheotomy. If this was done, they could immediately take out the respirator tube, and Sharon could begin breathing through an opening in her throat. How we hoped that this would not have to be done.

However, Dr. Jacob refused to perform the surgery. "We are only going to do a tracheotomy if it is absolutely necessary," he insisted. "I want you to completely disconnect her from the respirator for twenty-four hours and see how she does. If she is able to breathe adequately on her own, you can remove the tube from her throat. If not, then we'll do the operation."

How thankful we were for Dr. Jacob's intervention. We felt that once again, the pulmonologists were putting Sharon at risk because of their incompetence. They were proceeding at a snail's pace because several doctors were alternating in providing her care. Whenever a different doctor began working on her case, he would start the laborious process of weaning her off of the respirator all over again.

Since Dr. Jacob was in charge of Sharon's case, the pulmonologists had no choice but to follow his direction. Just as he had hoped, Sharon was able to breathe well during the entire twenty-four hours that she was disconnected from the respirator. The following day, August 6th, was the joyous day when the respirator tube was removed from her throat at last!

The same day that the respirator tube was finally taken out of Sharon's throat, we had to deal with a problem that had been virtually ignored by all of the medical personnel who were attending Sharon, but which we believed had the capacity to be life-threatening. Several days before Sharon's accident, she had visited a dentist to get a crown made for one of her molars. He had fitted her with a temporary crown to wear while the permanent one was being made. However, during the days immediately preceding the accident, the crown had fallen off into Sharon's mouth twice, and she had reattached it with Fix-o-Dent. As long as the respirator tube remained in Sharon's throat, it had protected her airway if the crown should fall off again. However, now that the tube was gone, we feared that the crown would come off and she might choke on it.

At our insistence, a dentist was summoned to remove the crown. When she arrived, Sharon was asleep, and her mouth was tightly shut. Within the short time that it took her to pry open Sharon's mouth, the crown had already fallen off and was lying on Sharon's tongue. She reached an instrument into Sharon's mouth and retrieved it. "You were very wise to call me," the dentist remarked. "Sharon could have either choked to death on this or it could have gone down into one of her lungs and caused aspiration pneumonia." Once again, we realized how important it was to keep a close watch on Sharon to make sure that she was receiving proper care.

The doctors had hoped that after the removal of the respirator tube, Sharon's lung congestion would improve. However, for the next few days, the mucous in her lung remained so thick that she was unable to cough it up. This made it difficult for her to breathe and caused her great discomfort. To alleviate this problem, a pulmonologist had to perform a bronchoscopy. This was a very uncomfortable procedure in which the doctor inserted a tube down into Sharon's lung and suctioned out the mucous. Once this procedure was done, Sharon was able to breathe much more easily and her lung inflated better and looked much clearer on the X-rays. However, within a day or two, the problem would return, and the whole procedure would have to be repeated. In all, six bronchoscopies had to be performed before the problem finally abated.

Other treatments were also prescribed to help loosen the congestion in Sharon's lung. A respiratory therapist visited her every few hours to give her medicated breathing treatments. Also, she was put into a special computerized bed, which periodically turned her from side to side and vibrated to shake loose the mucous. However, the bed created an unforeseen problem. Because Sharon was too weak to change positions in bed, the combination of the bed's vibrating while turning her from side to side caused her to be tossed against the railing on one side and wedged there. After finding her trapped in this extremely uncomfortable and awkward position, with a look of absolute terror in her eyes, I insisted that the bed be programmed to either vibrate her or to turn her, but not to do both simultaneously.

This is my first conscious memory – I have a vague memory of this terrifying bed. I remember being tossed from side to side with no way to control where I was being thrown. I was too weak to keep myself from moving and I had no way to communicate, so I was literally "held hostage" by this devious bed!

Within the next week, Sharon's congestion gradually began to clear up, and the same X-ray that showed that the pockets of fluid had disappeared from her chest cavity also showed that her lungs were clear, free of congestion, and inflating well at last. How we praised God that Sharon's life was no longer in danger. The crisis had passed, and although we knew she still had an extremely long hard road to recovery, we knew that she was going to survive.

How thankful we were for the encouragement of our dear family members and friends during this difficult time. Whenever they could get a day off from work, Carol, Robert, Janet, and Jeremy visited Sharon, and Paul, Nancy, and Ernie phoned every day. Even though Sharon couldn't answer him, Ernie never failed to talk to her for several minutes each day to assure her of his love for her. We were encouraged to see by the expression on Sharon's face that she recognized family members and friends when she saw them or heard their voices on the phone. How we rejoiced when, on August 12th, one month after the accident, Sharon smiled as she listened to Ernie's voice on the telephone. Since her left side was almost paralyzed, it was a one-sided smile, but it was the first time that she had smiled since her injury.

Since Albuquerque is a five-hour drive from our home, it wasn't practical for many of our church family to visit us there, although our pastor, John Soden, and his wife Janet came to visit us twice. However, each day Pastor John, or his secretary, Gyanne, who is one of my dearest friends, called for an update on Sharon's condition, and then passed it along on our church's "prayer chain" to many other concerned friends. Adeline, another close friend who attended a different church in Cortez, also called regularly so that she could pass along our prayer requests to the people there. And because we are missionaries, and had sent out a letter telling everyone on our mailing list about Sharon's accident, we knew that people all around the globe were praying for her. In addition to this, Glenn and Bev, dear friends who lived in the Albuquerque area, came to visit several times a week, and took us out for dinner at least once a week to give us a break.

One of the greatest blessings, however, came from a retired missionary friend, Thurley, who made her guest cottage available for us to stay in for as long as we needed it. Since Thurley lived only a mile or two away from where Sharon was hospitalized, this was an ideal location. Each day, we would arrive at the hospital early in the morning and spend the day with Sharon, leaving only to eat our meals. Then late each night, we would return to the guesthouse, where we would pray and cry together before we fell into an exhausted sleep.

On August 15th, after spending more than a month in intensive care units at three different hospitals, the wonderful day finally came when Sharon left the ICU and was transferred to the sub-acute care unit at Presbyterian Hospital. What a day of rejoicing that was. We realized that we had passed a significant milestone, and that the critical first phase of Sharon's recovery was over at last!

As we said goodbye to the ICU nurses there, we reflected on what special people they were, and how tenderly they had cared for Sharon. Diana had lovingly nursed Sharon as if she were her own younger sister. She and Heather, a young student nurse, had even taken time to fix Sharon's hair, shave her legs, and do her nails, so that she would look her best whenever Ernie came for a visit. Maureen and Ann were always ready with an encouraging word for us when we felt especially discouraged. Katherine and Beth, who was the daughter of our friends Glenn and Bev, were also our dear sisters in Christ. It was such a blessing to know that they were praying for Sharon and for us, and relying on the Lord's wisdom as they cared for her. And all of the nurses worked together to make sure that everyone who entered Sharon's room knew that although she was unable to speak, she could understand everything that was said to her, and that she was to be treated with respect. How thankful we were that Sharon had received such outstanding care.

Part 2—Rehabilitation

Chapter 3

During the long weeks that Sharon struggled with her chest infection and her lung problems, we continued to learn more about the effects of her brain injury. The day that the respirator tube was removed from Sharon's throat was a joyous occasion for us. It was a very scary time also, because we knew that at last we would find out whether or not she was able to speak. As long as the tube had been in her throat, it had been impossible for her to make a sound. However, now that it had been taken out, we knew that there was no longer anything hindering her from talking if she were capable of doing so. We stood by her bedside, eagerly waiting, longing to hear her voice again. Instead, she didn't make a sound and her lips remained firmly closed. She didn't even try to say anything. The awful silence that filled her room that day was one of the most devastating things that I have ever experienced. I wondered how we could ever bear it if Sharon was never able to talk again!

I thought that perhaps the reason Sharon wasn't talking was because she had an extremely sore throat from having had the tube in her throat for so long, so I asked a respiratory therapist if this was possible. She informed me that this was highly unlikely, and that Sharon's brain damage was probably preventing her from speaking. I then questioned a neurologist about what Sharon's chances of regaining her ability to speak might be. He informed me that Sharon's entire brain had been affected by her injury, and that it was impossible to tell if Sharon's speech would ever return, but that it was not hopeless. However, he said that it would probably take a long time for her to recover it—possibly even a year or two. Later that same day, Sharon began moving her lips and tongue slightly, and she made an extremely faint "h" sound. And two days later, when Joe said, "I love you" to her, she attempted to mimic his lip movements, although she was still unable to make a sound. Most of the time, however, her lips remained closed and motionless.

Since it was obvious that Sharon was not going to be able to speak anytime soon, her occupational therapist, Christy, sought to develop another means of communication that Sharon could use. Christy took a large piece of cardboard, covered it with white paper, and wrote "yes" on one half of the paper, and "no" on the other half. If Sharon were still able to read, she would be able to answer questions by touching the appropriate word.

On August 15th, the day that Sharon was transferred from ICU to the sub-acute care ward, she used her communication board for the first time. How thrilled we were to realize that Sharon still possessed the ability to read. However, because her motor coordination was so poor, all she was able to do was to slap haphazardly at the half of the board that she wanted to touch. Because of this lack of coordination, it was often difficult to tell which word she was indicating, even though the board was so large. But at least she was able to answer questions. What a joyful day that was!

Christy also discovered that Sharon remembered how to appropriately use various objects. Although she was extremely weak and uncoordinated in her movements, she attempted to use a tissue to wipe her mouth and a pick to comb her hair. And when Christy gave her a pen and asked Sharon to autograph her paper isolation gown, Sharon reached toward her gown and made weak scribbling movements. The speech therapist, whose name was also Sharon, found that our Sharon was able to understand and follow simple commands, such as "Touch the bed," and "Touch your head."

I have a foggy memory of Christy asking me to sign her gown. I was amused and encouraged by her kind gesture – assuming I understood even though I was unable to communicate.

Sharon, the speech therapist, also made another discovery that was not as encouraging, however. When she attempted to feed our Sharon some ice chips, she was unable to swallow them, and she began to choke on them. Also, when a nurse attempted to give

Sharon some medicine by mouth, she encountered the same problem. It was obvious that the brain injury had affected Sharon's ability to swallow, and that she would probably have to continue to be fed through the tube which was inserted into her nose for a long time to come.

Shortly after Sharon's brain injury, we had been informed that waking up from a coma involves going through eight physical and mental stages, beginning with a state of deep "sleep" and unawareness of surroundings and gradually progressing to a state of wakefulness and purposeful and appropriate behavior. In between those two states, however, we were warned to expect a prolonged and heart-rending period of confused, agitated, inappropriate behavior, as Sharon slowly progressed through the other six stages. We were also informed that there was a possibility that she might remain "stuck" in one of the stages for a long time, and that there was no guarantee that she would ever reach the final stage. By the time Sharon had begun using the communication board, the medical personnel were speculating about whether Sharon was now in stage 3—the "inconsistent response to stimuli" period, or stage 4—the "confused, agitated" phase.

However, as we observed Sharon's consistently appropriate answers to questions and responses to commands, and saw a look of definite recognition and understanding in her eyes as we talked to her, we began to wonder whether or not she was already at stage 8—the "purposeful and appropriate" stage, which was the last and highest stage. One day, Sharon had a special visitor, Mary, who is the daughter of two of our former co-workers. Mary is a talented rehabilitation nurse, and we posed this question to her. "Yes," she responded, "it's possible that Sharon is at stage 8. It may be that most of the effects of her brain injury are physical, rather than mental. If that is true, she is much like a stroke victim. Although her left side is almost totally paralyzed, and she is unable to swallow or speak, she is still able to understand everything that is said to her and to respond appropriately." As the days went by, Mary's evaluation of the situation proved to be correct. How we rejoiced that, even though Sharon was so severely handicapped physically, the Lord had miraculously shielded and preserved her mental abilities and her personality—the unique qualities that make her the special person that she is.

As Sharon gradually recovered from her infections and regained her strength, she began moving more. Her right arm and leg became a "perpetual motion machine", as she continually moved them up and down and back and forth, and she regained some movement in her left leg. However, her left arm remained paralyzed and motionless.

Sharon's stamina also increased, and she was able to sit up for increasing lengths of time in a chair by her bedside, although her head still sagged down and to the left because she was unable to hold it up. And on August 17th, two days after she was moved out of the ICU, we were able to take Sharon outside for the first time since the accident. She was seated in a cardiac chair, which resembles a recliner on wheels. What a joy it was to be able to take her out into the hospital courtyard where she could enjoy the beautiful summer day.

I have to say, I absolutely loved getting to go outside! Imagine, if you can, what it would be like to stay indoors and lie flat on your back for an entire month – never going outside. It was very liberating, to say the least – to feel the warm sunshine on my face and the cool breeze!

One day as she was sitting in the chair beside her bed, she crossed her right leg over her left one, as she often did. "Wouldn't it be wonderful if she could cross her left leg over her right one?" Joe commented to me. A moment later, to our joyful surprise, Sharon did that very thing. She had heard what Joe had said and followed his directions. How we rejoiced that she was now able to move her left leg enough so that she could cross it over her right one.

Sharon's loving personality and sense of humor began to reappear also. When Ernie, Robert, Carol, and Janet visited her, she greeted them with a one-sided version of her radiant smile, and she eagerly reached up her right arm to encircle them each in a one-armed hug.

And when Ernie jokingly asked her if she wanted him to say "Hello" for her to one of her college professors whom she had particularly disliked, she slapped her communication board to respond with a resounding, "No!"

I didn't realize that this had actually happened until my mom was reading her journal to me. I have a very definite memory of this, but I had thought it was just something I dreamed. Imagine my delight to discover this really occurred! He actually asked me two questions – first if I wanted him to say hello to one of my favorite professors to which I responded with a hearty, "Yes!" Then he asked me if I wanted him to say hello to one of my least favorite professors eliciting my profound response of, "No!" In retrospect, the most compelling aspect of this event was two-fold. First, I communicated the fact that I remembered people from my college and second, my sense of humor was intact!

In addition to visits from family members, Sharon also enjoyed visits from many friends during those days. Rieko, one of her former roommates from high school, surprised Sharon with a visit as she passed through Albuquerque on her way back to college in Arkansas. As Rieko was "gowning up" to enter Sharon's room, a nurse asked if she was the technician from ultra-sound. Rieko, for whom English is a second language, thought that the nurse was asking if her name was "Ultrasound", and she responded with, "No, I'm Rieko!" Sharon, who was listening to this exchange from her bed, was heartily amused.

Yes, I was highly amused! Again, I had thought this was something I dreamed.

To our amazement, several of Sharon's co-workers from Christina's Restaurant, where she had worked prior to the accident, made the long trip to Albuquerque to visit her, bringing her presents, cards, and greetings from the entire staff. One of these visitors was Shoni, the girl who had been in the accident with her. We knew that it was extremely difficult for Shoni to see how seriously Sharon was injured, since she still blamed herself for the accident, but we deeply appreciated her coming.

Livi, one of Sharon's best friends since their early childhood, came bearing a very special present. Livi is a talented pianist, and she had teamed up with Gary, another dear friend of Sharon's, who is a gifted trumpeter, to make an original tape of Christian praise choruses for Sharon. Gary's mother, Gyanne, had printed a special "program", which had the words of the songs that they had played, to go along with it. What a blessing it was for Sharon to have a tape of beautiful music that was made especially for her.

On August 19th, almost a month after she had entered Presbyterian Hospital for her chest surgery, Sharon was finally well enough to be transferred to the low-tolerance rehabilitation hospital where she had been hospitalized prior to her operation. Because Sharon had received such poor care when she had been there before, we strongly objected to her being taken back there again. We argued vigorously with Sharon's doctors and tried desperately to find another alternative. However, Dr. Jacob informed us that there was no other option for Sharon at this point in her recovery. She needed to be at a facility where she would be exposed to fewer germs and would receive more therapy than she could get at Presbyterian, but she was not yet strong enough to do the three hours of therapy per day which was required at St. Joseph's Rehabilitation Hospital. Until she was stronger, she would have to remain at the Transitional Hospital Corporation (THC), because it was the only hospital of its kind in the area. How we prayed that she would swiftly regain her strength, so that she wouldn't have to stay there very long.

Since Sharon's life was finally out of danger, Joe was now dividing his time between working and visiting Sharon. He spent most of each week working in Cortez, Colorado and then made the long trip each weekend to Albuquerque, New Mexico to spend a couple of days with Sharon. I remained in Albuquerque all the time, however, and spent every day and most of each evening with Sharon. I usually arrived at the hospital between eight and nine in the morning, and stayed until nine or ten each night, leaving only for meals. I was the only family member that was able to do this, since I didn't have a job. How thankful I was that I was available to be with Sharon full-time.

When Sharon was moved back to THC, I was especially glad that I could be with her, because just as we had feared, the nursing care there proved to be very poor. Also, since Sharon was not yet physically able to even call a nurse if she needed help, it was critically important that a family member be with her to make sure that her needs were being met and that she received adequate care.

The events of the day that Sharon was transferred back to THC were a vivid illustration of the substandard care in that facility. She was placed in a room at the end of a long hall, so that the nurses in the ICU ward could monitor her vital signs and watch her with a video camera, even though she was no longer in intensive care. However, the nurses who were actually responsible for her care were located at the other end of the hall. They were extremely slow to respond when I summoned them, and sometimes they didn't even see that Sharon's call light was on, and I would have to leave her room and go find them.

Although Sharon's only source of food and water came through the tube that was inserted into her nose, it was not until five hours after she arrived at THC that she was given any fluid or nourishment. Also, she missed two doses of the antibiotic that had been prescribed for her, because the doctor who admitted her refused to believe that she was being given that medication until I finally insisted that he call Dr. Jacob and find out. And she missed two of her respiratory therapy treatments because the respiratory therapist was extremely late in making his rounds. I had to stay at the hospital until eleven o'clock that night before I felt satisfied that Sharon's needs had been met.

However, when I arrived the next morning, I was appalled to find Sharon lying there soaked with her own urine. When I pointed this out to the nurse on duty, she found that Sharon's catheter had been inserted in the wrong place, allowing her urine to continuously flow out onto her gown and into her bed. I wondered angrily how the woman who had made this terrible error had ever become a nurse, since she obviously must have flunked her course in basic anatomy.

I also vividly remember this incident. After the catheter tube came out and needed to be reinserted, I knew it didn't feel right, but was unable to communicate this to anyone. Now, I'm not a nurse, but I am a woman and I don't know how a woman who is a nurse could be so incompetent! When asked why she had improperly inserted the catheter tubing into my vagina rather than my urethra, she responded with, "Well, it looked like the only place it could go. I wondered why I didn't get any urine back." Brings to mind Abraham Lincoln's well-known saying, "Better to remain silent and be thought a fool than to speak out and remove all doubt!"

Several days later, Sharon's catheter was finally removed, after being in place for six weeks. Because of Sharon's lack of muscle coordination, it was impossible for her to use the regular call button to summon the nurse if she needed to use the bedpan, so the nurses rigged up a special call button for her. It was called a "soft touch" button, and was taped to the railing of her bed. It worked if Sharon barely brushed it with her hand or arm. This caused a number of "false alarms" because Sharon often bumped into it accidentally as she moved her arm back and forth in bed, but at last Sharon was able to call a nurse if she needed one.

As my mom mentioned earlier, I was regularly moving my right arm and leg. I guess I was just doing this because I could, and I would often accidentally hit the soft touch call button. I remember one nurse answering my accidental call numerous times, and when I couldn't tell her why I had called, she jokingly suggested, "Oh, you were you just exercising?" I communicated to her that indeed this was the case, and I greatly appreciated the humorous exchange.

Since Sharon had had a catheter in for so long, her bladder had to be retrained, and she sometimes had "accidents" before the nurse could get to her room and put her on the bedpan. Most of the nurses were kind and understanding when this happened, but the day after the catheter was removed, Sharon had a callous, lazy, uncaring nurse who epitomized all that is worst in the nursing profession. This particular woman, Katrina, was quite overweight and whenever she was called, she could be heard lumbering down the hall, her arrival heralded by loud sighs and groans. She refused to believe that Sharon was capable of calling her, or of using the bedpan, so she insisted on putting Sharon in adult diapers. This disastrous decision reinforced Katrina's false belief that Sharon wasn't able to use the bedpan, because by the time that she reached Sharon's room and removed her diaper, she had already had an "accident".

I was further humiliated by the responses of nurses when I called them to have them come change my diaper because I had gone to the bathroom. By the time they finally figured out why I had called them to come – by me grabbing my crotch, as I did not have a symbol on my communication board that signified "change my diaper" they would open up the diaper and say, "You're not that wet." and close it back up!

After several hours of this embarrassing and demeaning treatment, big tears began rolling down Sharon's cheeks, although she was still unable to make even the faintest sound. It was the first time that she had cried since the accident. Even with all the agony that she had been through, nothing else had ever brought tears to her eyes. I determined then that I was not going to allow my daughter to be humiliated in this way any longer. I hurried out of Sharon's room, found the nursing supervisor, and informed her of Katrina's incompetence and uncaring attitude.

"My daughter is a 20 year old woman who is fully aware of everything that is happening to her," I told the nurse manager firmly. "She deserves to be treated with respect. She is able to call the nurse and to use the bedpan, and I refuse to allow her to be diapered like a baby!" The supervisor heartily agreed with me and gave a stern reprimand to Katrina. She forbade her to put any more diapers on Sharon and ordered her to ask Sharon every hour if she needed to use the bedpan.

I must take a moment to note how incredibly difficult and virtually impossible it is when one has very limited physical abilities to perform the acrobatics required to raise oneself off the bed and position oneself precisely just so, in order to actually USE a bedpan! Not an easy task, let me tell you!

With this problem resolved, I decided to try to find some humor in this depressing experience. "Honey," I said to Sharon, "I know that it isn't funny now, but I hope that someday we'll be able to look back at this day and laugh about it together. I hereby proclaim that henceforth, this day will be known in history as 'The Great Diaper Fiasco Day'!" And I was rewarded with the joy of seeing a smile on Sharon's face and an amused twinkle in her eyes. Even though this day was a difficult day, I praised the Lord that the worst thing that we had to be concerned about was an incompetent nurse who insisted on putting Sharon in diapers!

I have to make note of what a lifesaver and saint my mother is. I would not have been able to make it through without her unending, loving support and humorous approach. We have looked back on this day many times over the years and laughed at the incredible experiences we shared through this ordeal!

However, although THC had some major problems, many of which were caused by the fact that it was in the midst of being taken over by the Vencor Corporation, we were thankful that this time when she was hospitalized there, Sharon had a wonderful, caring doctor, and competent, skilled therapists. Since she was now healed from her chest and lung problems, Dr. Jacob turned over her care to Dr. Elizabeth Spaulding, a physiatrist, (a doctor of physical rehabilitation who is trained in working with patients who have suffered strokes, brain injuries, and spinal cord injuries). In contrast to how the pulmonologists had tried to prevent the therapists from working with Sharon, Dr. Spaulding immediately prescribed physical, occupational, and speech therapies for her. When we met Dr. Spaulding, we were thrilled to learn that she is not only a gifted physician, but also a dedicated Christian, who sees her medical practice as her mission field.

After her initial evaluation of Sharon, Dr. Spaulding motioned for me to join her out in the hall. "Mrs. Mehesy," she said gently, but seriously, "Based on what I observed in my examination, it will be a miracle if Sharon is ever able to return to college, or to become a teacher, or to function normally as a wife and mother. But our God is a God of miracles, and I've seen miracles in my practice—some of them just within the past few weeks!" Then we reentered Sharon's room, and she took Sharon's hand and my hand, bowed her head, and said, "Let's pray." She offered a simple, but heartfelt, prayer asking the Lord for healing for Sharon and for wisdom for herself in treating Sharon. What a comfort it was to have such a dear sister in Christ as Sharon's primary care physician, and to know that her doctor was regularly seeking help and guidance from the Great Physician—"Dr. Jesus", Who was really the Chief Doctor on Sharon's case.

The following day, when Dr. Spaulding came in to examine Sharon, we all received a thrilling surprise. "Sharon," she questioned, "Have you ever met me before?"

Sharon, using her communication board, replied, "Yes."

"Did you meet me yesterday?" Dr. Spaulding asked.

Sharon again answered, "Yes."

"Did you ever meet me before yesterday?" the doctor inquired.

"No," Sharon said.

"This is amazing!" Dr. Spaulding exclaimed excitedly. "Most patients with a brain injury have severe problems with their short-term memory, but Sharon's memory seems to be fine. Many people with an injury like hers wouldn't be able to remember that I came to see them the previous day, or that they had never met me before that, but Sharon recalled exactly what happened."

Based on what Dr. Spaulding had discovered, we were able to determine from Sharon that she now knew that she was in

Albuquerque, New Mexico in the hospital and that she had been in a car accident, and that she even knew what day and month it was. How grateful we were to know that she was now oriented as to place and time.

However, we also found out that her continuous memory of events had only resumed after she was admitted to THC for the second time. Before that, she remembers only tiny bits and pieces of things that happened while she was at Presbyterian Hospital, and she doesn't recall anything at all about the accident, or about her hospitalization in Durango or her first stay at THC. Amazingly enough, though, she lost only one day of her memory of the time before the accident. Altogether, she lost about 5 or 6 weeks of continuous memory. She said that she felt as if she had gone to sleep in the summer and awakened in the fall, since the accident happened on July 12th and it was now late August. However, her memory loss was actually a tremendous blessing, because it was during that period that she underwent her chest surgery and many other painful medical procedures. How thankful we were that she had no recollection of that extremely painful time. The nurses in the ICU had assured us that Sharon would not remember all the pain that she was going through, and what they had said now proved to be correct.

At the time I didn't realize how significant my memory of Dr. Spaulding was, but since I've learned more about brain injury, I've realized it is simply astonishing that my short term memory was intact after such a severe injury!

Since Sharon was still unable to make a sound, Stephanie, her speech therapist, helped us to devise a method by which she could make known her basic needs, rather than having to rely totally on questions that could be answered with "Yes" or "No". Using the communication board to discuss it, Sharon and I planned the making of a picture board. Stephanie had given us several sheets of paper with different illustrations on them, and Sharon chose what needs were most important for her to communicate and which picture she wanted to use to represent each of them. When we were finished, we had a communication board with about 20 pictures on it. In addition to replying "Yes" or "No" to questions, Sharon could now tell us when she was in pain, nauseated, or dizzy, and when she was hot or cold. She could let us know when she wanted to be read to, to listen to music, or to watch TV, and when she wanted to sit up in her chair, go outside, or go back to bed. And she could tell us when she wanted the light on or off, when she wanted her mouth to be moistened with a sponge, and when she needed to use the bedpan. We were so thankful that by this time, Sharon's motor coordination had improved enough that she was able to point to the picture that showed what she wanted. What a joy it was to us that Sharon could now "talk" to us and let us know her needs!

However, although most of the nurses used Sharon's communication board enthusiastically, a few of them refused to use it. They would not believe that Sharon was really "there" mentally and that she was capable of communicating. Because Sharon was unable to speak and her eyes weren't working together properly, these insensitive women treated her as if she were merely a "body in a bed." One night, a nurse came in and said to Sharon very slowly, "If you can understand me, blink your eyes once for 'Yes' and twice for 'No'." Angry at this demeaning treatment, Sharon totally ignored her and began blinking both eyes continuously, as rapidly as she could. This nurse then responded with, "Oh, you really don't understand what I'm saying to you, do you?"

When I answered her in this manner, I was thinking, "Have you ever heard of sarcasm?!? Lost on you!!!"

In contrast to the callous attitude of these uncaring women, we especially appreciated the loving concern of two very special nurses, Roni and Donna. Roni, who is a Christian, liked to joke with Sharon and tried to encourage her in any way possible. Donna had been motivated to go into nursing because she was in a motorcycle accident at the age of fifteen and was hospitalized for five months. She understood well the feelings of a young person who was in Sharon's situation, because she had been there. One night, she brought Sharon a special gift—a lovely plaque with a picture of an angel on it to put beside her bed.

Roni and I developed a game of sorts. I accidentally hit her in the butt with my foot one time when I was moving about and she indignantly responded with, "Hey! Are you trying to kick me in the butt?" I felt bad because it had been an accident, but then every time she came into my room, I tried to "kick her in the butt" to tease her. She was so much fun, and I truly valued Donna sharing her personal story with me and was so encouraged by it!

In addition to these two dear ladies, Sharon was blessed to have well trained, creative, and caring therapists. We were surprised to learn that speech therapists do many other things in addition to helping a person relearn how to talk. Stephanie also began retraining Sharon to swallow, so that she would be able to eat and drink again. Because of Sharon's brain injury, her swallowing reflex was dangerously slow. The first time that Stephanie measured it, thirty seconds passed before Sharon swallowed an ice chip that was placed in her mouth. Stephanie said that for a young woman of Sharon's age, the normal time was only one or two seconds. Therefore, if she were to try to take anything by mouth, she would either choke, or else it would go down into her lungs, causing aspiration pneumonia.

To stimulate Sharon to swallow, Stephanie used a cold spoon that had been dipped into lemon water. She inserted it into Sharon's mouth and pressed down on Sharon's tongue with it. She then watched to see when Sharon swallowed and timed how long it took. She also showed me how to do the "cold spoon" therapy, as well as other mouth, lip, and tongue exercises, which I did with Sharon several times a day. As the days passed, Sharon's swallowing time gradually got faster—first ten seconds, then six, and then down to four. Finally, the wonderful day came when Sharon swallowed perfectly ten times in a row.

Can you imagine not tasting anything for over a month?!? I loved the cold spoon therapy using lemon water! However, I was greatly dismayed at how long it took my swallowing reflex to respond. I had to relearn how to swallow – something you never have to consciously learn in the first place. So try to imagine having to learn the mechanics of swallowing. I was thankful I was able to do it, but incredibly frustrated at how long it was taking. Slowly but surely I made progress. I was definitely the tortoise in this race, but I was determined to win this competition with myself!

However, even though Sharon was making great progress, her swallowing ability was still not consistently good enough for her to be able to safely take food or water by mouth. Because of this, Dr. Spaulding recommended surgically implanting a tube in her abdomen that would allow liquid nourishment and medications to be poured directly into her stomach. This would enable Sharon to quickly be fed an entire liquid "meal" at specific times, thus freeing her from being continuously attached to the machine that had been feeding her through the tube in her nose. This surgery would be done just before she was ready to leave THC and go to St. Joseph's Rehabilitation Hospital, so that she would be ready to participate actively in the therapy there.

I remember Dr. Spaulding asking me if I wanted to have the tube removed from my nose and I indicated to her that I did, but when she asked me if I wanted to have the stomach tube inserted, I replied that I did not. I did not realize that I had to have one or the other. When I indicated that I didn't want either tube, Dr. Spaulding told me that I had to have one of these devices, so I reluctantly agreed to have the stomach tube implanted.

The surgery to implant my feeding tube was minor by comparison to the other surgeries I underwent, but thankfully it was the only surgery I remember. I had to have assistance with sitting up due to the painful incision in my abdomen and was in pain much of the time, but it was nothing compared to the major chest surgery – the thoracotomy. I have been told that is one of the most painful surgeries as it cuts through so many major muscle groups. I am truly grateful that I have no memory of this. My mom tells me she remembers enough about this time for both of us!

In addition to speech therapy, Sharon also received treatment from two other dedicated young ladies—Nicole, the physical therapist, and Kristen, the occupational therapist. Sometimes they worked together with Sharon, and at other times they worked with her separately. We learned that the goals of occupational therapy are to help a patient to regain the use of her arms and hands and to retrain her how to do her personal care and basic activities of daily living (ADLs). We also found out that the purpose of physical therapy is to work with a patient's legs and feet, and to help her relearn skills such as balance, sitting, standing, and walking.

Sharon's progress continued to be measured in tiny steps. How we rejoiced on August 22nd, when she was able to stand up for the first time since the accident, even though she was very weak and her balance was still not good. (In order to keep from falling over, she had to lean on a table, and also be supported on each side by a therapist.) We were also thrilled when she confirmed that she could recognize letters and numbers and that she could read, even though it was necessary to patch her right eye to enable her to do this, since she had severe vision problems.

We were ecstatic when she began regaining a little movement in her left hand, so that she could open her fingers, which had been curled tightly into a fist, hold her thumb and forefinger up, and also make a knocking motion with her fist. To combat the spasms in Sharon's left hand, Kristen, the occupational therapist, designed a resting hand splint for Sharon to wear each night, so that her fingers could be held in an outstretched, functional position, rather than being clenched up in a fist.

It was a great day when Kristen helped Sharon to get dressed in regular clothes, rather than in a hospital gown. (Although Sharon couldn't help much with her personal care or with getting dressed, she was now able to wash her own face) And it was wonderful when Sharon was strong enough to be helped to the bedside commode, rather than having to use the bedpan.

However, it was heartrending to see how hard Sharon struggled during her therapy sessions as she tried to accomplish even the simplest tasks, such as using her right hand to place plastic rings on a wooden dowel or to put plastic clothespins onto a yardstick. Because of her vision problems and her poor muscle coordination and weakness, it was terribly frustrating and almost impossible for her to do either of these things, but she never gave up.

Each night before I went to bed, I took time to write down the day's events and my feelings about them in a journal. So much had happened since Sharon's accident that I knew that I would never be able to remember everything unless I wrote it down, although at the time it all seemed unforgettable. On August 21st, I decided to take stock of Sharon's situation at that time. The following is a portion of my diary entry for that day, "Sharon's main problems at this point—Not able to swallow, eat, or drink. Not able to speak or make a sound. Left arm almost completely immobile. Left side much weaker than right. No fine motor coordination. Has only half a smile. Hard for her to hold her head up. Very weak. Eyes not working together well. Very poor eye-hand coordination. Great praises—Cognition, intelligence, mental ability, personality, emotions, and memory seem to be intact. Has age-appropriate behavior and responses. Can read and can communicate with picture board. Healed from infections. Able to move both legs and her right arm. Getting better every day!"

Chapter 4

On August 28th, the day after Sharon had the surgery to place the feeding tube in her abdomen, Dr. Spaulding said that she was finally strong enough to leave THC and be transferred across the street to St. Joseph's. For the first time, she was transported in a wheelchair, which was put into a van that had a lift, rather than on a stretcher in an ambulance. That was a wonderful day, because we knew that, barring any unforeseen complications, this would be her last hospitalization, and that in 4 to 6 weeks, she would be going home!

The next day, Sharon met her new therapists and was evaluated by them, so that they could determine her strengths and weaknesses and plan her therapy. We were impressed with all three of Sharon's therapists. To our surprise and delight, we learned that Sharon's physical therapist, Tim, was the husband of Sharon's primary care doctor, Dr. Spaulding, the physiatrist. It was wonderful to know that he, like his wife, is a Christian, and we were also glad to know that Sharon's physical therapist and her doctor would obviously be consulting together about Sharon's case on a very regular basis. Sharon instantly liked Tim, because he reminded her of her high school basketball coach, whose name was also Tim. And she certainly needed a good coach, as she was facing the biggest challenge of her life – trying to relearn how to sit, stand, and walk.

I cannot adequately describe to you how it feels to go from being an athletic, independent, active young woman to instantly have everything ripped out from under you – causing you to have to relearn everything from walking, to talking – even to swallowing! It was quite an adjustment, to say the least, because I had to relearn how to do things that I never consciously learned in the first place – like swallowing. So yes, I desperately needed a good coach – thanks Tim!

Sharon's occupational therapist was a lovely young woman named Debbie. Besides helping Sharon to regain the use of her arms and hands and to relearn how to dress and groom herself, she also tested Sharon's vision and did activities to evaluate and improve her cognitive abilities. As we watched Debbie interacting with Sharon, we could sense that she would soon become Sharon's friend, as well as her therapist.

Sydney, Sharon's speech therapist, was a creative, enthusiastic woman who worked with her on swallowing, and sought to determine what was hindering her from speaking. She also worked to improve her attention span, concentration, and other cognitive abilities. She immediately recommended that her vocal cords should be scoped by an ear, nose, and throat specialist to find out exactly why she was unable to make a sound.

We felt much more comfortable with the quality of nursing care that Sharon was receiving at St. Joe's. She was placed in a small ward designated for patients with brain injuries. Her bed was located right across the hall from the nurse's station, and she was given a call button that beeped, in addition to lighting up, whenever she pushed it. Most of the nurses and techs were very caring and competent professionals. We quickly learned to appreciate the tender, loving care that Sharon received—especially from Karen, Valerie, Cecile, Pam, Jennifer, and Ed.

The day after she was transferred to St. Joseph's, we received a delightful surprise. For the first time since her accident, Sharon began nodding and shaking her head to answer "Yes" or "No" when she was asked a question, and she also began mouthing words. It was as if her brain was very gradually waking up and remembering that in order to speak, her lips must move! How we rejoiced that she was still able to think of and form words. But even though her lips were going through the motions of speech, she was still unable to produce even the slightest sound. Although I was thrilled that Sharon was mouthing words, it was terribly frustrating to me, because I am totally unskilled at reading lips, and I couldn't understand what she was trying to say. Fortunately Carol and Janet, who were visiting during the Labor Day weekend, are very proficient in lip reading, so their sister was able to carry on a conversation with them for the first time since her accident, and they were able to relay her messages to the rest of us.

It is important to note here that you never think about how much your head weighs and how HEAVY it is! Up to this point, I had been unable to hold my head up because my neck muscles had gotten so weak from lying motionless in a bed for six weeks. I was so thankful to be able to hold my head up and answer questions with a nod or a shake rather than having to rely on my Yes/No communication board!

Also the main reason my parents were not skilled at lip reading was because they did not have the years of practice that my sisters and I had. This was how we communicated during dinner when we didn't want my parents to know what we were saying. Tee hee hee! So yes, my sisters were excellent translators!

My problem was alleviated the next day, however, when Carol suggested that Sharon be given an alphabet board, so that she could spell out whatever she wanted to say. By this time, Sharon's coordination had improved enough so that she could point accurately to the various letters on the board, and I could often guess what she was spelling before she finished the word. Sharon was overjoyed to have this new way of communicating, and many times she spelled out words so rapidly that the only way we could keep up with her was to write them down as she spelled, and then read what she had said. How thankful we were for this new evidence that her reading and spelling skills were intact.

Another exciting development occurred that day also. Sharon was able to eat almost a cupful of ice chips without choking—showing that her swallowing ability was improving, and that she would soon be able to begin eating during her sessions with Sydney, the speech therapist. Sydney recommended that Sharon should undergo a video swallowing test, in which they would x-ray her throat as she attempted to swallow various types of food. This would be used to determine how well she was able to swallow, whether or not she was capable of eating, and what kinds of food would be the safest for her when she began eating again.

In occupational therapy, Sharon surprised us by revealing that she knew the entire sign language alphabet. Since she was unable to speak, Debbie suggested that when she needed to use the bedside commode, she should make the sign for the letter "t" and move her right hand back and forth – the sign for "toilet" in American Sign Language. This proved to be a very effective way of communicating that important message. And that night, Sharon reached another milestone in her personal care, when she was able to sit in a shower chair and receive her first shower since the accident.

Sharon was greatly encouraged that Labor Day weekend by the arrival of some very special visitors from Oklahoma—her fiancé Ernie, her two roommates Tara and Angie, and one of her closest friends, Erin. Since Sharon had now been given her own wheelchair, she was able to go outside and visit with them on the hospital patio. We rejoiced to see Sharon "talking" to them, through a combination of mouthing words, using the alphabet board, and gesturing. How glad we were that Sharon's picture board was no longer needed. And Ernie was overjoyed at her special surprise for him—when she mouthed, "I love you!"

As we all sat there that day, seven weeks after the accident, we were thrilled to see that Sharon's head was no longer sagging down and to the left. At last, she had the strength to hold her head up and look at us. And as she visited with her friends, it was a joy to see her smile and shake with silent laughter as they joked together.

I thoroughly enjoyed this visit. What a joy it was to finally be able to communicate as well as to go outside with my friends. It was so wonderful to be able to hold my head up and indicate "yes" or "no" with my head, rather than relying on the communication board. Tera and Angie brought some shiny purple nail polish and painted my nails! What good friends.

September 2nd was a day of very strong, but opposite, emotions! We were filled with joy at the wonderful progress that Sharon was making in physical and occupational therapy. For the first time since her accident, even though she was still quite weak and wobbly, she was able to stand without assistance and to sit on the edge of her bed unaided. And she was able, at last, to wash her own face and to brush her teeth by herself. How we rejoiced to see Sharon growing stronger every day, now that she had been healed from all of her infections.

However, this was also the day that Sharon was taken to Dr. Ray, the ear, nose, and throat specialist for an examination, and the news we received from her was quite discouraging. Dr. Ray inserted a lighted scope through Sharon's nose and down into her throat and asked her to try to say "e", but even though she strained with all her might and turned red in the face, she was unable to make a sound. Dr. Ray told us that her vocal cords were extremely weak—almost paralyzed, and that they were stuck in a slightly open position, barely quivering and unable to touch each other. She explained that it was very fortunate that they were open, because if they had been frozen in a closed position, Sharon's airway would have been cut off, and she would have died. However, since they were continuously open, there was another great danger. If she tried to eat or drink anything, it might go down into her lungs and cause aspiration pneumonia. Dr. Ray recommended some exercises to try to strengthen Sharon's larynx muscles, and also suggested that she try to use an electronic larynx—a mechanical device that is held up to the throat and which produces sound when the lips are moved. She also said that if her voice didn't return within the next year, she might be able to perform an operation which would move the weaker vocal cord closer to the stronger one so that they could meet again.

I wondered sadly if I would ever hear Sharon's sweet voice again. In my sorrow, I looked in the Bible to try to find the verse that the Lord had used on the day of the accident to assure me that Sharon would survive. When I found it in Psalm 118:17, I read the entire verse for the first time, "[She] shall not die but live, and tell of the works of the Lord." As I read the second half of that verse, the Lord soothed my aching heart with the calm assurance that Sharon would regain her ability to speak!

The following day was another day of emotional "ups and downs". Sharon reached another major milestone in her recovery when she took her first steps, using a walker. Our overwhelming joy that she was able to walk once more was mixed with deep sadness, as we saw the exhausting effort that she had to exert just to take a few halting steps. Only a parent who has been through such an experience can understand the conflicting emotions that we felt as we watched our 20 year old daughter as she began learning to walk all over again.

In occupational therapy that day, Debbie gave Sharon some visual perception tests, and found that she didn't seem to be able to see objects that were located to her left. It was as if her vision was abruptly cut off at that point. This was confirmed when Sharon told Debbie that she was unable to see her left shirt sleeve when Debbie helped her get dressed each morning. The tests also seemed to indicate that she might have other visual perception problems that were similar to those experienced by people with certain types of learning disabilities. Upon learning of these problems, Dr. Spaulding made an appointment for Sharon to be seen by a neuro-ophthalmologist, in order to determine the exact nature of her vision problems.

Later that same afternoon, Sharon was given the video swallow test to find out exactly how well she was swallowing and if she could begin eating something during her speech therapy sessions with Sydney. She did quite well with swallowing yogurt, and fairly well with canned fruit, but when she tried to eat some honeydew melon, she couldn't handle it and had to spit it out. Also, when she tried to drink water, she coughed and choked and it went right down into her lungs. However, when she drank water using a "chin tuck" she was able to swallow it better. In order to perform a chin tuck, the person takes a sip of water, holds it in her mouth, lowers her chin to her chest and then swallows. We were told that this was a manual way of closing the vocal cords thereby protecting the airway while swallowing.

Based on the results of the test, Sydney concluded that Sharon could begin eating pureed food of the consistency of yogurt, and that she could drink liquids if she used a chin tuck. As we talked with Sydney, we learned a surprising fact. She told us that the most difficult and dangerous task for a person with swallowing problems is to drink thin liquids such as water, and that the safest and easiest is to eat pureed food that has the consistency of pudding. The next day, almost two months after the accident, Sharon ate her first "meal," raspberry yogurt, during speech therapy. She also drank water for the first time—taken in tiny sips using the chin tuck.

How amazing and wonderful to finally be able to eat again! It was as if my sense of taste had been heightened – the raspberry in the yogurt was especially tart – how delicious! You never think about all the acrobatics your tongue automatically does to push the food over to your teeth so you are able to chew it. When the honeydew melon was placed in my mouth, my tongue had no idea what to do with it, which is why I ultimately had to spit it out. I needed to retrain my tongue muscles so they would be able to push food to my teeth so I could chew it.

After Sharon had finished her "breakfast", Sydney began teaching her to use the electronic larynx. This task is extremely difficult to master, because the larynx must be held in just the right spot on the throat, with exactly the correct amount of pressure, or it won't work at all. Sharon's poor coordination made success with it almost impossible, but at last, after much fruitless effort, I heard a vibrating electronic voice convey a message from Sharon that was more beautiful to me than the sweetest music that I had ever heard—"I love you, Mom!"

Joe also found another way to help Sharon communicate. He brought in a portable computer, so that Sharon could type what she wanted to say. Her first message was, "Breakfast was good!"—a fitting message from someone who had just begun to eat and drink again after two months of not being able to take anything by mouth. Then she typed, "Thank you for being here every day!"

Later that day, as Sharon mouthed the words, "Thank you," I heard the very first tiny speech sound come from her lips—the "th" in "thank." Sharon was beginning to combine breath with her lip movements as she attempted to say words. The next day, she was able to make several other consonant sounds, such as "c" and "t", and on the following day, September 6th—eight weeks after the accident—she finally began talking in a faint whisper. How wonderful it was to hear Sharon actually saying, "I love you, Mom", rather than her having to rely on a mechanical "voice" to say it for her. And how happy Ernie, Carol, Paul, and Janet were that Sharon was finally able to talk to them on the phone when they called her.

Since Sharon's voice was still such a quiet whisper, Joe devised an ingenious way to amplify it. He created a unique contraption—using two plastic headbands, a lapel microphone, and a battery-powered amplifier. He fastened the headbands together in such a way that one of them fitted over Sharon's head and the other one was positioned in front of her mouth. He attached the lapel mic to the headband that was in front of her mouth, and connected the microphone to the amplifier which sat on a table nearby. As Sharon spoke into the mic, her voice was amplified, so that it was much easier to hear.

However, there were still times when it was a bit difficult to understand her. Since she could only whisper, it was impossible for her to correctly pronounce the voiced consonants. For this reason, it was often hard for us to distinguish between "b" and "p", "d" and "t", "k" and "g", "f" and "v", and "s" and "z", so we occasionally had to resort to the alphabet board. However, a little more than a week later, Sharon began making some actual voice sounds. Her voice was still very quiet, and it was hoarse and squeaky, like that of someone who has extremely bad laryngitis, but it was definitely a voice. How we all rejoiced that day.

As part of Sharon's occupational therapy, Debbie worked with her to determine whether she could still follow directions, whether she had the ability to read and understand a calendar and a map, and whether she could do simple math. She also checked to see if she remembered such basic personal facts as her full name, her address, and her date of birth, and whether she could write them down. It was soon obvious that Sharon had lost none of these skills, for which we were very thankful. However, it was heartbreaking to watch her as she struggled to write. Because of her almost total lack of fine motor coordination, her weak, unsteady, squiggly attempts at writing were hardly legible, and they resembled the scribbles of a preschool child.

As Sharon settled into her daily therapy routine, we could finally understand why it would have been impossible for her to come to St. Joseph's any sooner. Her day began at 7:30 each morning, when Debbie came in to help her relearn how to do her personal care and get dressed. Then at 8:30, she had speech therapy for half an hour, which included eating "breakfast". After a short rest time, she had thirty minutes of physical therapy at 10:30, followed by occupational therapy from 11:00 to 11:30. After a midday nap, she had another session of physical therapy at 1:30, and more speech therapy at 2:00.

In addition to this she had Oral Aerobics class twice a week. This was a group that practiced various mouth and tongue exercises, under the direction of a speech therapist, in order to improve their speech and swallowing. Also, she did handcrafts several times each week with Rebecca, the recreation therapist, to work on redeveloping her fine motor coordination skills. As we saw how exhausted Sharon became from this grueling schedule, we realized that she would not have had the strength any earlier in her recovery to endure three to four hours of therapy each day. However we were so thankful to see that she was now able to do it, and to watch her growing stronger and improving each day, even though her progress was agonizingly slow.

I have thoroughly enjoyed telling people about my class called Oral Aerobics since I have been out of the hospital—especially men. When I tell them the name of the class, inevitably there is an impish smile followed by some comment like, "I think my wife could use a class like that." It loses some of its appeal when I explain what the class entailed, but I always enjoy the exchange none the less.

Each day, I arrived at the hospital early in the morning and stayed until late at night. Since Sharon's therapists gave her exercises to do in her "spare time", I spent several hours every day helping her do her "homework". Debbie told her to use her right arm to bring her left arm, which was still completely immobile, up to the level of her chin, and then back over her head. Although Sharon was able to bring it up as far as her chin, she needed help to bring it over her head, because the muscles in her left shoulder were still extremely tight, and she wasn't able to lift her right arm that high either. There were also hand and finger exercises to be done, and Tim assigned various leg, foot, and toe exercises for her to do. In addition to this, I did range of motion exercises to make sure that all of Sharon's muscles and joints were moved in every direction, just as I had done when she was in the ICU.

Although I may not have enjoyed doing my "homework," this combined with the passive range of motion exercises my mom faithfully performed, have given me the full range of motion I currently have. I must say I am forever in my mom's debt for faithfully exercising my every joint. Thanks, Mom!

However, the most interesting exercise was the larynx-strengthening exercise. To do that, Sharon would sit facing me, and she would interlace her fingers with mine. Then she would push against my hands with all of her strength, while attempting to "yell" out the numbers one through ten, as I resisted her. Sydney explained the reason for this unusual exercise. She told us that scientists had discovered that people who have no larynx are unable to lift heavy loads, because when a person lifts things, his throat muscles tighten up, and a person who doesn't have a larynx is no longer able to do this. As a result of this discovery, it was found that resistance exercises strengthen the larynx, as well as the throat muscles.

Since I spent so much time at the hospital, the nurses began training me to help with various aspects of Sharon's care, in preparation for the time when we would be taking her home. I began learning how to transfer her from her bed to her wheelchair, the bedside commode, or the shower chair, and then back again into her bed. At first, this was a very scary thing for me to do, because I have never been good at understanding directions or learning skills that involve physical activity, and I was very concerned that I might do it incorrectly and cause Sharon to fall. However, as time went on, I became more and more confident and comfortable about my ability to transfer her safely. I also learned how to give her a shower while she was sitting in the shower chair, and soon I was able to take over the responsibility of giving her showers. The nurses also instructed me in feeding Sharon through her stomach tube. This involved attaching a receptacle to the end of the tube, opening a valve at the end of the tube, pouring in a can of liquid nutrition, and then closing the valve. Although I had a few accidents, in which the food leaked out onto her clothes, instead of going into her stomach, it wasn't long before I felt quite competent to feed her correctly.

Let me tell you, this is the strangest sensation – to be starving, have a nurse come and open a valve at the end of your stomach tube, pour in a can of Ensure, close the valve when finished, and all of a sudden you feel full – with nothing ever crossing your lips!

I also took Sharon to her various therapies. One extremely irritating and annoying aspect of doing this was the fact that she was still in isolation, due to the penicillin-resistant bacteria that she carried within her body. Although it no longer had any effect on her, it could be dangerous to the other patients, many of whom were elderly people who had suffered strokes. To prevent it from spreading, she was required to be dressed in a yellow paper gown and to wear latex gloves whenever she left her room for any reason. So each time she went to therapy, I had to help her clothe herself in the proper attire—an extremely difficult task, since her left hand and arm were paralyzed. Trying to put a glove on her left hand was always an especially frustrating and time-consuming endeavor.

However, we had some fun times too. I often took Sharon outside, and I tried to spend some time each day reading to her and playing games with her. Also, Karen, one of the nurses, brought in several Disney movies for Sharon to watch—including one starring "Winnie the Pooh", who had been Sharon's favorite storybook character since childhood. How thankful I was that I had the privilege of being with Sharon all day, every day—to keep her company, to make sure that she received good care, and to try to help her get the most benefit possible from her rehabilitation.

Although most of the nurses at St. Joe's gave Sharon excellent care, there was one nurse there who vied with Katrina, the nurse of "The Great Diaper Fiasco Day," for first place in our personal "Nurses' Hall of Shame!" Her name was Marie, and once again, the trouble that we had with her involved Sharon's using the bathroom. On the very first day that Sharon was at St. Joseph's, Marie insisted on putting adult diapers on her. I immediately protested her humiliating treatment of Sharon, and this problem was promptly resolved.

However, about a week later, we experienced another difficulty with Marie. Since Sharon had recently had her catheter removed, after having it inserted for six weeks, there were times when she would experience "false alarms". She would feel like she needed to go to the bathroom, but when she was placed on the bedside commode, she would find that she didn't need to use it after all. Then a bit later, she would experience an urgent need to go.

One morning about eleven o'clock, Sharon called Marie and told her that she needed to urinate, but when Marie sat her on the pot, it turned out to be a "false alarm". At noon, she called Marie again, telling her that she desperately needed to use the commode. However, Marie responded, "No. I'm not going to put you on it now. You've got to wait until one o'clock. Your bladder needs to be retrained, and I think that you need behavior modification to do it! I'm putting you on a schedule. You'll be placed on the pot every two hours whether you need to use it or not, and whenever you feel like you've got to urinate, you'll have to wait until it's your next scheduled time."

*I was completely taken aback at Marie's attitude and wondered why on earth she insisted that I was in need of behavior modification. I felt that **she** was the one who needed behavior modification!*

I was furious at Marie's callous, uncaring attitude. I knew that Sharon <u>couldn't</u> wait for another hour. If she tried to, I was sure that she would have an "accident" in her bed, and I didn't intend to let her suffer that uncomfortable embarrassment. At that time,

Sharon was still very weak, and she needed a lot of help with getting from the bed to the commode. Also, I was just beginning to learn how to transfer her from one place to another, and I was very concerned that I wouldn't be able to do it correctly and that she might fall. However, I breathed a silent prayer for strength and protection and successfully assisted Sharon in getting onto the commode, where she quickly proved that she could not have waited much longer to use it.

After I got Sharon back into her bed, I walked angrily out into the hall and over to the nurses' station, told Marie what had happened, and confronted her about her totally inappropriate behavior, but she refused to admit that she was wrong. "Mrs. Mehesy," she said haughtily, "I have been a nurse for more than twenty years, and I always trust my instincts about my patients, because ninety-nine percent of the time, my instincts are right!"

Not to be outdone by her, I retorted icily, "Marie, I have been a mother for more than twenty-five years, and I have learned to trust my instincts regarding my children. I certainly can't claim that I'm right ninety-nine percent of the time, but this is one time that I know I am!"

After a long, fruitless argument on the subject, I finally gave up and went in search of Debbie, Sharon's occupational therapist, to ask her advice on the matter. Debbie was appalled when I recounted to her what had happened. "Marie was totally 'out of line' to act like that!" she said firmly. "I want you to come with me right now to the nurse manager's office and tell her your story."

When the nurse manager heard about Marie's behavior, she agreed with Debbie's assessment of the situation. "You can be sure that this problem will be taken care of immediately, Mrs. Mehesy," she assured me. "It won't happen again." And indeed it did not, for within a few days, Marie was removed from her position in the brain injury unit.

Just as we had done on the day when Sharon was forced to wear adult diapers at THC, we decided to laugh about this unhappy situation. "Sharon, we now have another important day to remember in the history of your hospitalization," I announced. "From now on, this day will be known as 'Potty Paranoia Day'!" And from then on, when I needed to go to the bathroom, I would often look anxiously at my watch and jokingly ask Sharon, "Is it time for me to go yet, or do I have to wait until later?"

One day, when I asked that question barely an hour after my last trip to the bathroom, Sharon grabbed her alphabet board and spelled out, "Mom, I think that you need behavior modification!" As I laughed and Sharon shook with silent giggles, I rejoiced to see that Sharon still had her sense of humor!

I thoroughly enjoyed this humorous exchange with my mom. We have since laughed about these days of infamy many times over. I am so thankful for my mom's presence during my hospitalization as well as her advocacy on my behalf!

On September 15th, after eleven days in which Sharon had eaten yogurt, cheesecake, cooked cereal, and pureed scrambled eggs during her speech therapy, she reached another milestone in her recovery. She was able to begin eating three meals a day, and just four days later, her stomach tube feedings were discontinued, because she was taking enough food by mouth to provide adequate nourishment for her. However, at first she was required to eat all of her meals in a "swallowing group", which was made up of people who had difficulty swallowing, and who ate their meals under the supervision of a speech therapist. As they ate, the therapist would remind them to use correct swallowing techniques, and she would watch carefully to make sure that no one was choking or aspirating their food. Most of these people were elderly men and women who had suffered strokes that had impaired their ability to swallow. Sharon's presence among them was like a ray of sunshine, especially since by this time her beautiful smile had been fully restored, even including the dimple in her left cheek. Often the men in the group would argue with each other over which one of them would have the privilege of sitting next to Sharon at the meal.

Although Sharon was very thankful to be able to eat again, she quickly tired of the pureed consistency of the food that she had to eat. How we all rejoiced when just one week later, she was able to totally skip the next stage of swallowing therapy—eating a diet of foods that are classified as "slippery soft", such as regular scrambled eggs, cottage cheese, canned fruit, green beans, and chopped meat. Instead of being limited to only those types of food, she was able to move up to a "mechanical soft" diet, which included all foods except for leafy vegetables, rice, grains, and nuts. To Sharon's great delight, she could once again eat pizza! And just four days later, on September 26th, after Sydney had tested Sharon's ability to eat a salad, all restrictions were removed, and Sharon could once again eat a regular diet.

Then on October 2nd, Sharon was finally cleared to leave the "swallowing group" and eat by herself in the hospital cafeteria. However, just as Sharon and I were celebrating her release from the swallowing group, a nurse suddenly hurried over to where we were eating. "Sharon," she reprimanded sternly, "Don't you know that you're supposed to be wearing a mask whenever you're out of your room to keep you from spreading germs to others?" Sharon and I were heartily amused as we contemplated the nurse's ludicrous idea of expecting Sharon to feed herself, with only one working hand, while wearing a mask that covered her nose and mouth!

As Sharon continued to make progress in eating, speaking, and walking, she often admonished her visitors, "Be thankful that you can walk, talk, and eat!" And we all realized how often we take our physical abilities for granted, how quickly they can be taken away, and what an excruciatingly slow and painful process it is to regain them once they have been lost!

Chapter 5

Now that Sydney no longer had to work with Sharon on swallowing during speech therapy, she began trying to help her improve her voice and her cognitive skills. Sometimes, she had Sharon read aloud a passage from a book and then answer questions about it. Although she was able to read and to do well on the comprehension questions, reading was extremely difficult and laborious for her because of her vision problems. In addition to the problems caused by her double vision, her left eye was also making tiny involuntary movements that made it difficult for her to focus on what she was reading and that often caused her to lose her place.

Sydney also did exercises with Sharon to improve her concentration abilities and attention span and to test her knowledge of certain concepts. Some of these activities involved concepts that were extremely elementary, such as identifying objects that were round, square, or rectangular, and things that come in pairs. Sharon did well with these tests, but as I watched my twenty-year-old daughter being tested on concepts that I had taught to children in kindergarten, I was reminded once again, that when someone has suffered a brain injury, no ability can be taken for granted.

Other tasks were extremely boring. Sharon would be required to push a buzzer whenever she heard the number "2" read during a series of numbers, or when she heard a number in a series which was one more or one less than the number preceding it. Because Sharon had difficulty in responding correctly during these tests, Sydney concluded that she was having difficulty concentrating and paying attention, but I strongly doubted it. I had never noticed that Sharon was having difficulty with concentration when I read a book to her, or when she was engaged in an activity that she enjoyed. I was sure that I also would have had trouble concentrating if I were required to perform tasks similar to those that Sharon had to do. Instead, I felt that, rather than showing concentration or attention problems, Sharon's difficulty in responding was due to an overall slowness in her response time—partly caused by her lack of coordination, and partly due to a decrease in the speed at which her brain was processing information.

My theory was supported by Sharon's behavior during her recreation therapy sessions. Her first project was a copper etching of two kittens and a ball of yarn. She had to repeatedly rub a small wooden pencil-shaped tool over a thin piece of copper, which was stretched out over a pattern that became etched into the copper as she put pressure on it. The purpose of this exercise was to help improve her fine motor coordination and to regain her ability to apply pressure to an object while grasping something with her thumb and her other fingers. However, the reason for this task was never explained to Sharon, and the recreation therapist never showed her what the finished product would look like. As a result, she worked at it half-heartedly and often commented on how boring it was. Later, after the project was completed, resulting in a very attractive wall plaque, Sharon said, "If I had known ahead of time what this was going to look like, I would have been much more interested in doing it."

In contrast to this, Sharon worked eagerly on her next craft project, because this time she was shown a completed model of it before she started working on it. Her assignment was to make a jewelry box covered with various colors and shapes of tile. Since she knew what it was to be, she carefully picked out the tiles that she wanted and used them to create a unique and beautiful design to decorate her jewelry box.

In addition to this, in her free time, Sharon made a necklace with beads on it for herself. Prior to the accident, she had been an expert at making macramé necklaces using hemp, waxed linen and beads. In fact, the night of the accident, she had been wearing one of these creations, which had to be cut off of her neck after she was taken to the hospital. Now, although she only had the use of one hand, she managed to string some beads to make a necklace.

Then, through trial and error, and using her mouth along with her right hand, she managed to secure the beads in place and tie knots to keep them from slipping and then make a loop to fit over the bead that she was using as a clasp. She worked steadily on this project for an hour and a half, persevering even though it was extremely difficult, and she was not in the least bit distracted by the noise of people continually passing by and talking to each other. When I saw her ability to do this, I felt confident that my theory was correct, and that Sharon's difficulty in doing her exercises in speech therapy was not due to a lack of concentration or attention.

On September 25th, Sharon was examined by a neuro-ophthalmologist to determine exactly what type of vision problems she had. His report was not encouraging. "Sharon has had damage to three of her cranial nerves—the third, fourth, and sixth. In addition to this, she has had generalized damage throughout her brain," Dr. Carlow explained after he had done extensive testing and examination of Sharon's eyes. "Because of these injuries, she has five different visual impairments. Her right eye can no longer look down, and it has lost its ability to accommodate and has become farsighted. Her left eye can no longer look out to the left side, it makes tiny involuntary movements that make it hard for her to focus on things, and she is unable to see anything that is past a certain point on her left side. This is called a 'left visual field cut'. Also, because of the inability of her right eye to look down at the same time that her left eye is doing so, she has double vision. When she looks at something, she sees double, but the two things are not side by side; one is on top of the other. For example, if she looks at you, she sees a person with two heads—one above the other." In addition to all of these problems, Dr. Carlow also informed us that Sharon's left eye had become extremely nearsighted, although he didn't feel that it was related to her injury. He felt that this condition would have developed anyway, irregardless of the accident, because it runs in our family.

"Will these problems improve with time?" I asked hopefully, even though my mind was still reeling from learning the extent of Sharon's visual disabilities.

"Some of them will get better, but others probably won't," Dr. Carlow replied. "For example, the 'left visual field cut' is quite serious, and most of the time an impairment such as that is permanent, but there is a chance that it may improve. Her right eye may regain some of its ability to look down, but it is too early yet to tell whether or not it will heal enough to eliminate her double vision. If it does not, there is an operation that may be able to help her. However, I believe that the farsightedness in her right eye and the involuntary movements of her left eye will be permanent. I would like to see Sharon again in six to eight weeks, so that we can determine how much progress she has made."

"But can't glasses help her?" I questioned.

"Not at this point," Dr. Carlow answered. "It wouldn't be practical to fit Sharon with glasses now, because her vision will be changing a lot over the next few months. For now, the best thing that you can do is to buy a pair of inexpensive sunglasses with light-colored lenses and put tape on the inside of the right lens. This will keep her from having the double vision, because she will only be using her left eye."

That very day, I purchased some sunglasses and taped the right lens, and Sharon began wearing them. Although they kept her from seeing double, it was overwhelming to me to think of all the serious visual problems that she was struggling with. As I had often done since the accident, I appealed to the Great Physician on Sharon's behalf. Once again, I prayed the same familiar prayer that I had prayed so many times in the past two and a half months, "Dear Lord, You made Sharon's brain, and You can heal it. Please do!"

As I wore my sunglasses all the time, my sister Carol would jokingly call me a "movie star!" ☺

After Sharon took her first few steps on September 3rd, nearly two months after the accident, she continued to make painfully slow, but steady, progress in walking. However, she had a number of serious problems as a result of her injury that made it impossible for her to walk normally. One of her major problems was balance. Because of her poor balance, she was still unable to stand for more than a few seconds without support, and as she practiced walking with her walker, she had to wear a cloth gait belt fastened around her waist. Tim, her physical therapist, held onto the gait belt, and also braced Sharon as she walked, to keep her from falling.

Another problem was the extreme weakness of her left side. Although her left leg and foot were no longer paralyzed, they were still very weak, and many times as she was trying to walk, her left knee would almost give way under her. Her left hip and her left ankle were also weak, and muscles that were in spasm caused her to have a condition called drop foot. This meant that her left foot was turned in an unnatural direction—pointing down and in, and she was unable to lift it up or to position it so that she could walk on the sole of her foot. This forced her to walk on the outside of her foot. In addition to this, her toes were curled under, because of muscles that were in constant contraction – spasticity. Also, since she still didn't have the use of her left arm and hand, she could only hold onto her walker with one hand as she walked.

I remember talking to various people during this time and telling them I was learning to walk again. They attempted to encourage me by saying things like, "Well, you already learned how to walk once, so this should be easy for you." Although well-meaning, their comments were not helpful, since they did not seem to realize how complex walking is. Not only was I learning to walk again, but this time I had to learn the mechanics of walking – something I never had to do in the first place.

In spite of all these obstacles, however, she began walking longer and longer distances during her physical therapy. On September 9th, she only managed to walk 15 feet, but by the 17th, she was able to walk 170 feet, and on the 25th, she walked 450 feet! By mid-September, she began practicing walking sideways and backwards, and going up and down stairs. And by the beginning of October, she took her first few steps without the walker.

However, Sharon's weak ankle and drop foot continued to be a major problem that hindered her from walking properly. Finally, Tim decided that it was necessary to fit her with a brace that could be steadily tightened to stretch her tight calf muscles and force her foot and ankle back into the proper position. Sharon's foot and ankle fitted into this brace and it extended up to the middle of her calf. At first, she was to wear it for just two hours at a time, and the pressure was to be kept light, but as she got used to the brace, she was to wear it for longer periods of time, and the tension was to be gradually increased. Unfortunately, though, this brace was very hard to adjust, and it failed to function properly. It sometimes irritated Sharon's ankle and foot and threatened to cause skin breakdown, and it often spontaneously lost its tension after the pressure had been set. As the time approached for Sharon to leave the hospital, I became very concerned about whether or not I would be able to adjust it properly when this responsibility fell on me after we had returned home.

In addition to working with Sharon on walking, Tim also spent a lot of time having her do exercises to strengthen her muscles and activities to improve her balance. He would have her try to keep her balance while she was sitting or kneeling on a mat or sitting on a large ball, and at the same time, hit a balloon that he tossed to her. As time went by, her balance and strength gradually improved. By the middle of September, she was finally able to sit up in bed without assistance and then swing her legs over the edge and sit on it.

As Sharon increased in strength and her balance improved, she was able to do more and more of the work of transferring from her bed to the wheelchair, or from the wheelchair to the toilet. She would use the bed rail or wheelchair to support her as she pulled herself to a standing position, and then turn and sit down. Although she still needed someone to steady her, she didn't need nearly as much help as she had previously. And then at last, Tim gave his approval for Sharon to use her walker to walk from the bed to the bathroom, with a nurse holding on to her gait belt and bracing her to keep her from falling. However, in spite of the progress that she was making, her main means of locomotion was still her wheelchair, which Tim had taught her to drive by using her right arm and her right foot. Even though her improvement had to be measured in "baby steps", we rejoiced as we saw each new accomplishment.

As Sharon continued to recover, she also regained more and more feeling in the left side of her body. One day, she told Debbie, her occupational therapist, that her entire left side felt "asleep", and had a "pins and needles" sensation, such as a person has when his foot is "asleep." Debbie tested her to see if she could distinguish between hot and cold, and between sharp and dull objects. Although she was able to do so, her response to these sensations was a bit delayed on her left side. As time passed, however, the tingling gradually subsided from most of her left side, although it remained for a long time in her left hand and foot.

At the same time that Sharon's left leg and foot were improving, her left hand and arm were also gradually getting better, but at a much slower pace. At first, she was unable to move them at all, and she had to use her right hand to pick up her left one and place it wherever she wanted it to be. And every night, I had to fit her left hand into her Resting Hand Splint, stretch out her fingers, and fasten them in place, so that her hand wouldn't involuntarily tighten up into a fist. By the second week of September, however, she finally began getting some movement back in her left hand and lower arm, although her muscles were still very weak.

And on September 24th, during Sharon's rest time, while I was sitting quietly nearby and asking the Lord to restore her ability to move her left arm, hand and ankle, I suddenly heard Sharon calling me in her hoarse whisper. "Mom," she exclaimed excitedly, "I can move my arm, hand, and ankle!" She had suddenly discovered that she could lift her arm from the bed, move it from side to side, move her wrist and open and close her fingers, and that she could also move her ankle. How I rejoiced in this wonderful and immediate answer to prayer.

I vividly remember this moment. I was supposed to be sleeping and as I lay there wondering if I could move my hand, I was ecstatic to find that I was not only able to move my hand and fingers, but also my arm and ankle!

Sharon's left shoulder muscles continued to be extremely tight and painful, however, and her shoulder joint was almost immobile. Her occupational therapist, Debbie, worked diligently on Sharon's arm and hand—stretching her tight muscles and applying heat to them, as well as having her do many exercises herself. To exercise her hand and fingers, Debbie gave Sharon a ball of Theraputty – a thick, pliable substance that she could practice squeezing, in order to develop her ability to grasp things, hold onto them and then let go. At first, it was much easier to grab an object than it was to release it, but as time went on, her ability to open her left hand improved.

Debbie also gave Sharon a piece of stretchy, rubbery material called TheraBand. One end of this material would be tied to an object that provided resistance, and Sharon would hold onto the other end and pull it to strengthen her muscles. Also, during therapy, Debbie would sometimes place Sharon's left arm in a sling-like device called a Deltoid Aid that supported the weight of her arm, so that she could move it back and forth even though she didn't have the strength to hold it up herself. She also had Sharon do various exercises, such as picking up plastic cones and stacking them on top of each other, moving her arm back and forth on the table to make a "figure eight", and removing objects that were stuck to a board with Velcro and then replacing them. As time passed, Sharon's tight shoulder muscles finally began loosening up, and by late September, she was able to shrug both shoulders, use both arms to pedal an "arm bicycle" exercise machine, and hold onto her walker with her left hand.

When Debbie used the deltoid aid to facilitate movement of my left arm, she expressed excitement at the fact that I was able to move my arm. At the time, I didn't realize how amazing it was that I was initiating these movements and I just felt like it was perfectly natural for me to be able to move my arm. In retrospect, it was nothing short of a miracle for me to be initiating movements with my left arm – to go from immobile to voluntary movement – how amazing!

Now that Sharon's strength and her ability to use her left arm and hand were improving, she became able to care for her personal needs with only minimal assistance. By the end of September, she was once again able to get dressed, fix her hair, and put on make-up, with very little help, as well as wash her hair and most of her body as she sat in the shower chair. Her handwriting also improved, and on September 25th, when she visited the neuro-ophthalmologist, she was able to sign her name in shaky, but legible, cursive writing for the first time since the accident. How we rejoiced to see the progress that she was making toward eventually being able to live independently again.

About three weeks after Sharon had been admitted to St. Joseph's, a new patient was brought into the room next to hers. He was a nineteen-year-old boy named Robert, and he had been in a multiple-rollover car accident just twelve days after Sharon had hers. Like Sharon, he also had a severe brain injury, and was experiencing many of the same effects from it. However, he had not yet progressed as far as Sharon had, and he was still unable to speak or to swallow, and he had balance problems and weakness on one side. When his mother Teresa and I met, we formed an instant bond because of the similar circumstances that we were in. As mothers, we each knew instinctively what the other was feeling, and it was a great comfort to us both to talk together about what we were going through and to share hugs and tears.

Since Robert was still not able to talk, we gave him Sharon's old picture communication board, which she no longer needed. His family was overjoyed when their son promptly demonstrated that he could understand them and that he could still read, by pointing to the words "yes" or "no" on the board, in response to their questions. Also, they were greatly encouraged to see Sharon's progress, because it gave them hope for their son's recovery! As they saw her relearning how to walk, observed her eating, heard her voice, and saw her radiant smile, they were encouraged to believe that someday, Robert would be able to do the same. Teresa and I decided that even after our kids had left the hospital, we wanted to keep in touch with each other and let each other know how our children were progressing.

A very unique event occurred during the same week that Robert was admitted to the hospital. Sharon was asked to pose for a picture with Dr. Elizabeth Spaulding, her physiatrist. Manzano Medical Group, the doctors with whom Dr. Spaulding worked, was planning to print a brochure describing their practice, so they wanted pictures of each of their doctors treating a patient. So Sharon's hospital room was briefly turned into a photography studio, and numerous pictures were taken of Dr. Spaulding standing by Sharon's bedside exercising her arm. Dr. Spaulding is a beautiful young lady with shoulder-length blonde hair, sparkling blue eyes, and a brilliant smile, and Sharon has beautiful brown eyes, a radiant smile, and naturally curly hair, which had been cut short after her accident, giving her a "Shirley Temple" look. Together, they made a lovely picture! After the photo session was over, I remarked to Sharon, "No one who sees your picture with Dr. Spaulding will believe that you two are a doctor and her patient. They'll think that you are professional models."

Several times during Sharon's hospitalization, a family conference was held. This was a meeting that included Dr. Spaulding, all of the therapists who were working with Sharon, a member of the nursing staff, all family members who could be present, including Ernie, and also Sharon herself. Each of the medical personnel would give a report on Sharon's progress in the particular area that he or she was working on with her, and then they would set goals for the future. How thrilled we were when, during one of these conferences, Sharon's discharge date was set for October 10th. It was a joy to know that, almost three months after the accident, we would finally be going home!

September 15th was a very special day for all of us, because now that Sharon had improved in strength and stamina, we were allowed to take her on her first outing. We were only gone from the hospital for a few minutes, but we had time enough to visit Thurley, the lady in whose home we were staying, and then to stop for some chocolate ice cream. How wonderful it was to see Sharon enjoying it with us.

The following Saturday, we took Sharon on her first trip to the mall—to buy some pants with stretchy waistbands, which would be easier for her to put on, since she could not yet zip up zippers. With a little help from me, she was able to try on clothes in the dressing room and even stand up to look at herself in the mirror.

I must take a moment to comment on how amazing it was to not only eat ice cream again, but also to wear clothes that were of my own choosing. Just try to imagine, if you can, experiencing each of these for the first time in over two months!

And the following morning, Sharon was able to attend church with us for the first time since the accident. It was such a joy to have her there, and to see her praising God for sparing her life and being with her in the severe trials that she was going through. However, there was one thing that was extremely frustrating to Sharon. "Mom," she said to me, "I wish I could sing!" As my precious daughter sat next to me, quietly whispering the words to the songs, I prayed fervently that her voice would be completely restored, and that someday she would again be able to sing praises to the Lord.

Appropriately, the message, which was from Psalm 84, dealt with how we should respond to trials. The pastor said that when we go through hard times, we have two choices. Either we can "grit our teeth and bear it" and "hang on till heaven", or we can transform the trial into a joyful experience by focusing on the Lord's Presence with us. It was a great encouragement to me, and it confirmed to me two things that I had learned in desperation, and by necessity, on the day of Sharon's accident. In my overwhelming sorrow, I quickly realized that the only way that I could endure this tragedy was to focus on Jesus, rather than the circumstances, and that life is much too hard for me to live it in my own strength—I had to let Christ be my Life. Sharon was also learning these same lessons. Her radiant smile and her cheerful, thankful attitude amazed everyone around her, as they considered all that she had already endured, and the tremendous struggles that she was experiencing in doing even the simplest tasks. Often she would remark, "God is good." or "God has been good to me."

That weekend began a routine that continued until Sharon was released from the hospital. Since she had no therapy on weekends, and Ernie, Carol, Robert, Janet, and Jeremy would often come to visit then, we would take Sharon to the mall on Saturday, to church on Sunday, and also eat out together several times during the weekend. It was a wonderful relief for her to be able to leave the hospital for a while, and as she got stronger, she was finally able to go out for six or seven hours at a time.

*What a joy it was to be able to not only "go out to eat" with my family, but to also **eat** with them as well! After being unable to take anything to eat or drink by mouth for TWO MONTHS, this was especially delightful!*

In addition to giving Sharon a break from hospital life, our outings were also valuable for another reason. It gave her, and us, an opportunity to practice skills that we would need when her hospitalization was over. We learned how to transfer her from her wheelchair to the car and back again, and how to do bathroom transfers under various conditions. Also, we quickly found that the outside world is an extremely challenging obstacle course to a person with a disability—particularly someone in a wheelchair! Bathrooms, especially, were an example of these difficulties—as we encountered doors that were too narrow to allow a wheelchair to enter, and toilet stalls that were supposedly "handicapped accessible", but were too small to allow a wheelchair to turn around in them. One of the most maddening things that happened to us occurred one morning when Sharon needed to use the restroom, and I tried to take her to the bathroom in two different business establishments, only to find that in both of them, the "handicapped accessible" toilet was out of order! As a result of these experiences, we gained great understanding and empathy for those who are forced to spend their lives in wheelchairs.

Because the problems we encountered would only be evident to a person using a wheelchair, such as either not being able to turn around once inside the stall, or not being able to get into the stall to begin with, I would routinely comment that handicapped accessible stalls need to be designed by people who actually USE wheelchairs!

Besides going out with us, Sharon also had the opportunity to go on excursions that were sponsored by the recreation therapy department of the hospital. One night, we attended a performance of the musical comedy, "How to Succeed in Business Without Really Trying", that was being presented in the University of New Mexico auditorium. It was a very funny play, and Sharon thoroughly enjoyed it, but unfortunately, she was still physically unable to laugh at this point. All she could do was smile, so she spent the entire evening wearing a huge grin! Also, since her voice was still just a whisper, she was unable to make herself heard in such a noisy environment when she tried to talk to me, so she had to once again use her alphabet board to communicate. And as she sat there watching the play, her left arm and leg began aching terribly from sitting in the same position for several hours. No one had thought to tell us that a person in a wheelchair needs to shift his weight periodically to prevent a problem such as this from developing.

I thoroughly enjoyed the play though I was unable to express it through laughter. It was extremely uncomfortable not being able to shift my weight, something that the average person does automatically without even thinking about it – a concept I soon realized applied to a variety of situations.

In October, the city of Albuquerque had its famous annual hot air balloon festival. On October 9th, the night before Sharon was to be discharged from the hospital, Gina, who was one of the recreation therapists, took us to the "balloon glow." It was a beautiful sight, as colorful balloons in all kinds of imaginative shapes were illuminated in the early fall twilight. Though we had a wonderful time, I realized again, as Gina wheeled Sharon's chair along the bumpy ground from one balloon to another, what a tremendous challenge lay ahead of us.

Again, the bumpy ground would most likely have gone unnoticed by the average person without mobility impairments, but it presented a tremendous obstacle to a person using a wheelchair for locomotion! Thankfully I was traveling with people who were skilled at navigating such challenges, but I soon realized the world outside the hospital was not nearly as user-friendly.

During the last few days before Sharon was discharged from the hospital, she was given a series of neuropsychological tests. The purpose of this was to determine how her brain injury might have affected her ability to think, learn, and behave appropriately and safely. Several weeks earlier, Sydney, Sharon's speech therapist, had shown us a video that described how even a relatively minor brain injury can seriously damage these abilities. Since Sharon's brain had been severely injured, the hospital psychologists wanted to determine what problems she might experience because of her injury.

When we received the test results, on October 8th, just two days before Sharon was to leave the hospital, they were extremely discouraging. The neuropsychologist told us that Sharon had slow mental processing, difficulty in paying attention and concentrating, trouble with problem-solving, and also that she would tend to be uninhibited and impulsive, so that she might act inappropriately or put herself in danger by her actions.

However, as frightening as the report sounded, I didn't believe most of it. I did agree that Sharon was temporarily experiencing slowness in her mental processing, but I felt sure that this would improve in time. But I had not observed her having trouble with concentration or attention, and I had watched her solve some very challenging problems as she tried to cope with only having the use of one hand. And I had certainly not seen her exhibit dangerous or inappropriate behavior.

In fact, Pam, who was one of the techs who helped care for Sharon in the brain injury unit, had remarked one night, "You know, Sharon, every other patient in this ward has a yellow folder in which we record all of their inappropriate behaviors, but you don't have one of those folders. And do you know why you don't? It's because you don't have any inappropriate behaviors."

And Sharon abundantly demonstrated her ability to act appropriately in the way that she responded to the doctor's report. To our amazement, he was extremely rude to Sharon when he gave her the test results. There was one test which was particularly hard and confusing for Sharon, and on which she had done poorly. It was a card-sorting test, in which the cards had to be matched either by color, shape, or number. However, she was not told how the cards were to be matched, and as the test progressed, the way in which they were to be matched changed several times. The examiner would tell Sharon whether each answer was right or wrong, but not why she had made a mistake. When the neuropsychologist was talking with Sharon about her performance on this test, he put his face right next to Sharon's and yelled, "When the examiner kept saying 'Wrong! Wrong! Wrong!', you should have thought, 'Hello! Hello! Hello!' and realized you were making a bunch of mistakes and done something different!"

Sharon had already been discouraged by her performance on this particular test, because she realized that she hadn't done well, and now she felt insulted, humiliated, hurt, and angry as well, because of his extremely rude behavior. The following day, Sharon went and talked to Dr. Padilla, another psychologist, and reported how the neuropsychologist had treated her. Then, with sarcastic understatement, she added, "You might want to tell him to abandon that approach!" Dr. Padilla was outraged by his actions, and she agreed with Sharon wholeheartedly. As I thought about the situation, it occurred to me that it was the neuropsychologist, and not Sharon, who seemed to have a problem with inappropriate behavior.

I had been a good student prior to the accident and was already feeling down on myself for doing poorly on the test, so the neuropsychologist's inappropriate assessment of my performance merely added insult to injury, literally!

However, this maddening episode was totally overshadowed by the great joy that filled our hearts when only two days later, on October 10th, almost three months after the accident, Sharon was discharged from the hospital! The therapists did their final evaluations and gave Sharon her home exercise programs, Dr. Spaulding examined her for the last time, and we packed up Sharon's belongings and put them into the car. We also loaded up all of the paraphernalia that would be needed for Sharon's life at home as she continued her recovery—her wheelchair, her walker, a raised toilet seat, and a shower bench. After five grueling hours of travel, including several stops in which we navigated obstacle courses that were otherwise known as restrooms, we finally arrived home at ten o'clock that night. We were joyfully welcomed by Carol, Robert, Janet, Jeremy, and Ernie, who had recently moved to Durango, Colorado from Tahlequah, Oklahoma, so that he could be near Sharon as she recovered. How we all rejoiced that Sharon was home at last!

It was so encouraging to finally be home, not to mention to be greeted by my loving family! My lengthy stay in the hospital had seemed never-ending, so imagine my delight when it was finally over! However, I was now facing a challenge of a different sort – learning to live in the world outside of the hospital.

Sharon Mehesy and Eberly Mehesy

Part 3—Home At Last

Chapter 6

Sunday, October 12[th,] was a great day of rejoicing for us, as Sharon, Joe, and I joined our church family at Arriola Bible Church for the first time since the accident. Sharon spoke briefly, using a microphone. She thanked everyone for praying for her and expressed her gratitude to God for sparing her life. Then I sang "All is Well". That song had been a special blessing to me throughout all the time since the accident, as it reminded me that, no matter what happened, God was with me, and that He was in control, and that therefore, "all is well." I had sung it nearly every day as I drove to the hospital to visit Sharon. What a joy it was to be able now to sing it with Sharon sitting there in the audience smiling at me, and to share it with our dear brothers and sisters in Christ, who had upheld us so faithfully in prayer during the past three months.

However, the joy of being home again was mixed with the depressing reality that we were actually only there for a short weekend visit, before Sharon and I had to move to Farmington, New Mexico so that she could begin her outpatient therapy the following day. The next morning, after driving for an hour and a half, Sharon and I checked into the motel where we would be living while Sharon did her therapy. We had decided that we would live in Farmington during the week and come home on weekends. We planned to move to a motel in Durango several weeks later, after Sharon had regained more of her strength, so that she would be able to see Ernie, Carol, and Robert more often. After we moved to Durango, we would then make the one-hour drive from there to Farmington for therapy three times a week.

Knowing what I know now about brain injury and the lengthy recovery that follows, looking back on the above proposed scenario it seems absolutely ludicrous that we would live in a motel during the week and come home on the weekends. I was entirely too weak to gain anything from therapy while attempting to travel back and forth on the weekends, not to mention the idea that we would commute to Farmington three times a week after moving to a motel in Durango!

However, as I considered what lay ahead of us, I felt overwhelmed at the thought of caring for Sharon under those conditions. Sharon was still very weak and she tired very easily, and I was physically and emotionally exhausted from being away from home for three months and spending long hours at the hospital with her each day. How I wished that it had been possible for Sharon and me to be at home permanently. "If only the therapy that she needs were available in Cortez," I thought wistfully. But I quickly dismissed that unrealistic thought from my mind. "I want Sharon to get the best possible therapy, and if this is what it takes for her to get it, then this is what we'll have to do." I concluded.

My discouragement was greatly increased by the maddening discovery that, although we were placed in a room that was supposedly "handicapped accessible," our room was actually more like a challenging obstacle course for the disabled. We needed a bathroom that was big enough to allow a wheelchair to enter and turn around in it, and we also needed a shower that was large enough to accommodate Sharon's shower chair. However, the bathroom had such a narrow doorway that the wheelchair would not fit through it. The only way that the wheelchair could go into the bathroom was if the door was taken off! Even when Sharon used the walker, the only way she could get into the bathroom was to walk in sideways, while dragging the walker in with her, which was extremely awkward and dangerous. And the shower stall was very small also. The shower chair took up so much room in it that Sharon either had to walk backwards into the stall, or else step in sideways, and then walk around in front of the shower chair before sitting down on it. In addition to that, there was a big ceramic hump to step over, in order to enter the shower. We were extremely concerned, because these problems presented a very real safety hazard, which could cause Sharon to fall and injure herself further. Sharon and I promptly christened that motel the "Obstacle Course Motel."

In the midst of this depressing situation, there was one bright spot, however. Three of Sharon's friends from Oklahoma--Erin, Vicky, and Nate--had come for a visit, and they came over to see Sharon in Farmington. Even though they could only stay for a couple of days, it was a real encouragement to Sharon to have her friends sitting there with her in the motel room. It was wonderful to watch them eating pizza together and joking and clowning around, as one of them sat in the wheelchair, and Sharon posed behind the wheelchair, as if she were pushing it and her friend was the patient.

How amazing and touching it was to have these encouraging friends visit! They didn't treat me any differently, but simply joked and laughed with me as if nothing had changed. We took pictures of me "pushing" them in my wheelchair and once again, we used humor to combat these overwhelming circumstances.

That same day, Sharon began her outpatient therapy at Interface, the outpatient rehabilitation center there in Farmington. She was evaluated by three therapists—Sharon Hess, a speech therapist, Jami, an occupational therapist, and Traci, a physical therapist. All of them had encouraging news for us. Sharon Hess tested Sharon's visual memory by showing her drawings and then asking her to reproduce them without looking at them, and she tested Sharon's auditory memory by reading a set of numbers and having her repeat them. She also did some tests to measure Sharon's reaction time. Sharon did better on these tests than she had done while she was hospitalized, and was able to reproduce three of the five drawings correctly and to remember a sequence of six numbers, rather than only four, as she had done the last time that she was tested. When the testing was concluded, the speech therapist remarked, "You know, I don't believe that Sharon has problems with attention and concentration. She concentrated and paid attention throughout the entire testing period, and didn't get distracted, but she performed better when I was testing her at slower speeds than she did at faster speeds. I think that her main problem is slowness in mental processing, and that will get better with time, as her brain continues to heal." She also gave Sharon a computerized visual fields test to see whether or not her ability to see things that were on her left had improved, and to our great joy, it had gotten much better. In fact, that problem appeared to be almost gone.

Jami, the occupational therapist, tested Sharon's grip and found it greatly improved. She now had the ability to exert 58 pounds of pressure with her right hand and 17 pounds with her left, and her pinching strength had improved also. Then Jami gave Sharon the same visual perception test that Debbie had given Sharon at St. Joseph's. This time, rather than getting only one-third of the questions right, as she had done when she was first tested, she got all but two of them right, and then she recognized her errors and corrected them.

Traci, the physical therapist, evaluated Sharon's walking with her walker, and was impressed with the amazing progress that she had made in just three months, after such a severe injury. There was one thing on which all three therapists heartily agreed. After evaluating her, they said to us, "After looking at Sharon's medical records and then seeing her today, all we can say is that she is a walking miracle."

The following day, Sharon had her first appointment with Dr. Chiodo, the physiatrist who would be supervising her outpatient rehabilitation therapy. He tested her eyes and announced that her cranial nerves were beginning to heal and that her ability to look out with her left eye and to look down with her right eye had improved. He also decided to replace the leg and foot splint that Sharon had received at St. Joseph's with another brace, that would be individually made for her and that would be able to fit inside her left shoe. He said that she would probably have to wear it for four to eight months so that it could stretch the muscles in her left calf, ankle, and foot and bring them back to their correct position.

We told Dr. Chiodo of our plans to live in Farmington during the week so that Sharon could receive therapy and to travel home on the weekends, and to eventually move to Durango and commute to Farmington from there, and we received a tremendous surprise. "Where are you from?" he inquired.

"Cortez, Colorado," I replied.

"Well, what in the world are you doing over here?" he asked in shocked amazement. "Sharon can get all the therapy she needs right there in Cortez at Southwest Memorial Hospital. I've just started going over there twice a month to see patients, so I can still supervise her treatment. You should go home."

Sharon and I could hardly believe this wonderful news. We were actually going to be able to go home and rejoin Joe and Janet there, after three long months of being away. Sharon could live at home, in her own room, and still receive the therapy that she needed. What a marvelous answer to prayer this was. The very next day, we returned to Cortez and made arrangements for Sharon to begin therapy at the hospital there the following day. What a relief it was to pull into our driveway that afternoon---home at last! It was October 15th—three months and three days after the accident.

For the rest of that week and the first part of the following week, Sharon was evaluated by the therapists at Southwest Memorial Hospital, and they all had encouraging news to share with us. Her occupational therapist, Julie, found that Sharon's ability to track things with her eyes had improved, and that she was now able to move her eyes in all directions. She also found that Sharon's strength and range of motion in her left arm were now about three-fifths of what is normal. Rosie, her physical therapist, discovered that the range of motion and strength of Sharon's left leg had improved even more than that of her left arm—to four-fifths of normal. And Ann, her speech therapist, found out that Sharon's vocal cords were now closing completely when she hummed. The therapists agreed that Sharon needed three hours per day of therapy—one hour of each kind—five days a week. How thankful we were that we lived just nine miles drive from the hospital, and that after completing each day's exhausting therapy, Sharon could come home and rest in her own bed.

During her first few days at home, Sharon reached some significant milestones in being able to care for herself. At last, she could completely dress herself, including tying her own shoes, without help. And she could also bathe herself without assistance, (except for washing her right arm, because her left arm was still too weak to do it), and wash and fix her own hair and apply her makeup. She was now able to move around in all directions in bed, sit up, and then transfer herself from the bed to the wheelchair, and from the wheelchair to the bed, the toilet, or the car, without help. Then, within just a few days, she began using the walker, rather than the wheelchair, to move about the house and to go to the bathroom. As we observed her doing this, we rejoiced to see how her ability to stand up, to keep her balance, and to walk with her walker was steadily improving. And one morning, several days after we returned home, she found that she could stand at the sink and lean on it as she brushed her teeth, without any other support at all. And only two weeks after she was discharged from the hospital, she shaved her own legs for the very first time since the accident.

Sharon continued to make progress in her therapy also. We were especially impressed with the expertise of Rosie, her physical therapist, who had been working in that field for thirty years. Unlike most physical therapists, who work primarily on a patient's legs and feet, Rosie worked with Sharon's entire body. In addition to helping her regain her ability to walk, she was also concerned with Sharon's balance and posture, and with the many muscles throughout her body that were still in spasm. To release the tight muscles in Sharon's neck, shoulders, and trunk, Rosie spent a lot of time massaging and stretching them. And to improve her posture, Rosie had her stand in front of a mirror to see if her body was properly aligned, and then adjust her posture so that the two sides of her body were symmetrical.

*Now I'm sure when you read that Rosie was massaging my muscles, you probably thought, "Massage? I could use some therapy like that!" Rest assured that you do not want to experience **this** type of massage. My muscles were extremely tight and this massage was anything but pleasant. But, pardon the pun, this intense massage was sorely needed!* ☺

To help Sharon with her balance, Rosie had her work with a machine called the Balance Master. This machine was a computer that analyzed Sharon's balance and weight distribution as she sat, stood, and walked on a track that was similar to that of a treadmill. Because of the weakness in her left side, she had developed a pattern of compensating for it by putting most of her weight on her right foot, thus throwing her off-balance, and giving her poor posture. The Balance Master assigned exercises for her to do, to help correct the bad habits that she had acquired, and then it gave her feedback by showing her performance on its computer monitor. Sharon's goal, as she exercised, was to cause the "man" on the Balance Master's screen to go into a little box, which was the target that would be reached if she did the exercises correctly. Her actual performance was then shown by a squiggly line that told her how near or how far she was from her goal. Although Sharon worked her hardest, it was extremely difficult for her to make her body cooperate, and she rarely measured up to the standard set by the machine. It was heartbreaking for me to watch her, as she struggled to perform those simple actions that had been so totally automatic before the accident. However, as time went by, she gradually improved.

Once again, you never think about how many movements you automatically make because they are just that – automatic! You never think about how many muscles you enlist in order to stand up straight or to self-correct when your body is out of alignment.

Rosie also worked tirelessly on Sharon's left leg—using ultrasound, stretching, and heat to try to loosen up her tight calf muscles, and then had her practice walking with her walker. And, rather than having her come to therapy in the wheelchair, she required Sharon to use her walker to walk down the long corridor from the outside door to the outpatient rehab department when she arrived each day. On October 23rd, Sharon was able, for the first time, to walk back and forth between the parallel bars in the rehab department gym, while holding onto them with both hands. By the end of October, Rosie had Sharon begin practicing walking with a Quad Cane, and then later with a regular cane. And by the middle of November, Sharon was walking forward, backward, and sideways up and down the hall, while only holding onto Rosie's hands for support.

However, for safety reasons, until her strength and balance improved, Rosie advised Sharon to continue to use the walker when she was walking short distances, and to ride in the wheelchair when she had to go a longer distance. When we went to the store, though, Sharon found that she could hold onto a shopping cart instead of using her walker, and that she was also able to reach out and take items from the shelves and put them in the cart as she walked along.

In addition to practicing walking, Rosie also had Sharon working out daily on various pieces of exercise equipment. During each therapy session, Sharon would spend part of her time riding the stationary bicycle and exercising on the Total Gym, a machine on which she reclined in a slanted position and used her legs and feet to push her body up and down. All of these exercises served to increase her strength and coordination. Sometimes Rosie supervised Sharon as she worked out, but often one of her assistants—Aimee, Sena, Stacy, or Brandi would take over this part of Sharon's therapy. Sharon especially enjoyed her time with Brandi, because she and Brandi had been friends before the accident, and now their friendship was renewed as Brandi worked with her in rehab. And Stacy, who was doing her internship in physical therapy, under Rosie's supervision, soon became a valued friend also.

What fun it was to get reacquainted with Brandi through this new venue. She helped me in more ways than simply attending to me during therapy – it was so encouraging to have her support as a friend also.

In occupational therapy, Julie divided her time between working with Sharon's left arm and hand and doing cognitive therapy that was geared toward helping Sharon with the practical tasks of everyday living. She tested Sharon's ability to use a phone book, to write a check, and to do simple math problems with a calculator. Sharon had no problem with any of these tasks, and was able to do

26 math problems in 11 minutes, with no mistakes. Julie also gave her a reading comprehension test that emphasized picking out the main idea and differentiating between the main idea and the details of the selection, and Sharon did well on that test also.

Then in the middle of November, Julie came to our house to check for safety hazards and to observe Sharon in her home environment, and while Julie was there, Sharon made lunch for her. Holding onto her walker, Sharon moved about the kitchen, gathered the ingredients that she needed, and prepared a meal of grilled cheese sandwiches and cream of tomato soup. Julie remarked that Sharon had demonstrated, by her ability to successfully do more than one thing at a time, that she didn't have a problem with short-term memory, concentration, or dividing her attention between two tasks. To me, that simple lunch was some of the most delicious food that I have ever eaten, because it was the first meal that Sharon had prepared since the accident.

During occupational therapy, to help Sharon's left hand and arm, Julie had her do various activities that were designed to improve her strength, range of motion, coordination, and balance. To improve her ability to move her left arm, Julie had Sharon pick up a wooden dowel with both hands and try to raise it above her head and also move it back and forth to the left and to the right. And to help with her fine motor coordination, Sharon was given various tasks to do with her left hand—such as stringing beads, or sorting a collection of rubber washers according to size and then putting them onto wooden rods of corresponding size. Other activities included handwriting exercises, picking up little pegs and putting them in holes, pushing beans through holes into a container, and putting clothespins on a pole. To improve her strength and balance, Julie had Sharon play balloon volleyball, play catch with a small ball, and bounce it and try to make baskets with it in a miniature basket. She also had her practice keeping her balance while she was seated astride a large pillow. Even though I rejoiced to see the steady progress that Sharon was making, it was also heartrending to see my daughter, who had been a star athlete, struggling so hard just to accomplish these simple tasks.

It was very discouraging to realize that I had lost so much and struggled to perform the most basic tasks—to look at various parts of my body and recognize that they no longer obeyed my commands.

In speech therapy, Ann spent most of her time working with Sharon's voice, but she also did some cognitive testing. These tests were designed to evaluate Sharon's understanding of various concepts, such as time, space, and historical information, and to test her reading comprehension and her ability to recall the names of objects and the definitions of words. We were greatly encouraged to learn that Sharon had scored in the 99th percentile on the vocabulary test, and that her scores on all the other tests ranged between 80 percent and 95 percent. This showed that, in spite of her brain injury, she still retained the knowledge that she had accumulated prior to the accident, and was still on the mental level of a 20-year-old.

Even though Sharon could now talk, her voice was extremely soft and whispery—making it hard to hear her. Although she was no longer speaking in a monotone, her vocal range was still very limited, so she didn't have much variation in her speech. To try to help her voice improve, Ann had Sharon hum, sing simple songs, whistle, and practice reading with expression. Ann's goal was for Sharon's voice to become stronger and less breathy, to have a more natural rhythm, and to vary more in pitch, so that it could be more expressive.

I often worked with Sharon at home using some of these techniques, and before long she could hum most of the notes of the scale and sing simple songs such as "God Is So Good". We also did "echo reading", in which I would read a line from a poem with expression, and she would attempt to mimic me. However, although she improved somewhat, her voice quality was still very poor, and her range was very limited. This was very discouraging to her, because before the accident she had been involved in various kinds of drama, and she had also enjoyed singing. But now the sounds coming from her throat didn't even remotely resemble the beautiful, richly expressive voice that she used to have.

It was a devastating loss to not have the ability to convey meaning by simply using the inflection in my voice. It is difficult to describe and for anyone to imagine if they have never experienced it themselves. I had now become a "robot," only able to communicate in a monotone with no expression.

In addition to Ann, another speech therapist, Marcia, also began working with Sharon. She added diaphragmatic breathing exercises, "yelling" exercises, (although Sharon couldn't actually shout), pushing exercises, and resistance exercises, which involved pulling on a piece of TheraBand, which is made of a material resembling that in an inner tube. Although her suggestions helped some, any improvement in Sharon's voice was so gradual that it was almost imperceptible, and it continued to be one of the most discouraging aspects of her recovery.

About a month after Sharon began therapy in Cortez, her therapists informed me, gently but firmly, that it was time for me to stop doing so much for Sharon and to begin "backing off" and letting her do things for herself whenever she could. They told me that the time had come for me to leave her at the hospital for her therapy sessions, rather than staying there with her. They also said that I should quit sleeping in the same room with her, which I had been doing in case she needed help in the middle of the night, and that I should stop helping her go to the bathroom. Since it was Sharon's long-term goal to be able to once again live on her own, I knew that what they were saying was true. Also, I was overflowing with gratitude to God that Sharon's desire to live independently was now actually a realistic and attainable option. That this was even possible was nothing short of miraculous.

I believe the suggestion that my mom needed to stop sleeping in my room at night originated with me, but I was relieved to have my desire validated by my therapists, who obviously carried more weight than me at this point.

However, it was still difficult to begin "letting go" of Sharon, after coming so close to losing her. Although my desire to protect her from any further injury was very strong, I also realized that it was beyond my ability to do that, and that I must leave her safety in God's Hands. "After all," I reasoned, "I couldn't protect her from the accident in the first place, so I certainly can't keep her safe now. I'll just have to trust God to do that." And several days later, I saw this truth illustrated when Sharon fell as she was attempting to transfer herself from her bed to her wheelchair. Fortunately, she merely sat down hard on the floor and didn't hit her head or injure herself in any way. How I praised the Lord for protecting her.

Another area that created tension between us during this time was my desire to encourage Sharon to concentrate on speaking as loudly as she was able to, on using her left arm and hand whenever possible, and on faithfully doing the homework that each of her therapists assigned to her. Although my desire was to remind her to do things that would help in her recovery, I found it very difficult to walk the fine line between encouraging her and what she interpreted as nagging. Unfortunately, there were many times when Sharon felt that I had crossed that line, even though I didn't realize that I had. And if I asked her to speak more loudly because I was having difficulty hearing her, Sharon was convinced that either I wasn't listening to her, or that I was becoming slightly deaf. So, as time passed, I learned that I had to let Sharon take the responsibility for her own recovery, and for deciding when, and if, she would do her exercises.

*This time was definitely taxing on our relationship as I felt my mom was on my case all the time to do my exercises. I also felt that when she asked me to repeat myself or to speak more loudly, she was merely not paying attention. I was reluctant to do my home exercise program because I felt that therapy was already occupying most of my time and therefore that was **all** I was doing. I was still a twenty year old young woman who wanted to have a life.*

Even though it seemed as though therapy consumed all of Sharon's time in the days following her discharge from the hospital, she did manage to fit in some fun also. At least once a week, she went to Durango to spend time with Ernie, Carol, and Robert. And on Halloween, she was invited to a party at her friend Brandi's house. She decided to dress up as a cat, and she designed and made her own costume. She wore a black turtleneck with black pants, and she made "ears" out of construction paper, which she attached to a headband and wore on her head. For her "tail", she stuffed black socks into a pair of black panty hose and tied it around her waist. And for the finishing touch, she used eye pencil to draw whiskers on her face and lipstick to make her nose pink. And she discovered that she could purr. I thought that I had never seen such a cute "cat", and I was thrilled to see how creative Sharon had been in coming up with her costume.

Sharon also began trying to resume some of the hobbies that she had enjoyed before the accident. She had always liked baking, and less than two weeks after she got out of the hospital, she decided to make chocolate chip cookies. She was able to read and follow the directions without any problems, and even doubled the recipe in her head, so that she could make twice as many cookies as it normally made. The cookies were absolutely delicious, and she took some of them with her to rehab and shared them with her therapists, who were all astounded, when they learned that she had made them herself. A few days later, she made a rhubarb pie, with the same delectable results.

Another encouraging development took place when Sharon decided to write to some of her friends and was able, on November 7th, to write the first letter that she had written since the accident. It was an excruciatingly slow process, because her left hand wouldn't cooperate and it was also hard for her to apply the correct amount of pressure to the keyboard, even with her right hand. This often resulted in her typing a whole string of identical characters where she had meant to type just one. However, in spite of the difficulties, she finally managed to complete the letter by "hunting and pecking."

However, not all of Sharon's attempts to engage in activities that she had formerly loved to do were so successful. One day toward the end of October, she decided that she would try to make an ankle bracelet. Before the accident, Sharon had been very skilled in creating beautiful necklaces out of hemp or waxed linen, by using macramé knots. This day, I helped her to cut the lengths of cord that she needed, and she managed to tie a knot on the end of them, put a bead on them, and then tie another knot. However, no matter how hard she tried, she was unable to continue any further with it, because her left hand was not yet coordinated enough to handle the long cords and tie the knots.

After giving up in frustration, she then tried to play her flute, which had always been a comfort to her when she was upset—only to find that although she could still produce a good tone, she was unable to do the fingering with her left hand. That day was a very depressing day for Sharon, as she struggled fruitlessly to make her body obey her commands and then realized how very limited her abilities still were. My heart ached for her as I saw her sadness and frustration.

*I wrestled with utter discouragement and disillusionment as I continually bumped up against my numerous losses on any given day. This day was especially difficult when I attempted to soothe myself by using formerly loved activities—only to discover I now no longer possessed the ability to perform **any** of them!*

Another source of tremendous sorrow to Sharon during this time was the steady deterioration of her relationship with Ernie. Although he had moved all the way from Oklahoma to Durango, Colorado to be near Sharon as she recovered, we all began to notice that he was calling less and less frequently, and that when he did call, he would only talk to her for five or ten minutes. Also, he always seemed to be "too busy" to make the hour's drive from Durango to our house to visit Sharon. And on November 2nd, the night of his birthday, he called and said that he was just "too tired" to come over and pick Sharon up and take her to his party. Because I knew how much Sharon wanted to be there, I was the one who finally took her to Durango, so that she could go to his birthday celebration.

I couldn't help contrasting Ernie's actions that day with his behavior in the weeks immediately following the accident, when he had called daily and talked to Sharon, even though she couldn't yet speak, and when he had made several thousand-mile trips, just to be by her side. Sharon was angered and deeply hurt that he seemed to be losing interest in her, and I was extremely shocked and confused by his uncaring attitude toward her. I had thought that since he had been so loving and caring to her during her hospitalization, he would remain faithful and committed to her during the long process of her recovery.

I soon became aware Ernie was pulling away from me and that our relationship was ending, despite everything we had been through already. I would recount to him the story my mom had told me about the morning of the accident when they called his parents in an attempt to get in touch with him. Fred, Ernie's father had answered the phone and when they told him of the accident and my subsequent injuries, he began crying and said, "Sharon is just like our daughter." Each time I would tell him the story in an effort to elicit some type of emotion, he would respond with irritation, "Well how do you think I felt?" But I never had the courage to say, "I don't know because you have never told me."

While Sharon had been at St. Joseph's, the staff there had shared with us a sobering statistic regarding the ability of romantic relationships to survive the trauma of a serious injury to one of the parties involved. They had said that, following a severe accident in which a woman is injured, 90 percent of men will leave their partner, even if they are married. They also told us that if the man was the one injured, a much greater percentage of women will continue in the relationship. I had always thanked the Lord that Ernie was one of the minority of men who would stay with their partner, but now I was beginning to wonder if he might be one of the majority instead. How I prayed that he wouldn't leave Sharon, after all that she had been through. My own heart broke as I thought of the terrible heartbreak that she would suffer if that should happen.

As November dragged on, Sharon became more and more aware of the seriousness of her injury and the extent of her disabilities. She also faced up to the fact that it was uncertain if she would ever fully recover and be able to do all of the things that she had enjoyed doing before the accident. In addition to dealing with these sobering realities and the daily frustration of struggling to do even the simplest tasks, she also sensed the heartrending possibility that her three-year relationship with Ernie might be coming to an end.

The combination of all of these factors caused her to become extremely depressed and at times to even talk about suicide, although she admitted that it would be a real waste to kill herself after all that she had been through. Many times she asked angrily, "Why did God cause my accident? I had a great life! I was doing well in school, I loved playing sports and acting, and Ernie and I were planning to get married next summer. And why did God force me to live, if I'm going to be so disabled? I wish that I had died in the accident! I would have been better off, and so would Ernie. He deserves someone with two good arms and two good legs—not a cripple."

*I would often angrily demand to know, "Why did God **cause** my accident?!?" To which my mom would calmly respond, "God didn't **cause** your accident. He **allowed** it." I would always say, "Cause/allow, semantics! Same thing! He could have prevented it, but he didn't!"*

I spent much of this time in the depths of despair as I routinely compared myself to who I had been and no longer was. Depression is a strange animal...you think you are indulging yourself by feeling bad, but before you know it, you have been caught in this monster's suffocating stranglehold of emotions and escape seems virtually impossible.

It broke my heart to hear Sharon talk like that, because I was so very thankful that her life had been spared, and that we still had her. And I had no answers to her "why" questions either. For myself, I had learned that there are no good answers to questions like that, and that I couldn't even allow myself to ask them. Instead, in times of deep trial and sorrow, the only way that I was able to survive was to focus on Jesus and to recognize that since I know that He is trustworthy, I don't have to understand His purpose in allowing a tragedy to happen. I sought to share these truths with Sharon, but she wasn't in any mood to accept them. She was too depressed and too angry with God. All I could do was cry with her and pray for her and hold her in my arms as she wept. And in my own prayers, I begged God, through my tears, not to allow us to lose her through suicide, after she had survived the accident and made such a miraculous recovery.

Sharon's therapists noticed her depression also, and they recommended that she begin meeting with Carolyn, a social worker who was trained in crisis counseling. Talking to Carolyn and sharing her thoughts and feelings with her was a real help to Sharon. Carolyn gave Sharon her pager number and told her that she wanted her to call anytime that she had suicidal thoughts, which Carolyn referred to as "stinkin' thinkin'" She also suggested to Sharon that she should keep a journal and write down her feelings, and that she should join a support group, where she could interact with others who had had similar experiences.

Since there wasn't a brain injury support group in the Cortez area, Sharon's therapists developed a creative alternative. There was a young man named Leo who had suffered a traumatic brain injury (TBI) in a car accident two years before Sharon's injury, and he was also undergoing therapy at Southwest Memorial Hospital. Sharon's therapists suggested that he and Sharon could meet together weekly with Marcia, the speech therapist, and share their experiences and their feelings, as well as receive speech therapy. This weekly meeting became a real encouragement to Sharon, as she was finally able to interact with someone who truly understood her emotions. When she told Leo that she wished that she had died in the accident, he responded, "I used to feel that way too, Sharon, but I don't anymore. Now I'm glad I'm still alive." As she talked to Leo, Sharon began to see a tiny glimmer of light at the end of the long tunnel of depression that she was in, although she continued to have many dark days.

*It was a relief to finally talk with someone who had an experience similar to mine. It was nice to be able to express my feelings and to have the other person say, "Yeah, I know what you mean." It was so encouraging to hear Leo say, "I **used** to feel that way, but I don't anymore." I was so thankful to Carolyn and Marcia for listening to me and not judging me.*

Another experience that enabled Sharon to gain a different perspective on her injury was meeting Shelly, another patient at outpatient rehab. Shelly was the same age as Sharon, and she had sustained a brain injury four years previously, when she was only sixteen years old. Even though it had been so long since her accident, she was still confined to a wheelchair, and she had uncontrollable muscle movements, like a person with cerebral palsy. She needed total care, she could only say a few words, and her short-term memory was so bad that she couldn't remember what had happened the previous day. And it appeared that she would be in that condition for the rest of her life. As Sharon observed Shelly, she realized that, in spite of the struggles she faced, she still had a lot to be thankful for.

I knew I still had a lot to be thankful for, but this did not negate the losses I had suffered. I needed to find a way to grieve the multitude of losses I had experienced and then find a way to move forward. I finally found a forum for this grieving process in my sessions of psychotherapy many years later. I cannot stress the vital importance of psychotherapy enough here. I would not be where I am today without the patient listening ear of Pam, my psychotherapist and her ability to steer me through the maze of emotions I desperately needed to navigate.

Chapter 7

On November 18th, we took Sharon to Albuquerque to see the ear, nose, and throat specialist and the neuro-ophthalmologist. Dr. Carlow, the eye doctor, found that the vision in both of Sharon's eyes had improved, and that she could now read with her right eye without a lens. He also repeated the visual field test that he had previously given her, and we were delighted to find out that her ability to see things on the left had almost returned to normal. The only remaining area of impairment was very far up and to the left—a direction in which most people don't look very often anyway. Sharon's ability to look outward with her left eye had also improved, but her right eye's ability to look downward had not gotten any better. Dr. Carlow said that her inability to look down with her right eye was the cause of her continuing double vision, and that if it had not improved by nine months after the accident, she would require surgery to correct the double vision. He then tried putting a prism lens on the right lens of her glasses to see if it would help her double vision, but it didn't help. Dr. Carlow also informed us that, after studying her CT scan, he was amazed that she hadn't suffered more damage to her vision due to the extensive hemorrhaging in that area of her brain. Once again, we thanked God for His miraculous intervention on Sharon's behalf.

Later that day, as Dr. Ray, the ear, nose, and throat specialist, examined Sharon's vocal cords, she was amazed at the progress that Sharon had made. "I've never seen anyone with an injury this severe make such rapid progress as Sharon has made!" she exclaimed. She explained to us that Sharon's right vocal cord now appeared normal, and that her left cord was also working, although it was still weak. "Sharon's vocal cords are both vibrating, and they are almost meeting, but there is still a two millimeter gap between them. The air that is escaping between her vocal cords is causing her voice to be breathy and hoarse," she explained. "With time, I believe that her voice will return to normal."

I have to note here what actually happens when an ear nose throat doctor examines (or "scopes") one's vocal chords. To the lay person the idea of scoping doesn't mean much and you probably think if they are going to look at your vocal chords they would likely stick the scope in your mouth. I thought this as well, so I was shocked when they stuck a tiny camera on a cord up my nose, dangled it at the back of my throat, and then instructed me not to swallow. Not an easy task, I must tell you, especially since the swallow response is primarily a reflex!

While we were in Albuquerque, we stopped by St. Joseph's Rehab Hospital so that Sharon could visit her former doctor, therapists, and nurses, and they were all amazed at the marvelous progress that she had made. We also had a chance to see Robert, the young man who had occupied the room next to Sharon in the brain injury unit there. It was a great joy to see that he was not only improving physically, but that he was also mentally on an adult level, just like Sharon. It was wonderful to see Teresa, Robert's mother, again also. We embraced like old friends and eagerly shared with each other the latest developments in our children's recoveries. Teresa was greatly encouraged to see how much progress Sharon had made since she had left the hospital, and we rejoiced with her in the good news that she was finally going to be able to take Robert home from St. Joe's the following day.

Again, I knew I had very much to be thankful for and I knew that I was doing remarkably well compared to others who were in similar situations. However, since I was the one experiencing it, my progress seemed anything but fast. Looking back and knowing what I know now, I can definitely say I made an amazingly speedy recovery, but it sure didn't feel like it while I was going through it!

Since Ernie had made the trip to Albuquerque with us, albeit reluctantly--at Sharon's insistence, and the next day, November 19th, was the third anniversary of the day that he and Sharon had started dating, we planned a special celebration for them. We took them to dinner at the Olive Garden, one of Sharon's favorite restaurants, and made sure that they were seated together at a table far across the room from where we were sitting. We assumed that they would enjoy being alone, so we were shocked when Ernie acted as if he would prefer that we all sat at the same table, rather than separately. Although he finally agreed to the seating arrangement that we suggested, and Sharon enjoyed the evening, Ernie seemed less than enthusiastic about their "date." Once again, we were puzzled and saddened by Ernie's strange behavior.

Again, I was keenly aware that Ernie was pulling away from me and I longed to prevent the impending separation. Tragically, there was no way to stop this from happening and since I knew it was happening now, the only question was not if, but when.

On the way back from Albuquerque, we stopped in Farmington, New Mexico, and Sharon had an appointment with Phyllis, who was a voice specialist that was recommended to us by Sydney, who had been Sharon's speech therapist when she was at St. Joe's. Phyllis is Sydney's friend, and former teacher, and is one of the top ten voice specialists in the United States, and Sydney felt that if anyone could help Sharon's voice, Phyllis would be able to do so. After evaluating Sharon, Phyllis told us that she had difficulties in two areas that affect speech—with respiration and with the vocal cords themselves, although her articulation was quite good. She said that the difficulties were a result of nerve damage and muscle weakness, as well as some atrophy due to lack of use during the time when Sharon was unable to make a sound. She also said that Sharon was probably unable to discern and adjust how loudly she was speaking, because the part of her brain that knew how to do this had probably been "wiped clean" by the injury and had lost the ability to do it. She said that she wanted to use a scope to look at Sharon's vocal cords, and that she could do this in Durango at the office of Dr. Wiley, an ear, nose, and throat specialist there. We were very impressed with Phyllis' expertise, and also thankful that Sharon would no longer have to travel to Albuquerque to see an ear, nose, and throat doctor, since there was one in Durango.

Phyllis then told Sharon that she needed to do breathing exercises and lip, tongue, and mouth exercises, and to consciously try to talk loudly and to concentrate on articulating her words—even to the point of exaggeration. Phyllis had also wanted to work with Sharon on strengthening her vocal cords and neck muscles, but she was unable to do so, because just the week before, a neck x-ray that Sharon had revealed an injury that had been missed by all the doctors. She had a fracture of the seventh, (and lowest), neck vertebra, which is known as C-7. Fortunately, though, the bone itself wasn't completely broken. It just had a chip broken off of it, on the outside of the bone, so her spinal cord was not in danger. The chip was free-floating, and there was nothing the doctor could do to treat it. Dr. Chiodo said that it would heal on its own, with time. However, he did advise Sharon to be very careful not to fall, or even to sit down too hard, and also restricted some of the exercises that she was allowed to do in therapy. So Phyllis was unable to do the strengthening exercises that she had wanted to do with Sharon until they were approved by the doctor.

Phyllis also told us that if Sharon's voice didn't improve within a year after the accident, there were a few surgical possibilities that might help her. One was to take a small piece of fat from another area of Sharon's body and transplant it into Sharon's weaker vocal cord—thus literally making it "fatter", so that it could touch the other cord more easily. Another option would be to surgically move the left cord closer to the right one. Both of these operations sounded horribly painful and risky to me, so I prayed fervently that Sharon's voice would continue to improve so that no surgery would be necessary. And when Phyllis scoped Sharon's vocal cords on December 11th, we received the marvelous news that her vocal cords had dramatically improved. They were now working normally, and the paralysis and weakness were gone from both cords. Dr. Wiley said that Sharon no longer needed the services of an ear, nose, and throat specialist, and that surgery wouldn't be needed after all.

However, even though Sharon's vocal cords now appeared normal, her voice was still far from restored. Phyllis said that Sharon needed to continue working on the various exercises that she had given her, and that hopefully, with time and practice, her voice would improve. Phyllis was eager to consult with the speech therapists at Southwest Memorial Hospital, and give them her suggestions for Sharon's treatment. However, although one of them was open to Phyllis' advice, the other one was not. She acted insulted that we even suggested such a thing, and absolutely refused to take any direction from Phyllis. Although I tried to point out to her that we didn't doubt her ability, but merely wanted to involve Phyllis in Sharon's care, since she is a voice specialist, she was still adamantly opposed to receiving any input from Phyllis. After seeking the help of her supervisor in the situation, we still remained at an impasse, so we eventually had to request that this speech therapist should discontinue treating Sharon, and that Sharon should begin seeing a different speech therapist instead. It saddened us that a speech therapist would allow pride and professional jealousy to interfere with what was best for Sharon, her patient, and that she also deprived herself of a wonderful opportunity to learn from someone else who was an expert in her field.

Although Sharon's physical therapy enabled her to make steady improvement in her ability to walk, it was still not enough to correct the problems that she had with her left leg and foot. She also needed an ankle brace to stretch her tight calf muscle and bring her foot back to its proper position. A week after we returned home from Farmington, Joe took Sharon back there to get the brace that had been designed to correct this problem. However, from the moment that she began wearing it, it began causing another difficulty. Although it held Sharon's leg, ankle and foot in a better position, and enabled her walking to improve, it was so poorly designed that it pressed on Sharon's foot and irritated it, creating red marks that Rosie said could soon cause Sharon's skin to break down and develop open sores. Although numerous adjustments and changes were made to the brace during the next month, this problem was never completely corrected, and Sharon was never able to wear it for an extended period of time.

The people who made the brace were insistent that there was no problem with it. After numerous trips back and forth to

Farmington – an hour and a half one way - for adjustments, each time they would tell me that the problem was with me, not the splint. While I was seated on the exam table, they would point to the gap between my ankle and the splint saying, "Look at all that space." I tried futilely to explain that the gap was no longer there once I stood up and put weight on it.

Finally, Dr. Chiodo, Sharon's physiatrist, decided that the splint was not going to be able to correct Sharon's problem after all. He said that Sharon needed serial casting of her leg to stretch the muscles and force her foot back into the correct position. He explained that he would stretch Sharon's muscles as far as possible and then he would put her leg and foot in a cast to hold them in that position. A week later, he would remove that cast, stretch her muscles a bit more, and put on a new cast. After this process was repeated three or four times, and the final cast was removed, her leg and foot should then stay in the correct position.

On the afternoon of December 4th, the first cast was put on Sharon's leg. First, Dr. Chiodo numbed her leg with Novocain, and then he did three nerve blocks to cause the muscles to relax. He said that the nerve blocks would last for 6 to 12 months, and that, hopefully, by that time, her muscles would no longer be in spasm. After the nerve blocks were done, Rosie used ultra-sound on Sharon's leg and applied heat to it while stretching the muscles as much as possible. Then Dr. Chiodo put the cast on and he then gave Sharon a cast shoe to wear over it, in addition to a plastic shower bag to put over the cast to protect it from getting wet when she took a shower.

The cast was extremely uncomfortable, however, and put a lot of pressure on Sharon's ankle and toes. Since her toes were still in spasm, the cast made the pain worse, and I would often reach in under the cast and massage the bottom of her foot to try to relieve the muscle spasms. Sharon soon found that it was almost impossible for her to walk with the cast on, because in addition to the ankle and toe pain that she was experiencing, the cast also caused her knee to "lock", so that she couldn't walk normally. She soon found herself once again confined to the wheelchair most of the time, and this made her feel as if she had experienced a major setback in her recovery. Her ankle also began to swell, and it finally reached a point where we had to go to the emergency room and have the doctor there cut a "window" in the cast and remove the part of it that was pressing on her ankle. This relieved some of the pressure, but the cast was still extremely uncomfortable.

Extremely uncomfortable—to put it mildly! I felt I had lost some of my independence as I was once again relegated to the wheelchair. Imagine going from finally being able to walk again, unaided, to being forced back into the wheelchair – dependent on others for mobility. Miserable indeed!

After two very miserable weeks, Sharon's cast was finally removed and replaced with another one, only to encounter the same problem which required another trip to the ER to have a "window" cut in the new cast. About ten days later, that cast was removed, and replaced with the third, and final, cast. And at last, on January 2, 1998, after a very long depressing month of painful discomfort and extremely limited mobility for Sharon, the final cast was taken off, and Dr. Chiodo pronounced the treatment a success. What a wonderful day of rejoicing that was!

However, even though the treatment was successful, Sharon would still need to wear a brace on her left leg for many months. At first, her skin was too irritated and her ankle was too sore and swollen from the cast to tolerate the brace, but the day finally came when she was able to wear it consistently. The brace was too large to fit inside a shoe that was Sharon's regular size, so we ended up buying two pairs of shoes, and using one from each pair—the left shoe from the larger pair and the right shoe from the smaller one.

Sharon continued to have another problem also. The muscles in her left leg and foot were still in spasm, causing the toes on her left foot to curl under, and making it impossible for her to straighten them. This was very painful, and also kept her from being able to walk normally. Dr. Chiodo informed us that he could inject Botox, which is made from botulism toxin, into the muscles of her left leg and foot to cause them to relax so that her toes could function normally. However, he decided to wait for a month or two before doing that, to see if the brace would help to correct the problem.

In spite of these hindrances, though, Sharon's walking improved enough so that she was able to use a cane, rather than a walker, for going short distances, though she continued to use the wheelchair when she had to go longer distances. On January 12th, 1998, six months after the accident, we celebrated her progress in this area by returning the walker to the medical supply company, which had rented it to us, because she no longer needed it.

On December 10th, at the suggestion of Dr. Chiodo and her therapists, Sharon went to Farmington and had an appointment with Dr. Sherrill, a neuropsychologist. He gave her a battery of tests to determine how her brain injury would affect her ability to study when she returned to college, as she hoped to do the following fall. She was tested on her ability to define words, to draw pictures that she was shown, to remember stories that she was told, to arrange pictures in the right order to tell a story, and to match cards that were similar. She was also given an attention test and a personality test.

Several weeks later, we returned to Dr. Sherrill's office and received the results of Sharon's testing. "I've got some good news for you," Dr. Sherrill began. "Sharon's verbal skills and her memory are basically intact. That will be a tremendous help to her when she goes back to school. However, due to the damage to the right hemisphere of her brain, her visual-spatial skills have been affected, and she's also having some problems with attention, problem-solving, organization, initiation of activities, and speed of mental processing. And the personality test showed that she is depressed and has been having some suicidal thoughts."

He then told us how these problems might affect her performance in college. "Sharon's impairment in the visual-spatial area may affect her ability to learn things visually," he explained, "and her difficulty with attention and her slowness in mental processing may make it hard for her to focus on a lecture in class. Her initiation problems may interfere with her ability to begin tasks, and her decreased problem-solving ability may prevent her from thinking of more than one solution to a problem. In practical terms, Sharon may find it more difficult to find a theme in a piece of literature, to make an outline, or to write an essay or answer essay questions."

As you can imagine, I was more than reluctant to see another neuropsychologist following my traumatic experience with the doctor in Albuquerque, but was pleasantly surprised by the encouraging, kind report given by Dr. Sherrill!

"However," he continued, "all of these problems can be helped with therapy, practice, and medication. Sharon's therapists can give her exercises that will help her, and there are many excellent computer programs that can be used to retrain her in all of these areas. Consistent practice is the key. In fact, it would be good for Sharon to work on the computer for a couple of hours a day to improve her skills in attention, concentration, response time, visual-spatial skills, and problem solving. Also, I'm going to prescribe two medications for Sharon. I want her to take the antidepressant nortriptyline to help combat her depression, and amantadine to stimulate her brain and help her overcome some of the problems that have been caused by her injury. And I believe that it will be very helpful to Sharon if she audits a college course during the spring semester, to prepare her for returning to school next fall."

"Two more things," he concluded, "I would strongly recommend that Sharon receive neuropsychological counseling on a regular basis. This will help her to cope with the emotional pain that she's experiencing as she deals with her injury, and to learn about strategies that she can use to compensate for her deficits when she goes back to college. Also, Sharon and Ernie need to go to couples' counseling to work through the problems that they are having in their relationship because of the accident. I know of an excellent neuropsychologist in Durango—Dr. Ed Cotgageorge, who could help in both of these areas. Since you live closer to Durango than to Farmington, it would probably be more practical for Sharon to begin seeing him, instead of coming back here to me."

From that time on, some changes were made in Sharon's therapy. Rather than going to each therapy five days per week, she now went only three times to each one. This gave her more time to work on the computer exercises at home, to practice doing things for herself in preparation for the time that she would be living independently again, and to do the homework that each therapist assigned her. It was a great relief to Sharon to have her therapy sessions reduced, because being involved in such intensive therapy had totally drained her energy, leaving her with no strength for other activities.

What a relief to have my therapies reduced – to now have free time that I could devote to achieving my ultimate goal of once again living independently!

Another change involved her speech therapy. Sharon began going to Donna, a speech therapist who specializes in cognitive therapy, as well as continuing to go to Marcia for voice therapy. Donna worked with her on practical tasks such as filling out a checkbook register, figuring the balance, making a budget, and reading maps. She also read and discussed literature with her. Together, they studied the book The Bridge at San Luis Rey, since Sharon had been an English Education major before the accident, and she hoped to continue with her plans to become an English teacher. At each session, Donna gave Sharon a reading assignment, and had her take notes on it, look up unfamiliar words in the dictionary, and answer questions about it. Then, when Sharon went to therapy the next time, Donna gave her comprehension questions to answer, had her make inferences from what she had read, and talked with her about the meaning of the story.

It was a real challenge for Sharon to do this, because in addition to the learning difficulties that she now had, she also had vision problems that made it very hard for her to read. In addition to her continuing double vision, she also struggled with tiny flickering movements of her left eye that made it difficult to focus on what she was reading. However, she found that if she held the book at eye level rather than in her lap, the eye movements were not as bad.

In occupational therapy, Julie also began doing cognitive therapy with Sharon. She assigned her essay questions to do as homework, and Sharon wrote short papers on such subjects as "an event that changed my life", "how my life is different now than it was five years ago", and "my first job". And one day, she gave Sharon an actual college writing assignment that one of the aides in the rehab department had been given in a class that she was taking. To our great joy, Sharon's writing proved that she was still a very able and articulate writer. Julie also came to our house to help Joe install some cognitive therapy programs on our computer and to teach Sharon how to use them. From that time on, Sharon was able to do a lot of her cognitive therapy at home.

Even Rosie, Sharon's physical therapist, participated in her cognitive therapy by taking Sharon out to lunch to discuss literature with her daughter who was also an English Education major and who was home from college for the Thanksgiving holidays. We really appreciated the personal interest that all of Sharon's therapists showed in her, and the fact that they treated her not just as a patient, but as a friend. As Sharon worked on her therapy with them, she often confided her emotional struggles to them and related the latest difficulties in her relationship with Ernie, and was always assured of finding a caring, listening ear and receiving some wise advice.

I was deeply touched by how involved my therapists became in my recovery. I appreciated the opportunity to discuss English literature with Rosie's daughter very much and it truly made me feel as if I was going to recover from my injury!

Thanksgiving that year was a really special day for me, because in spite of all that we'd been through, we had so much to be thankful for. I took a few minutes that day to write down in my journal the things that I was grateful to God for. "Thanksgiving Day!" I wrote, "We have a lot to be thankful for! Sharon is still alive and is recovering well and making good progress! She's not in a coma anymore, and she isn't in a persistent vegetative state. She isn't on a lower mental level than she was before the accident. She has her personality, her intellect, her understanding, and most of her memory. Her mind is intact, even though her brain has been damaged, and she is still struggling with some of the physical effects of her injury. She isn't paralyzed in any way, and the only broken bone that she has is a small piece that is broken off of her seventh cervical vertebra, and fortunately this poses no danger to her spinal cord. Thank You, Father, for all that You've done!"

Several films that we watched during the holiday season also reminded us of how wonderfully God had intervened in Sharon's life to spare her from so many things that could have happened to her as a result of her injury and also to heal her. One night, we watched the film "Coma", which was a documentary on brain injuries. The film depicted several patients with brain injuries being treated with procedures similar to those that Sharon had undergone soon after the accident, and then followed them throughout their recoveries. Though we had told Sharon of the treatments that she had received immediately following her injury, it was helpful to her to see similar situations portrayed in the film. It was also encouraging for her to see a college-age girl who had a severe traumatic brain injury (TBI), and who had struggled with some of the same feelings that Sharon was experiencing, now living a normal life again just two years after her accident.

As we viewed the film, we also found a new reason to be thankful. We learned that inserting an intra-cranial pressure (ICP) monitor into the brain of a patient with a brain injury, as Dr. White had done for Sharon, to monitor the swelling of her brain, was an essential life-saving procedure. However, even though it can make the difference between life and death, or between the patient's returning to a productive life instead of being left in a persistent vegetative state, it is done in only about thirty percent of the hospitals nationwide. Just one month before Sharon's accident, Dr. White had moved to Durango from Los Angeles, where he had been a level-one trauma surgeon in an emergency room for five years, bringing his knowledge of this technology with him. And

Sharon was the first patient in Durango on which an intra-cranial pressure monitor had ever been used! My knees felt weak as I realized what might have happened to Sharon if God had not had Dr. White there at just the right time to treat her!

I am very grateful for Dr. White's presence in Durango, when I needed him most, and for his knowledge. How amazing to learn that I was the first patient in Durango to receive an ICP monitor, not to mention the astonishingly small percentage of patients who receive this vital form of treatment nationally!

Two other films reminded us that Sharon could have been left with much more severe consequences of the injury than she was. As we watched the film "Joni", which tells the story of Joni Eareckson Tada, who was paralyzed in a diving accident at age seventeen and has been confined to a wheelchair for the past thirty years, we praised God that Sharon didn't remain paralyzed. And as we viewed a film called "Erin", that traces the recovery of a young woman from the time of her traumatic brain injury until three years after her accident, we were filled with thanksgiving that Sharon still had her mental capabilities. Although Erin made a good recovery physically, her mental abilities were much less than they had been before the accident. She had severe memory problems and emotional difficulties, she didn't make sense when she talked, her personality had changed, and she needed constant supervision. How thankful we were that Sharon was still the same delightful person that she had been, and that she could realistically look forward to living independently again within just a few more months!

The holidays were an enjoyable time for Sharon, as some of her friends from the church youth group were home from college for Christmas. Livi, Gary, Joel, and Jarrod came over from time to time to visit, or to take Sharon out for a movie, dinner, or some other activity, and Sharon went over to Livi's house several times to hang-out and enjoy some "girl-talk." And in the middle of December, she had some very special guests. Two good friends from Oklahoma, Tera and Angie, who were her former roommates, came and spent several days with her—sharing the latest happenings in their lives, watching movies and playing games with her, and taking her to Durango to visit Ernie, Carol, and Robert.

*What true friends Tera and Angie were! They drove all the way from Oklahoma to spend time with me after my accident, multiple times. Their friendship reassured me that in spite of the serious injuries I had sustained, they still saw **me** and I had hope that I would fully recover!*

Christmas that year was a very special time for our family. Having Sharon still with us was the most wonderful present that we could have, and having Paul and Nancy come from Pennsylvania for a visit was an added joy. However, for Sharon, the joy of Christmas was mixed with deep sorrow, because Ernie didn't even come over for a visit on Christmas Day. When she confronted him about it the following day and asked if he wanted to continue in a relationship with her, he mumbled, "I just need some "space"— that's all." But his half-hearted response did nothing to ease her aching heart.

Fortunately, the New Year's holiday was more enjoyable for Sharon. Two more friends, Johnny and Rieko, came from Oklahoma for a visit. And on New Year's Eve, Ernie came and took Sharon to Durango for an evening of live music and "wheelchair dancing"--as Sharon was confined to her wheelchair since her foot was still in a cast. So as New Year's Day of 1998 dawned, Sharon was surrounded by a loving group of family and friends—Ernie, Carol, Robert, Janet, Jeremy, Rieko, and Johnny. And best of all, Sharon and Ernie were finally able to have a good talk about the problems in their relationship, and Ernie agreed to go see a counselor with her.

New Year's Eve was so much fun as I was wheeled around the dance floor and received kisses from multiple strangers! Ernie made the observation, "You are like a beacon! That is why everyone is drawn to you." The most humorous incident of the evening happened shortly after midnight as an old cowboy sauntered over to me asking if I had been kissed yet. I quickly responded with, "Yes!" hoping that he would accept this answer *and move on, but he casually drawled, "Well, **I** haven't!" and he proceeded to kiss me! I was mortified, while Ernie was highly amused!*

On New Year's Day, 1998, I heaved a great sigh of relief that 1997, which had been the worst year of my life, was finally over, and thanked God that He had seen me through that horrendous year. However, I also realized that, as awful that as it had been, it could have been much, much worse. And I was extremely grateful for the many blessings that the Lord had given us, even in the midst of our trials. But as I looked ahead to what 1998 would hold, I couldn't help but breathe a prayer that it would be a better year than the previous year had been and hope that my prayer would be answered.

One of Sharon's major goals for the year 1998 was to be able to live on her own again. She had desired to move to Durango and begin living independently again on January 2nd, but since the final cast was not taken off her foot until that day, that proved to be impossible. At a family meeting in December, all of Sharon's therapists agreed that there were several criteria that would determine when Sharon would be ready to leave home. She had to be able to walk well with a cane, rather than using a walker. She would also have to be capable of performing the many daily activities involved in caring for herself and for the place where she would live. And it would have to be determined that it was now safe for her to live on her own, without supervision. The therapists felt that it would be Valentine's Day at the earliest before these three important conditions could be met.

However, Sharon disagreed. She was eager to live in Durango, so that she and Ernie could spend more time together and work out the problems in their relationship. Also, the spring semester was just beginning at Fort Lewis College in Durango, where she planned to attend school the next fall, and she wanted to audit a class in Classical Literature there. She set the end of January as a target date for her move, and she began to work diligently toward this goal. She began making meals for herself and for our whole family—preparing such things as biscuits and gravy for breakfast;

bacon, lettuce, and tomato sandwiches for lunch; and lasagna for supper--and all the food that she made was delicious. She started doing her own laundry and putting away her clean clothes and doing the dishes.

I was very determined to be out on my own again, living independently, by the end of January. I was resolute in my goal and would not be deterred by any doubts of my mother or my therapists. I was committed to make this dream a reality and nothing would stop me!

Sharon's walking steadily improved, and by the middle of January, she was able to walk well with the cane and even do some walking without the cane for short distances around the house. She also made progress in being able to use her left hand. Rather than using only one hand, she began to consistently use both hands to do various tasks. And to her great delight, she found that she was once again able to do macramé and make jewelry out of hemp, waxed linen, and beads—just as beautifully as she had done before the accident. I also noticed that Sharon was doing much better at initiating activities and getting things done. The medications that she was taking seemed to be working.

Sharon also began getting ready to go back to college by applying to Fort Lewis, and by writing to request a transcript from Northeastern State University in Tahlequah, Oklahoma, where she had gone to school before the accident. She visited the Center for Students with Disabilities at Fort Lewis College to make arrangements to audit a class and to obtain the special help that she would need when she returned to college in the fall. And she learned how to arrange transportation to go to her therapy sessions, which would be continued at Mercy Medical Center there in Durango, and to her classes at Fort Lewis College. She would be able to ride on the Opportunity Bus, a special service for people with disabilities, which would pick her up at home and take her wherever she needed to go.

On January 7th, Heidi, who had been a friend of Sharon's since junior high days, found a two-bedroom apartment in Durango that she and Sharon could share. It was in a very good location—just two blocks away from where Carol worked and three blocks from downtown Durango. Sharon's moving day was set for January 31st, and she could hardly wait! By this time she had received a settlement from her car insurance company, which would reimburse her for a year's lost wages, and she had also begun receiving Social Security Disability (SSDI) benefits. So she was now financially able to live on her own. We bought Sharon a bedroom furniture set and arranged to have it delivered there, and also purchased some kitchen furniture and appliances for her. Fortunately, Heidi already had furniture for the living room.

During the last few weeks before Sharon moved, she and Ernie had several counseling sessions with Mindy, a woman who worked at People Helping People (PHP), an organization that helped people with disabilities to live independently in their community. In the counseling sessions with Mindy, Sharon and Ernie were able to express their feelings honestly to each other about how they felt about each other, and how the accident had affected them and their relationship. Sharon was able to tell Ernie how much he had hurt her by "backing off" and not calling her or coming to see her very often. She felt that they were making progress in rebuilding their relationship, and she could hardly wait to move to Durango, so that they could spend more time together.

After meeting with Mindy several times, I truly felt like Ernie and I were making progress toward understanding where each other were coming from – hopefully reaching some common ground. I had high hopes for being able to rebuild my relationship with him once I moved to Durango!

Sharon also began attending a weekly support group for women with acquired disabilities, and it was a great help to her to meet others who had experienced various accidents and illnesses. She soon found that these women could identify with her struggles and her feelings. One woman, Chris, who was paralyzed from the waist down due to a car accident, and whose husband had died of a brain injury which he had suffered in the same accident, became a special friend and encouragement to Sharon.

I gained so much insight, support and encouragement from attending this support group. I learned that I was not alone and that many others had experienced similar emotions and struggles. I so appreciated the personal interest Chris took in my life and the friendship she extended to me.

On January 20th, Sharon had another appointment with Dr. Carlow, the neuro-ophthalmologist, in Albuquerque. Once again, he had good news for us. Sharon's left eye was now able to turn to the left and look in that direction, and her problem with being able to see things on her left side was much improved. Her right eye's ability to look down had also improved enough that Dr. Carlow was able to give her a flexible plastic prism lens that adhered to the right lens of her glasses and corrected her double vision. After six months of seeing two of everything--one on top of the other, it was a tremendous relief for Sharon to see only a single image, and it also made it much easier for her to read.

It was a relief indeed to finally see only one image rather than two of everything, as you can imagine. Reading was far easier and much less of a chore, now that I didn't have to consciously try to ignore the extra characters when looking at a line of text.

However, Dr. Carlow warned us that Sharon's right eye might not improve much more than it had already done, and that she might still need an operation to correct her double vision. He recommended that, in three months, Sharon should see Dr. Durso, an eye surgeon, to find out if surgery would be necessary. And he also told us that the involuntary movements of Sharon's left eye were caused by her brain stem injury, that there was nothing that could be done to help this problem, and that these movements might never go away.

While we were in Albuquerque, we visited Robert, the young man who had been in the room next to Sharon's when she was at St. Joseph's Rehab Hospital. By this time, he was at home with his family, but he had progressed much more slowly than Sharon had. In contrast to Sharon, who was soon going to move away from home and live on her own, it would be a very long time before Robert would be able to do likewise. Seeing him again brought mixed feelings. On the one hand, we were overwhelmed with gratitude for the miraculous progress that Sharon had made, and on the other hand, our hearts went out to Robert and his family in the struggles they still faced.

At this time, I wondered if my presence bothered Robert. I thought that if I were in his shoes, I would resent me coming around. Because I knew how I would feel if I were him, I asked his mother to ask him if it was difficult for him to have me visit. He confirmed my suspicion that he did have a problem with me visiting him.

The following day, we went to Presbyterian Hospital, and Sharon met the intensive care nurses there for the first time that she could remember, and she thanked them for providing lifesaving care. Diana, Maureen, and Mindy were thrilled to see Sharon, and proclaimed that she was a walking miracle. And it was such a joy to eat lunch with Sharon in the hospital cafeteria there—the very place where Joe and I had often sat and wondered whether or not our dear daughter was going to survive. Before returning home, we also visited St. Joseph's and THC, so that Sharon could see Dr. Spaulding, her therapists, and the nurses who had cared for her there. They were all overjoyed at how much progress she had made since our last trip to Albuquerque two months before.

It was a thrill to meet these important people for the first time and see the others again who had served such a vital role in my recovery, as well as to be able to express my appreciation!

On January 30th, Sharon went to her last therapy appointment in Cortez, and that same day, we began moving her belongings to her apartment in Durango. The following two days were spent in helping her get unpacked and settled in her new home, and I stayed there with her until this task was completed. Early on the morning of February 1st, I left Durango and drove home alone. As I pulled out of Sharon's driveway, two conflicting emotions battled for control of my heart. Although I was overflowing with joy that Sharon had improved enough so that she could once again live independently, I was also deeply concerned for her safety. It was so hard for me to leave her by herself, after I had been by her side, caring for her, almost constantly for the past six months. However, I realized that Sharon's life, and her safety, were in the Lord's Hands—not mine, and that just as I was completely powerless to prevent her accident, or to heal her after it had occurred, I was also totally unable to protect her from any future danger. Knowing that I could depend on God to take care of her, I entrusted her to Him, and thanked Him with my whole heart that Sharon was on her own again at last!

How amazing and wonderful it was to finally be on my own again! There were many times I questioned whether or not I would ever be able to live by myself again, though I had desperately longed for this day. Imagine my delight when I was setting up my household for the first time and my mixed feelings as I said goodbye to my mom. I was finally going to realize my dream and meet my goal of living independently!

Sharon's high school graduation picture 1995

Totaled 1987 Plymouth Sharon was driving on July 12, 1997

Sharon with Dr. Spaulding at St. Joe's Rehab hospital fall 1997

Sharon at Cadence Therapeutic Horseback riding center 1998

D
u
r
a
n
g
o

Sharon with Mom and Dad on Durango & Silverton Railroad 1998

Sharon in front of her first apartment spring 1998

Univ of Northern Colorado
Commencement
May 10, 2003

Sharon 2011

Part 4—On Her Own Again

Chapter 8

The week after Sharon moved to Durango, she began speech, occupational, and physical therapy at the outpatient clinic at Mercy Medical Center, the same hospital in which she had been in intensive care immediately following her accident. Her speech therapist was Joyce, who was a friend and colleague of Phyllis, the voice therapist that Sharon had visited in Farmington, New Mexico. We were greatly encouraged by this development, because unlike the speech therapist in Cortez, Joyce would be consulting regularly with Phyllis and actively seeking and following her advice regarding Sharon's treatment. In addition to doing resonance, pitch and breathing training to help her voice improve, Joyce would also be doing cognitive therapy with her—to improve her attention, concentration, memory, and reaction time— to prepare her for returning to college in the fall. Her occupational therapist was a woman named Terri, who would be seeking to help her gain strength and coordination in her arms and hands, by doing exercises and handcrafts, and who would also be doing some cognitive therapy with her. Her physical therapist was Becky, who would be working on strengthening her leg and foot muscles and retraining her to walk properly.

Sharon also began attending the classical Greek literature course that she had decided to audit at Fort Lewis College in preparation for returning to school the following year. However, this class turned out to be more challenging than she had expected. By the time that she was able to start attending it, she had already missed several weeks, and they were in the middle of discussing the Iliad, which she had never read before. Joyce suggested that she not try to read the Iliad, but just go to class and listen until they began another piece of literature, and then try to do the homework from that point on. Sharon found it difficult to follow the professor's lecture, because she felt that he was talking too fast, and it was hard for her to read and to take notes, because of her involuntary eye movements. She did learn, though, that it was helpful to take a tape recorder with her and to record each class session, then listen to it at home, so that if she missed something, she could play it over again until she understood it. Another problem that Sharon faced was the fact that it was impossible for her to speak loudly enough so that she could ask questions or participate in class discussions. To help with this, she brought with her to class the little microphone and amplifier device that Joe had made for her when she was still in the rehab hospital in Albuquerque and could barely whisper. This made it possible for her to be heard by the teacher and the other students. As time went on, Sharon began being able to comprehend the literature that was discussed in class and even to write some short papers on it.

In order to get to class and to all of her therapy appointments, Sharon relied on the Opportunity Bus, a van that provided transportation for people with disabilities in Durango. Each week, she called the bus company and scheduled her rides for the following week. Then they would come right to her house, pick her up, take her where she needed to go, and then bring her back home again—for one dollar per ride. How thankful we were that this service was available, and that Sharon still had good memory and organizational skills, so that she was able to take advantage of it. Without it, she would have been unable to live independently.

However, just as Sharon was beginning to get settled in her new place and adjusted to her new schedule, she was dealt the most devastating blow that she had experienced since the accident itself. On February 8th, just one week after she had finished moving into her apartment, Ernie came for a visit and announced to her that he wanted to be free to date other people. At the same time, though, he told Sharon that he still wanted to date her.

For the next few weeks, Sharon tried to hold onto her relationship with Ernie, hoping that he would come to his senses and decide that he still loved her and wanted to marry her. On Valentine's Day, he gave her a rose, and she gave him some valentines, some poems that she had written about their relationship, and a letter in which she expressed her feelings about what he had said and done to her. They had gone to several sessions of counseling together, but Sharon was extremely depressed during this time—even to the point of talking about suicide. Since she was living on her own, an hour's drive away from us, I was very concerned for her safety, and I urged her to call someone if she felt tempted to commit suicide. She promised that she would do that, but she also assured me that, although she had thought about killing herself, she would never actually do it.

On Valentine's Day I gave Ernie the poem I had written about our relationship before—the True Love poem—contrasting it with another poem I had written for an ex-boyfriend lamenting the loss of his love. Although I did not say I was comparing and contrasting the poems, I hoped he would draw his own conclusions.

As Sharon struggled with her heartbreak, the support group that she attended each week was a real encouragement to her, as she shared her feelings with them. The ladies there sought to assure her that she was still a very special, beautiful, and valuable young woman, in spite of what Ernie had done to her. However, by the end of February, Sharon realized that she could not handle being in this excruciatingly painful and awkward situation any longer. Also, since she and Ernie had dated each other for more than three years and had been engaged, she recognized that it was totally unfair of Ernie to expect it of her. So she wrote him a long letter, telling him that although she still loved him with all of her heart, she loved him enough to let him go—thus breaking their engagement. It was a very loving, mature, well-thought-out, and heart-moving letter. I thought that surely it would melt Ernie's heart and cause him to realize what a precious gift he was throwing away when he chose to reject Sharon's love. However, he ignored Sharon's letter and began dating others, just as he had planned.

The letter I wrote Ernie was six pages long and essentially said that I loved him too much to share him with anyone else. I told him I still wanted to be in his life, but I couldn't date him if he was dating other people. He said that he was probably just going to have coffee with other people and that it would probably be more

in my mind than what was actually going on. We decided that he
would only share information with me if I asked for it and that was
how we left it for months.

Sharon was utterly crushed and heartbroken, and felt that she must
be completely unattractive, since Ernie didn't want her any more.
How my heart ached for Sharon. Once again, how I wished that it
was within my power to make things "all better" for her and take
the pain away. However, at the same time, my mind reeled with
disbelief that the same young man who had been so tender and
caring for months after Sharon's accident could now desert her and
be so callous and uncaring toward her. Though we had all realized
that there had been problems in Sharon and Ernie's relationship for
several months, we had hoped that after her move to Durango,
these difficulties could be worked out. So, when their engagement
was actually broken, it was a great shock and grief to us all.

One night, Chris, one of the women that Sharon had met in the
support group for women with acquired disabilities, invited her to
go and hear a man named Ron Heagy speak. Ron is a quadriplegic
who was paralyzed in a surfing accident when he was seventeen
years old. Since then, he has married, written a book called Life is
an Attitude, and become an inspirational speaker. He is a
dedicated Christian, and is also a gifted artist who draws and paints
by holding pencils and paintbrushes in his mouth. After hearing
him speak, Sharon purchased his book and asked him to autograph
it, which he proceeded to do—with a pen held in his mouth. She
then introduced herself to him and talked to him about her accident
and her break-up with Ernie. He encouraged her to trust God, even
though she couldn't understand why He had allowed the events
that had occurred in her life, and to realize that He had a good plan
for her future, even though she could not yet see it. She was
greatly impressed by Ron's faith in God and the positive attitude
that he had—in spite of his own extremely difficult situation.

I was inspired by Ron's story and encouraged by his wise words of
advice. It was amazing to hear how his life had been changed, but
that he had chosen to adopt a positive attitude in the midst of his
extremely challenging circumstances.

For the next several days, after she had written the letter to Ernie and had heard Ron Heagy speak, I noticed a tremendous difference in Sharon's attitude. She said that she liked and accepted herself the way that she was now, and that she hoped that she could be an encouragement to others someday, just as her friend Chris, and Ron, had been to her. She also said that since she had chosen to let Ernie go, she felt free, even though losing him still hurt her deeply. And she confided that she had begun to pray again, for the first time in a long while, and to pour out her questions and her feelings of anger and hurt to God. I was overjoyed by the transformation in her life.

However, in early March, Sharon experienced a significant reaction to a medication that she had been taking and had to be hospitalized briefly. This medication affected her brain function and caused her to be unable to sleep and to have racing thoughts. The effects of the medication reaction were compounded by the extreme stress and devastation caused by her break-up with Ernie along with the demands of auditing the college course at Fort Lewis – something which she was really not ready for at this stage in her recovery. This was our first experience with the fact that after brain injury, people tend to become very sensitive to the effects of medication, as well as to react quite differently to them than their peers without brain injuries would.

Several weeks after getting out of the hospital, Sharon told us that she had recently remembered something extremely unusual that had probably occurred at the time of the accident. She had what is commonly called a "near-death experience." She said that she had seen Jesus, and also her Grandmother Frazier, my mother, who had died when Sharon was only four years old. She said that she had been with them in a place of brilliant light and no pain, and that, instead of speaking with their mouths, they had communicated by "thinking" to each other.

I recalled that I had seen Jesus and talked with Him. When I had this memory, I felt a pain in my chest – where I had gotten a bruised lung from the accident. I remember begging Jesus not to

132

send me back because it hurt too much. He simply replied, "Don't you think it hurt when I died?" I was speechless in response to this question. My grandmother came to me and encouraged me saying, "It's okay, honey. You can go back now." I do believe that I died at the scene of the accident, went to heaven, spoke with Jesus and my grandmother, and then was sent back here because I still had work to do.

We don't know why Sharon recalled this occurrence at this particular time, rather than earlier. It may be that the Lord allowed her to remember it at this point in her recovery to encourage her in all the struggles and sorrow that she was going through. However, we do believe that her experience was real!

April 19, 1998 was Sharon's twenty-first birthday. What a day of joy that was—the birthday that we had feared we might never be able to celebrate. For her birthday present, we gave her a trip to Tahlequah, Oklahoma, the town where she had been attending college before the accident, so that she could visit her friends there. Since Sharon was still unable to make such a long trip by herself, I went with her. We flew to Oklahoma on April 14th, and returned to Colorado on April 22nd. During the time that we were in Tahlequah, Sharon stayed with her former roommates, in the trailer where she used to live, while I stayed with some friends who lived nearby.

Sharon's week in Oklahoma sped by in a whirlwind of joyful reunions with a multitude of friends from college, work, church, and the Campus Christian Fellowship in which she and Ernie had been active. And one of Sharon's former professors presented her with a medallion and a certificate honoring her for her recent induction into Sigma Tau Delta, the international English honor society. While we were there, we also made a trip to see Ernie's family, who lived in Spavinaw, Oklahoma. Then, on Sharon's birthday, all of her friends joined together in throwing a big party for her at Mazzio's Pizza, the restaurant where she had worked as a waitress.

What a fantastic birthday present! It was so much fun reuniting with old friends and coworkers. My old roommates took pictures during my time there and made a montage commemorating my 21st birthday, which they gave to me as a present – what fun!

On the way home, we had to pass through Denver, and rather than immediately returning home with me, Sharon stayed in the Denver area for five days with Tim and Ruth, a young Christian couple who are dear friends of hers. Tim had been her high school basketball coach, and Ruth had been her English teacher, whose example had inspired Sharon's desire to teach high school English. She spent an enjoyable five days with them, and they were a tremendous encouragement to her, as she shared her feelings and her struggles with them. And while she was there, she was also able to visit with several friends from her high school days. When she finally flew back home on April 27th, she had been gone for almost two weeks, and had enjoyed a refreshing and much-needed break from her therapy and from the stressful aftermath of her break-up with Ernie.

I so enjoyed spending time with Tim and Ruth and their words of encouragement were a balm to my aching soul. All in all, the trip was a welcome respite from the abysmal hospitalization and heartbreaking loss I had experienced prior to the trip.

Chapter 9

After Sharon returned from her trip, she resumed her therapy, but she did not continue auditing the literature class that she had been taking at Fort Lewis College, since the doctor felt that it would cause undue stress for her at this time. Instead, she began preparing for her return to college in the fall by continuing to do cognitive therapy with Joyce, her speech therapist, and by going to weekly counseling sessions with Dr. Ed Cotgageorge, a neuropsychologist, who is skilled in working with people who have had brain injuries.

"Dr. Ed" proved to be a tremendous help and encouragement to Sharon, as he led her through the difficult process of working through her feelings about the accident and about her break-up with Ernie. Although Sharon had recovered completely from the mental confusion that was caused by the medication reaction that she had suffered, she was still extremely depressed and would often say that she wished that she had died in the accident. She was also struggling with deep hurt and intense anger at all that had taken place in her life, and she was trying to deal with the unanswerable questions that she had about why God had allowed all of these things to happen to her. And it didn't help any when well-meaning Christians condemned her for her feelings and told her that she shouldn't feel that way, or gave her pat answers, such as "All things work together for good", or "Just think how much you will learn from all that you're going through." Such responses only made her even angrier, and I could certainly identify with how she felt, because such trite "answers" made me furious too!

These flippant responses only served to add insult to injury, literally, and made me feel worse than I already did. I really didn't care how much I would learn through these excruciatingly painful experiences and I could see no way out of the quagmire I found myself in!

In contrast to these "Job's comforters", Dr. Ed was like a breath of fresh air. He didn't minimize Sharon's feelings, but instead encouraged her to pour out her heart to God and honestly tell Him just how she felt—because He obviously already knew all about it anyway. Although he didn't pretend to have the answer to the "Why?" question, he sought to motivate Sharon to trust God by sharing his own spiritual pilgrimage with her. He recounted how, after he had studied all of the world's religions, he had chosen to become a Christian, because Christianity was the only religion that made a practical difference in people's lives. How thankful I was that Sharon was going to such a caring and competent Christian counselor.

Dr. Ed also constantly tried to help Sharon learn that she could choose to be happy, by deciding to be thankful for what she had, rather than focusing on what she had lost, and he often used humor to drive his point home. One day, when she was particularly depressed and said that she wished that she could die, Dr. Ed remarked sadly, "You know what, Sharon? I'd like to die too."

"You, Dr. Ed?" Sharon asked in shocked surprise. "Why would you want to die?"

"Because I'm short," he replied glumly. "I've always wanted to play basketball, but I'm way too short."

"But, Dr. Ed," Sharon protested, "you have many other talents. There are lots of things that you can do!"

"It doesn't matter," he responded despondently. "All that matters is that I'm short. I'll never be able to play basketball because I'm too short."

Sharon considered this sad pronouncement for a moment and then exclaimed, "Hey, now I see what you're doing, Dr. Ed. You're showing me how I sound. I've been focusing on what I can't do, instead of what I can, haven't I?"

"You got it!" he admitted with a hearty laugh, as Sharon joined in his amusement.

I truly enjoyed my sessions with Dr. Ed and was able to come to terms with many difficult realities as he steered me through this perplexing maze of emotions using his remarkable wit and outstanding sense of humor. He made the comment to me one day that the doctor who had the office next to his asked after one of his sessions with me what we were doing because there was always so much laughter. Dr. Ed said that this made our sessions unique, because he didn't spend many of his other sessions laughing with clients.

In addition to counseling Sharon, Dr. Ed also gave her some neuropsychological tests to find out what cognitive problems she still had as a result of her injury, and how they might affect her performance in school. The tests that he gave her were similar to the ones that she had taken the previous December—seven months earlier, and to our great joy, her performance had improved. "Your memory, attention, concentration, verbal memory, and verbal skills are good," he informed her. "However, your visual memory is mildly impaired, and you will have to use various techniques to compensate for this deficiency. Because of this impairment, you are no longer a visual learner, like you were before your accident. You are now an auditory learner, so you will need to tape record your professors' lectures and listen to them at home, and you should also listen to your textbooks on tape while you are reading them. Find someone else to take notes for you during class so that you can give your full attention to the professor's lecture. And get permission to take your tests in a quiet environment, allowing you to take as much time as you need to complete them, rather than during the regular class period."

"You know, Sharon," he continued, "in many ways you are very typical of most people who have had brain injuries similar to yours. However, in one very important way, you are dramatically different. Ninety-nine percent of patients who have suffered an injury like yours are no longer capable of carrying on a normal, intelligent, extended conversation, but you are still able to do that! You are a part of that very small, but fortunate, one percent who hasn't lost their ability to think and interact normally with others. And I see no reason why you can't return to college and successfully complete your schooling." When Sharon reported to us what Dr. Ed had told her, we once again lifted our hearts in fervent thanksgiving to God that He had miraculously spared Sharon's mind, personality, memory, and ability to think and communicate.

From February through August 1998, Sharon continued going to speech therapy and physical therapy. However, she reached an encouraging milestone in her recovery when she was discharged from occupational therapy on April 3rd. Her occupational therapist, Terri, felt that it was no longer necessary for Sharon to receive occupational therapy, but urged her to be faithful in doing her hand and arm exercises at home. Since Sharon is very talented at doing various types of handcrafts, Terri especially encouraged her to work at these in order to improve the movement and coordination of her left hand. Just two weeks before her discharge from occupational therapy, Sharon had proved that she was now able to resume her creative hobbies. For the first time since her accident, she was able to make a braided hemp and bead necklace. It took her only an hour and a half to make a double-braided necklace out of six strands of hemp, with twelve beads strung onto two of the strands. It turned out beautifully, and best of all, she was able to use her left hand, as well as her right, to do the weaving and to thread the beads.

I was very encouraged to be able to make necklaces again, as I had done before my accident – it was so rewarding to be able to express my creativity through this medium once more!

All throughout the spring and summer months, Joyce, Sharon's speech therapist, continued to do cognitive retraining with her to prepare her for returning to college in the fall, and also did voice therapy to help her improve the volume, pitch, expression, and quality of her voice. The cognitive retraining exercises involved doing a series of extremely boring and repetitive, but very necessary, exercises on the computer in order to improve her attention, memory, concentration, and reaction time. These exercises also sought to improve her ability to pay attention to more than one thing at a time, as well as to help her eyes to track objects faster, so that she would be able to read more rapidly.

For example, as the computer flashed a series of letters on the screen at random, Sharon was required to hit the space bar each time the letter "a" was followed by the letter "x", and at the end of the exercise, her reaction time was measured. Other programs involved Sharon either watching a series of colored boxes which marched across the screen and then choosing the ones that were identical in color to a set of two boxes that were displayed in the middle of the screen, or else counting how many boxes there were when a stack of blocks was arranged in various patterns. Still another program asked Sharon to quickly determine whether the sum of three numbers was an even number or an odd number. And as she worked on these exercises, Joyce would often read to her while she was doing them, in order to improve her ability to do two things at the same time, and then ask her questions about the reading selection—to test her comprehension. Even though these computer exercises were very simple, they were a real challenge to Sharon at this point in her recovery. However, as she diligently worked on them, both in therapy and on her computer at home, using first her right hand, and then her left hand—her reaction time, concentration, memory, and ability to pay attention to more than one thing at a time got better. And the coordination of her left hand gradually improved also.

Joyce also worked with Sharon on specific skills that she would need in school, such as reading speed and comprehension. By the time that the summer had ended, her speed had increased from one hundred forty words per minute to two hundred two words per minute, and when Joyce tested her comprehension, she usually scored between eighty and one hundred percent on the questions that Joyce gave her. In addition to this, Joyce gave Sharon literature assignments to read for homework, which they discussed during therapy, with Joyce playing the role of a teacher, in order to prepare Sharon for returning to her college classes that fall.

Sharon also practiced typing on her computer at home, in preparation for writing papers when she returned to school. However, she quickly found out that, although she could type well with her right hand, she lacked the coordination to be able to type with her left hand, since her left ring finger and little finger were still not functioning properly.

During the same period when Joyce was working with Sharon on cognitive therapy, she was also endeavoring to help her voice improve. She had Sharon read aloud and try to sing, in order to practice articulation, expression, and pitch. She had her do various exercises to help her relearn how to breathe from her diaphragm, to try to increase the loudness of her voice--including taking her to a park to practice trying to shout while she was swinging on a swing. However, although Sharon's voice did improve somewhat, it still remained very low, quiet, breathy, and whispery, as she seemed to have lost the ability to gauge how loud she was talking. The volume and quality of her voice varied from day to day. It was louder and of better quality sometimes, and softer and of poorer quality at other times.

I dutifully practiced the exercises Joyce gave me ad nauseum, but even though they were boring, the cognitive exercises especially paid off in preparation for my return to college in the fall.

On April 2nd, Phyllis, the voice specialist who was advising Joyce concerning Sharon's treatment, did a video-scoping of Sharon's vocal cords again and discovered that there was still one place where there was a gap of one sixteenth of an inch between her vocal cords. Both Phyllis and Joyce felt that this accounted for the breathiness in Sharon's voice. However, when they repeated the examination a month later, the gap was gone and Sharon's vocal cords appeared to be completely normal, although her voice had still not improved.

So the cause of Sharon's voice problem remained a mystery, and none of the therapy that Joyce tried seemed to help very much. Phyllis suggested several experimental surgeries that she felt might be a help to Sharon. However, since no one really knew what was causing the problem, or whether or not an operation would actually bring any improvement, Sharon decided against having any surgery. She feared that it might create more difficulties for her, rather than help her, and I thoroughly agreed with her decision.

At this time, Sharon returned to Dr. White, the neurosurgeon who had cared for her immediately following the accident, for a checkup, and he was thrilled and amazed to see the marvelous recovery that she had made. However, he said that he believed that her voice problem was caused by her brain stem injury, which had rendered her brain unable to remember and coordinate all of the components that go into speaking in a normal voice. This news was very discouraging to Sharon, who had been trying so hard to talk normally, and hoping that with time and practice she would improve. Sharon's voice problem also periodically created tension in our relationship with her, because we often had difficulty hearing what she was saying, and we would have to ask her to repeat herself. This made her feel that we weren't listening to her, when in fact we were straining to hear every word.

However, in spite of the bad news that we received from Dr. White, we were thankful that Sharon was even able to talk at all, and that she had no problem with pronouncing words correctly, although her voice itself still needed much improvement. And I reminded myself that Dr. White had been wrong about Sharon's prognosis several times before. He had thought that she was going to die the day of the accident, and he had also predicted that she would never wake up from her coma or ever be able to live independently again. And as time went by, Sharon's voice did gradually become louder and less whispery and breathy, although it still continued to be soft, low-pitched, and husky. It was a pleasant voice, but just a bit hoarse—like someone with a bad cold or mild laryngitis. However, it was music to my ears.

The fact that I was not able to speak louder, was a constant source of stress and frustration to me, in addition to making it difficult for me to communicate, especially in situations with a great deal of background noise.

During the same time that Sharon was working so hard in speech therapy, she was busily engaged in physical therapy. Because the spasticity in the muscles of her left leg and foot were hindering her from walking properly, her physiatrist, Dr. Chiodo, decided to try a Botox injection to help her muscles relax. (Botox is made from botulism toxin and is used to treat muscles that are in spasm and won't relax.) On February 12th, Sharon went to Dr. Chiodo, and he used a machine that measured muscle contractions to show him exactly where to inject the Botox. He stuck long needles into

Sharon's leg at various points, and then instructed Sharon to contract and relax her toes. After he had located the correct spots for the injections, he used a huge needle to inject the Botox into the back of her left calf and into the bottom of her left foot. It looked excruciatingly painful, but Sharon was very brave and barely flinched during the procedure. Dr. Chiodo said that it would take several days for the Botox to work, and that the effects of it would last for three to six months. However, although it helped somewhat, Sharon continued to have a lot of spasticity in her left leg, foot, and toes—especially her second, third, and fourth toes.

Sharon also had ongoing problems with the brace that she wore on her leg. It needed continual adjustment, and it often caused sores on her leg or foot, which made it impossible for her to wear it for days at a time. Finally, it became obvious that the brace had not been made correctly in the first place, and that it would not be possible to fix it, so we found another provider to make a new brace which was more effective and more comfortable for Sharon to wear.

When Sharon went to physical therapy, the therapists used ultrasound and heat to try to relax the spasms in her muscles, and then she did a variety of exercises that were designed to improve her walking, balance, coordination, and strength. She pushed weights up and down with her legs, and in and out with her arms, and pulled pulleys up and down with her arms to increase her strength and range of motion. She practiced standing on one leg, walking on a balance beam, and sitting on a large ball or cushion to improve her balance. She worked out on various exercise machines, such as the treadmill and the stepper to improve her walking, and also did gait training--as she walked back and forth with the therapist instructing her on how to walk properly.

By early April, she was able to begin practicing walking in therapy without her brace and her cane, although she still needed to use them when she was not in therapy. By late May, she finally regained the ability to lift up the toes of her left foot. This was a tremendous encouragement to Sharon, and a wonderful milestone in her recovery, because her toes had been the only remaining part of her body that was still not able to move properly. And by mid-August, she could walk well enough that she no longer needed a wheelchair when she had to go long distances, although she still had to use her cane, and she walked very slowly and with a limp. What a wonderful day of rejoicing it was when I was able at last to take the wheelchair back to the medical supply company.

I was ecstatic to bid farewell to the wheelchair once and for all, and felt it was reflective of the progress I was making. Although I still needed the cane when I was walking for stability, I was greatly encouraged!

In addition to her regular physical therapy, Sharon also had the opportunity to participate in two very special kinds of physical therapy—pool therapy and horseback riding therapy. She really enjoyed doing exercises in the swimming pool, since it was so much easier to exercise in the water. In fact, in the pool, she even found that she could run in place. And the horseback therapy was very beneficial as well. I was fascinated to learn that the gait of a horse is almost identical to that of a human being, and that horseback riding is very valuable in helping a person with a brain injury regain a feel for the rhythm and motion of normal walking. After being helped onto the horse, Sharon guided the horse around the ring and through a pattern of cones by shifting her weight from side to side, which helped to improve her balance. She also gave verbal commands to the horse, which was good for her voice, since she had to concentrate on talking loudly enough so that the horse could hear her. And it was so refreshing for Sharon to be outdoors.

I thoroughly enjoyed the hydrotherapy – water therapy as well as the hippotherapy – horseback riding therapy. I had so much more freedom in the water, a weightless environment, to be able to exercise in ways I would never be able to do on land. Being outdoors with the horses was so enjoyable and it was one of the first times I found that I was doing therapy without even realizing it!

As Sharon continued to recover, she began eagerly asking her doctors and therapists when she would be able to drive a car again.

"It all depends on when your vision and coordination are good enough, and your response time is fast enough," Joyce, her speech therapist, told her one day. "I don't think that you're ready to drive yet, and I'm afraid it will be a long time before that day comes. But if you want to, you can go to Albuquerque and be tested on the driving simulator at St. Joe's Rehab Hospital. That would give you an idea about how close you are to being able to drive again."

Imagine how devastating it was to hear Joyce say that she didn't feel I would be ready to drive again for quite some time! I desperately longed for the day when I would not have to be dependent on others for transportation, as well as the day when I would be able to fully regain my independence!

So, on June 18th, we took Sharon to Albuquerque and Vicky, an occupational therapist at St. Joe's, gave Sharon a driving assessment. First, Vicky gave Sharon a visual perception test—the same one on which she had scored only thirty-three percent when she had first taken it while she was in the hospital—and to our great joy, this time she scored one hundred percent! Then she gave her a vision test and a depth perception test, which involved showing Sharon three road signs and asking her which was the closest. After this the therapist gave her several simulated driving tests. The first one was a night driving test, in which the therapist shone "headlights" into Sharon's eyes and asked her to read letters on signs. Then her reaction time was tested by having her take her foot off the gas pedal and put on the brakes when a traffic light changed from green to red. Another test evaluated her ability to do two things at once, by requiring her to turn on the left or right turn signal at the same time that she stepped on the gas or the brake. The final test was a written driving test, on which she scored eighty percent.

To our great amazement, Sharon did well on all of these tests, and Vicky pronounced that she was ready to drive again. Her only limitation was that she could now only drive a car that had an automatic transmission, because the weakness of her left leg would make it impossible for her to operate a clutch. Sharon was thrilled that she could drive again, and could hardly wait to get behind the wheel! I was thankful that she was making such a wonderful recovery, but it was truly frightening to me to think of her driving again after coming so very close to losing her as a result of her injury. However, I realized that just as I hadn't been able to protect her from the accident, I couldn't protect her now, so I placed her in the Lord's Hand, and rejoiced with her in her miraculous recovery.

How thrilling to finally be told that I would be able to drive again—I could hardly wait to get back on the road again! I was so eager, I was "chomping at the bit," so to speak!

There were two more details that needed to be taken care of before Sharon could be out on the road again, however. She needed a new driver's license, because her license had expired on her twenty-first birthday, and she needed another car, since her old car had been sold after the accident. On July 6th, she went to the driver's license office, took her eye test, and received her license, and then we went car shopping and found Sharon's dream car. It was a dark red 1990 Subaru Legacy, in wonderful condition, with power steering and power brakes, air conditioning, a radio and cassette player, and power windows and door locks, and it only cost $4000—just the amount we were able to pay. So, on July 11th, Sharon drove her new car for the first time. And on July 12, 1998, the first anniversary of the accident, Sharon drove me to church. What a joy it was to have her sitting there in church with us that day. And what an encouragement it was to her, on what could have been a very sad, depressing day, to be able to drive again and to have such a beautiful new car.

WOW – a new car! ☺ I could hardly contain my excitement! Not to mention the new found freedom I would have now that I wouldn't have to depend on the bus to transport me to and from my appointments. Plus I would be able to drive myself to and from classes once I went back to college in the fall.

Before Sharon was ready to return to college in the fall of 1998, her continuing problem with double vision still needed to be addressed. On May 15th, she went to Dr. Durso, the eye surgeon who had been recommended by Dr. Carlow, the neuro-ophthalmologist. After the examination, Dr. Durso gave us the discouraging news that Sharon's problem with double vision had not improved since her last check-up in January. "You have two choices, Sharon," he said. "Either you can get glasses that are made with a prism in the right lens, which you will have to wear for the rest of your life, or you can have surgery on your left eye to help your eyes work together."

"Surgery on my left eye?" Sharon asked in confusion. "I thought it was my right eye that was causing the double vision, because it can't look down."

"You're right," Dr. Durso agreed. "It is your right eye that is causing the problem, but since it is a result of your brain injury – neurological, there is nothing that we can do to correct it surgically. The only solution is to operate on your left eye and make it so that it can't look down quite as far as it can now, and then your eyes will be able to work together and your double vision should be corrected. Hopefully, operating on your left eye will also help to somewhat reduce the involuntary movements that it makes as a result of your brain stem injury."

Sharon chose to have the surgery, so on July 17th, Dr. Durso did the operation, which was an outpatient procedure that took about an hour to complete. In order to keep her left eye from being able to look down more than her right eye, he made an incision in the bottom of her left eyeball, down under her eyelid, and loosened the muscle there. This made her left eye unable to look down any further than her right eye was able to, thus correcting her double vision. After the surgery, Dr. Durso was very optimistic that it had been successful. However, he warned Sharon that it would probably be a couple of weeks before she actually noticed a difference in her vision, since her brain had to get used to her eyes being able to work together again. The next week was a very painful time for Sharon, as she recovered from the effects of her eye surgery, but she was overjoyed when she began noticing some improvement on the very first day—both in her vision and in the involuntary eye movements she had been experiencing. By July 26th, she began having intermittent periods of single vision, and on July 28th, just eleven days after the surgery, she had her first full day of single vision. The operation was a success, and her double vision was gone.

I had been expecting to have the double vision corrected after the surgery, so I was disappointed to still be seeing double once the bandages were removed. However once it was explained to me that my brain had to relearn how to interpret the images being sent to it by my eyes, I was encouraged and I realized I just had to wait for another thing to resolve itself. They did warn me that although the surgery corrects the double vision, occasionally after several years the double vision can return for some people. I hoped and prayed I would be one of the lucky ones whose double vision would not return!

Dr. Durso told Sharon that while she was recovering from her eye surgery, she needed to take a break from all of her therapy and give her eye a chance to heal. During this free time, she and I traveled to Albuquerque to attend a "Women of Faith" conference with some ladies from our church. My heart overflowed with joy to see my daughter praising the Lord by my side—in the very same city where just one year before she had been fighting for her life!

Although it seemed to Sharon that her entire life consisted of therapy during the spring and summer of 1998, she also had a chance to participate in some enjoyable recreational activities from time to time. Carol and Robert often included her in their plans along with their friends, who soon became Sharon's friends too. We visited her often and enjoyed taking her various places. We often took her out to dinner, and sometimes went to the swimming pool at nearby Trimble Hot Springs, or to a musical play, or to play miniature golf. How thrilled we all were when Sharon made a "hole in one" during her first miniature golf game after the accident.

In mid-July, Ernie asked me to have coffee with him, and I wondered what had inspired his new interest. He told me that although we had agreed that he would only share information about the other people he was dating if I asked him, he felt he now had to force information on me. He told me that he had been seeing a girl named Samantha for a while and that she was planning to move to Iowa for grad school. He said that she had asked him to go with her, thus sharing the purpose for our meeting that day. He had come to tell me goodbye. My emotions were mixed at this news, because although he had not really been involved in my life for several months, I suppose I always had the thought in the back of my mind that he and I would somehow get back together. So now there was a finality that had not existed before. He really was out of my life – once and for all.

Sharon still saw Ernie occasionally, but at the end of July, he and his new girlfriend Samantha moved from Durango to Iowa—and out of Sharon's life, which was a relief to her. Sadly, however, Ernie was not the only person who abandoned Sharon during her long and difficult recovery. As time went by, we began to notice that several people, who had been among Sharon's close friends prior to the accident, had begun to distance themselves from her. They had been very supportive and caring in the early days after the accident; however, as the months passed, they always seemed to be "too busy" to visit her. And if Sharon mentioned that she would like to spend some time with them, they would respond with a feeble excuse about why they couldn't get together with her.

For some reason, these friends seemed to feel uncomfortable around Sharon. Perhaps being around her reminded them of the frightening possibility that they themselves could suddenly be seriously injured or killed in an accident. Or it may have been, since Sharon was still so full of questions about why God had allowed her accident to happen, that they felt, wrongly, that it was their responsibility to have all the answers for her. What they didn't realize was that all she wanted was to be able to hang out with her friends and talk—just like they used to do before the accident. They failed to grasp that what Sharon needed most was their friendship, acceptance, and understanding—not a deep philosophical explanation for the reasons behind the tragedy that had occurred. However, whatever the reasons were for their behavior, it was a great heartbreak to her, because it was one more loss that was heaped on top of all that she had already suffered. Although at the time we were totally shocked by how they acted, we learned later, from other people who have had brain injuries, that this type of behavior is rather common. Many times, a person with a brain injury loses most of the friends that she had before her injury and has to start all over again and make new friends.

For some reason, my friends felt like I expected them to be "my savior" but the only thing I wanted was their friendship just as I'd had in the past. Once again, I had to try to figure out how to start over on another front. I kept wondering how many other things I would have to lose and attempt to rebuild following this severe injury.

Another change that took place in Sharon's life during this period occurred when her roommate, Heidi, moved out in May. For the next three months, Sharon lived alone. It was expensive, as well as lonely, for her to live by herself, and I was very concerned for her safety also. However, Sharon wasn't totally alone during those months, since Carol had given her a cat, Mac A. Roo, whose companionship and unpredictable antics Sharon thoroughly enjoyed! We were all relieved, though, when she found another roommate, Cindy, who moved in with her in August and stayed until the end of the following school year.

Mac A. Roo was the best "companion kitty" I could have ever asked for! I didn't feel nearly as lonely as I would have been without him by my side. He had such a unique personality and we formed an immediate bond even though he was already 7 years old when he came to live with me.

As Sharon dealt with the many heartbreaking losses that she had experienced, she expressed her anguish by writing poetry, an activity that she had enjoyed before the accident, and which, thankfully, she still had the ability to do.

In an effort to process difficult emotions, I wrote a poem, as I often did. When I reflected on my old life and all that I had lost, I wrote the following poem to express my heartache.

WHAT IS REAL?

I wonder if my memories of my past life are real
*But what **is** real?*
If the memories are not real—then that suggests that
*I have a **very lively** imagination!*
What would it have been like to have been Sharon Mehesy,
As I imagined her?
I would have liked to know her
She had a wonderful life—lots of friends, good in sports,
4.0 in school, wonderful boyfriend—
*It is better that I find out **now** that it was all just a dream*
A mirage
It was all just too good to be true
*Who could actually **live** a life like that?!?*
Well, better now than later—as they say—
That the mirage was shattered
*To realize **now** that Sharon had been*
Dancing on her tiptoes for 20 years
It had to end sometime
It would have been better if it had a romantic ending
Like Romeo and Juliet
But no, the ending is just pitiful
Crippled, former athlete struggles to make it from day to day
She can't even scream—no voice!

I was so grateful that I still had this creative outlet for my emotions rather than having to keep them all bottled up inside me. I truly felt the ending was just pitiful because there was so much that I could no longer do – especially in athletic endeavors. Depression, coupled with anger, was my constant companion for many months.

After Sharon wrote this poem, she sent it to Joni Eareckson Tada, along with a letter telling Joni about her accident, her injury, and her questions about why God had let these things happen to her. In the letter, she also told Joni that perhaps her poem could serve to express the feelings of people with brain injuries, many of whom are incapable of speaking for themselves. Sometime later, Sharon received a very encouraging personal letter from Joni, telling her that she completely understood Sharon's feeling that her life before the accident had been like a dream. She said that she often asked herself the question, "What is real?", because her own life of activity before her injury seemed unreal, after being paralyzed and in a wheelchair for thirty years. However, she told Sharon that she had come to realize that the parts of her life before and after the accident were two different pieces of a whole reality—her total life. Through her trials, she said, the Lord was teaching her lessons of patience, trust, endurance, and caring for others. She also told Sharon that her life was just as active, or more so, on a deeper and more important level than it had ever been, on the surface, before her accident. Joni's caring, understanding letter was a great encouragement to Sharon during this hard time. Unlike some people who glibly told her, "I know what you're going through," as they sought to compare some incidental annoyance in their own lives to Sharon's immense and numerous losses, Joni understood because she had "been there"—since she was still living with her disability and dealing with her losses on a daily basis.

Another person who was a tremendous help to Sharon as she struggled through this part of her recovery was Rosie, a Christian friend of ours who herself had suffered a severe traumatic brain injury thirteen years previously. More than anyone else, Rosie understood what Sharon was going through. Rosie called her regularly to see how she was doing, and she told Sharon to call her at any hour of the day or night, if she needed to talk. How thankful we were that Rosie was lovingly reaching out to Sharon during her time of need, and giving her this special gift of understanding that no one else could give.

I appreciated Rosie reaching out to me on a deep level as she was the first person I had met who truly understood what I was going through! How amazing to meet someone who had also been through severe brain trauma, but was now living on her own and doing well in spite of all she had been through.

And Sharon herself began helping others by doing volunteer work at People Helping People (PHP), an organization which existed for the purpose of providing various services for people with disabilities who live in the Durango area. It was located six blocks away from her house, and she was excited to learn that she was now able to walk there—even though it took her thirty-five or forty minutes to do so.

As time went by, Sharon gradually began making some new friends—people who had never known her before the accident, and who liked and accepted her just as she was. At the beginning of the summer, she began attending a college Bible study, and soon found several friends there—Jill, Gretchen, and a girl whose name was also Sharon. They began including her in their various activities. And another friend, Tina, who was the driver of the Opportunity Bus that Sharon had ridden before she was able to drive again, invited her to go camping in the mountains the weekend before she started back to college. How exciting it was for her to be able to end the summer by camping out for the first time since her accident.

*When Tina invited me to go camping with her, I asked her, "**Can I go camping?**" questioning whether it was possible for me to do it, and she good naturedly responded, "Of course you can!" It was so liberating for me to be outdoors again and to be treated as an equal—as if there was nothing wrong with me. Tina's friendship did so much more for me than simply being a friend. She encouraged me to try new things, such as camping, and to push the envelope so to speak—expanding my horizons!*

Part 5—Back to School

Chapter 10

On August 31, 1998, Sharon started back to college at Fort Lewis College in Durango, Colorado. She enrolled in two courses— British Victorian Literature, a requirement for her English education major, and Southwest Studies, which was a course about the history and cultures of the peoples of the American Southwest, and was required as a part of her general education requirements. These classes together totaled seven credit hours and met on Mondays and Wednesdays, so Sharon only had to attend class for two days each week. In addition to going to school, Sharon also continued to go to speech therapy each Tuesday and to physical therapy on Tuesdays and Thursdays.

She also continued to attend the weekly meeting of the support group for women with acquired disabilities. However, as time went by, she felt that this group was too diverse to meet the unique needs of a person who had suffered a brain injury, because the people in it had such a wide variety of disabilities. So Sharon and several others decided to start a support group specifically for people who had sustained brain injuries, and it became a great source of encouragement to them as they shared their mutual struggles with each other, since they could each understand what the others were going through. One thing that they all agreed on was that it didn't help them when others tried to comfort them in the loss of one of their abilities by reminding them that there are many people who have never possessed that particular ability at all. Rather than being an encouragement to them, Sharon and the others in the group all felt that it made their heartbreaking losses seem unimportant and trivial. The reason for their grief was the contrast between what they could do now and what they had been able to do before their injuries—not the comparison of their abilities to someone else's. When Sharon shared this idea with me, I felt awful, because I realized that I had done this very thing, hoping that it might cheer her up. I had often pointed out to her that I have a learning disability that is similar to the visual-spatial impairment that she experienced as a result of her injury, and that I had managed to live with it, so she could too. I resolved to never make that mistake again.

This Brain Injury Support Group was a lifeline for me as I was finally with a group of people who truly understood where I was coming from and what I was going through! It was a much needed source of encouragement as I started back to college with a new set of abilities and disabilities. My fellow group members were like my cheerleaders – spurring me on with words of encouragement as I approached continuing my college career with fear and doubt.

In spite of the fact that Sharon was taking such a light load of classes, she found returning to college extremely challenging and discouraging. Although she did as Dr. Ed had suggested, and tape-recorded her professors' lectures and obtained someone to take notes for her during class, she still found it very difficult to comprehend the abstract ideas contained in the poetry that she had to read for English class. On her first test, she got a 65—a D—the lowest grade that she had ever received in her life. For Sharon, who had never gotten any grade lower than an A before her accident, this was devastating—especially since she got this grade in an English course, which made her seriously question whether or not she would be able to continue with the major that she had chosen. When she talked to Dr. Ed about her difficulty in understanding abstract concepts, he told her that this was not surprising, since her neuropsychological testing had showed that her abstract reasoning ability had been somewhat damaged by her injury, and that she was now more of a "concrete thinker."

I was utterly devastated to receive a D on my first essay exam! I was totally blown away by my professor's comments such as, "I am having a difficult time following what you are saying" or "I'm not really understanding the point you are trying to make." I had been used to receiving glowing responses to my writing prior to my accident and was completely caught off guard by comments implying that I was not making sense.

155

*It is important to note here that although by most people's standards, I was taking a "light load of classes," for me, going to school part-time most certainly felt like full-time! Because I had to include so many extra duties required of any student with a disability, in the form of academic accommodations, such as tape recording class lectures and having a note-taker, this significantly multiplied my workload. Tape recording class lectures essentially meant that I had to attend each class twice, as I had to listen to the lecture again following each class session, starting and stopping the tape as I endeavored to fill in the blanks in the notes I had taken during class. And when studying for a test, I had to study not only **my** notes, but also the notes of my note-taker in an effort to cover all of the material. So although it may have appeared that I was only taking a half-time load of classes, I was doing double the work which was equal to taking a full load!*

Later in the semester, though, when the class began reading novels, instead of the obscure poetry of Tennyson and Browning, Sharon's understanding of the material improved, even though reading them presented her with a different kind of challenge. Although the tiny side-to-side movements of her left eye, which were caused by her brain-stem injury, were imperceptible to anyone but her, they were a great hindrance to her in reading. This made it extremely hard for her to do the lengthy reading assignments that were required for the class. She found that it helped to hold the book in a position that was level with her eyes, but in spite of this, she was unable to read as rapidly as she could before the accident. Also, because her visual learning ability had been impaired by her injury and she was now primarily an auditory learner, it was difficult for her to comprehend and retain what she read. As the semester progressed, however, Sharon's grades steadily improved, in spite of all of the obstacles she faced, and she made an A on her final English exam!

In contrast to the English course, Sharon found Southwest Studies to be easier and more understandable. The assignments for this course consisted of writing short Reaction Papers to various topics that were discussed in class or on the assigned reading. As she wrote these papers, it became obvious that she still had the same outstanding writing ability that she had possessed before the accident, and she received A's and B's on all of them.

I had a much easier time with the Southwest Studies coursework. It was the concrete nature of the materials versus the abstract reasoning requirements of the British Victorian Literature course. I remember a conversation with my mom following the final grades from the semester. When I told her I got a B in Southwest Studies, she expressed enthusiasm but I dejectedly told her that B meant bad. I have always been a perfectionist, and when you combine perfectionism with TBI, you have a recipe for disaster! Perfectionism sets unrealistic expectations for the average person, but following TBI when abilities have changed and performance is altered, perfectionism is no longer even in the realm of possibility!

When the semester ended, Sharon received final grades of B in Southwest Studies and C+ in British Victorian Literature. Although she was disappointed by these grades, because they were not A's, I was more proud of her and more thankful for them than I had ever been for any of the A's that she had made in the past.

While Sharon was struggling through her first semester back in college, Joe and I were facing a different kind of challenge. Because we are missionaries, we have to regularly visit the churches and individuals that support us and report to them about our work. We had scheduled a trip to the East Coast, where most of our supporters live, for the fall of 1997. Since this trip had been canceled following Sharon's accident, it had now been five years since we had last visited our supporters, and we could wait no longer to do so. How hard it was to tell Sharon goodbye at the end of August, just before she started school—knowing that we would not see her again for three and a half months—in mid-December, when her semester was almost over. It was also frightening to be so far away from her for the first time since her injury, but I realized that just as I couldn't protect her from the accident in the first place, I couldn't protect her from any dangers that she might face now. So, as we drove out of our driveway and headed East, we committed her again to the loving care of her Heavenly Father, who was able to take so much better care of her than we ever could.

It was agony to be separated from our precious daughter by two thousand miles and only be able to hear of her difficulties, and to try to encourage her, via long distance phone calls. How heartbreaking it was to not be able to drive over to her house and visit her and to hug her close to our hearts when she was hurting. The scariest thing that happened during this time occurred when Sharon's psychiatrist decided to put her on Wellbutrin, an antidepressant which was also a mood stabilizer. (Sharon had been taking another medication—Paxil, but it had not seemed to help with her depression, and it also had the unwelcome side effect of causing her to gain weight.) After Sharon started on the Wellbutrin, she experienced several frightening symptoms. Her heart began racing, she became short of breath, her left arm began jerking, and she had difficulty in focusing her eyes. Since the doctor had warned that Wellbutrin might possibly cause seizures, and told Sharon that she should not drive for two weeks after she began taking it, we were concerned that these symptoms might be the precursors of a seizure. We wondered why the doctor had put someone who had a brain injury on such a medication.

Our concerns about the psychiatrist's competence increased when she attributed Sharon's symptoms to panic attacks and suggested that perhaps Sharon should take Ritalin to control them. Sharon had been given Ritalin when she had been hospitalized for the medication reaction that she had experienced the previous March, and it had greatly aggravated her problems. Fortunately, Sharon remembered this, and adamantly told the doctor that she wouldn't take it. Since Sharon couldn't tolerate Ritalin, the doctor insisted that Sharon continue taking Paxil to control the supposed panic attacks. After talking with a friend who was a nurse, we learned that Sharon's reactions to Wellbutrin were common side effects of that medication, and that they would probably go away with time. We were dumbfounded that a doctor would seek to create a diagnosis of psychiatric illness, and prescribe medicine to "treat" it, when the symptoms were obviously caused by the side effects of another medication. Fortunately, as time went on, Sharon's symptoms gradually disappeared, the Wellbutrin helped her depression, and she was able to discontinue taking Paxil. Although I was very thankful that the Wellbutrin was helping her, I prayed fervently that someday she would be able to be completely medication-free.

I was grateful that I <u>remembered</u> the reaction I'd had to Ritalin while I was in the psych ward and thankful I was able to communicate this to my psychiatrist. When I reminded her of my adverse reaction to it, she simply responded with, "Oh that's right. Ritalin made you go crazy didn't it?" "Shocked" and "dumbfounded" didn't even begin to convey my utter astonishment at her cavalier response.

On October 10th, the first anniversary of the day that Sharon came home from the hospital, I thought back over the events of the past year, and recorded my feelings in my journal. "Although Sharon's hospitalization was terribly hard—wondering if she was going to survive, and what her mental level would be, and watching her suffer so much, this past year has been hard in a different way," I wrote. "It hurts so much to watch her struggle to do simple things that used to be so easy for her to do, to see her no longer able to do some things at all, to see how <u>long</u> it takes her to do things, and how hard it is for her to do them now, and to see her struggling with depression, discouragement, heartbreak, and suicidal feelings! It hurts, Lord! But thank You for seeing us through this hard year, and thank You that You will be with us through whatever lies ahead. And thank You so much for sparing Sharon's life, mind, and personality! Please continue to heal every part of her brain and body. Only You are able!"

However, all of the news that we received from Sharon during this time was not discouraging. As the months went by, we could tell that her voice was continuing to improve, as it sounded progressively louder and stronger on the phone. And on November 15th, she told us the joyful news that she was able to walk without her cane at last! Now the only piece of "adaptive equipment" that she had was the small brace that fit inside of her left shoe and came up to the top of her ankle. Although we missed being with Sharon on Thanksgiving, we were glad to hear that she had invited Carol and Janet and some other friends over to her house for Thanksgiving dinner, and that she had roasted the turkey, prepared some of the other main dishes, and baked several pies herself.

What fun to have my sisters over for Thanksgiving! It was exciting to be able to roast the turkey and so much fun to bake again – always a favorite pastime!

What a joyful day it was when we finally returned home again and were able to see Sharon at last. It was wonderful to see how much progress she had made during the past three and a half months. We rejoiced to see her walking unaided for the first time since the accident and to see how much her strength and balance had improved. We were thrilled to see that the range of motion in her left shoulder had increased, so that she could now raise her left arm up over her head, and that the strength and coordination of her left hand and fingers had also improved. And we were overjoyed that her voice was now loud enough so that we could hear what she was saying, even when there was some noise in the background, and that she was able at last to sing a few notes of some simple songs.

When Sharon came over to spend Christmas with us, she brought with her several necklaces and a pair of earrings that she had made out of hemp cord or waxed linen and beads, as Christmas presents for various relatives and friends. It was wonderful to have her home for a visit, and as I thought back over the year of 1998, which was rapidly drawing to a close, I couldn't help contrasting this Christmas with the previous one. What wonderful progress Sharon had made in the past year! A year ago, she had been in a wheelchair and had one of the serial casts on her leg, and she was still living at home. Her voice was just a faint whisper, she had double vision, and the fingers of her left hand had been too uncoordinated to make the jewelry that she loved to create. Now, she was walking without even the aid of a cane, she was living on her own, she was driving a car, and she was back in college. Her voice was much better, her double vision was gone, and the coordination of her left hand had improved so much that she was now able to weave macramé necklaces that were just as intricate and beautiful as the ones she had made before the accident. How I thanked the Lord for these wonderful blessings!

I wanted to make Christmas presents for everyone and was so grateful to finally be able to do macramé again! I believe I made five or six necklaces and it was actually fun! What a contrast to the first time I attempted to make macramé jewelry following my accident!

During Christmas break, a reporter from the "Durango Herald" newspaper visited Sharon's brain injury support group, to find out more about brain injury so that he could write an article about it and about its impact on the lives of those who have experienced it. He told Sharon that he wanted to interview her, so he came over to her house and talked with her about her accident, and how her life had changed as a result of it. Then he took pictures of her and her cat. The two-page article, which was very well written, appeared in the paper on January 7, 1999.

I was happy to be a part of getting the word out about brain injury and its effects, so I didn't mind being the "poster child" for brain injury, brief though it was.

On January 11th, Sharon began her second semester at college. She took three courses, totaling eight credit hours—History of the Film, which was an English course, Southwest Studies II, a continuation of the class she had taken the previous semester, and a swimming course that was designed for people with physical disabilities. Sharon did well this semester—making A's and B's on most of her papers and tests, and her final grades were A in swimming, B+ in History of the Film, and B in Southwest Studies, giving her a grade point average of 3.21 for the semester.

I had finally come to terms with the fact that my expectations of myself now needed to be adjusted because of my injury, so I was actually proud of myself for making the grades I did during my second semester back in college. I could recognize that getting a B was more than equal to any A I ever received prior to my injury.

And the first time that she typed a paper, she received a very pleasant surprise. She found that the hours of weaving necklaces for Christmas presents had improved the coordination of her left hand enough so that she could now type with all ten fingers. Also, when she tried playing her flute, she discovered that she was able once again to do the fingering with all the fingers on both of her hands. "I guess when I made that jewelry, I was doing therapy without even realizing it!" she laughed excitedly, as she joyfully told me of her newly regained abilities.

What a wonderful discovery – to be able to type with all ten fingers again! That's my kind of therapy—the kind you are doing without even realizing it!

However, even though Sharon did well in her courses, she did not enjoy English as much as she had before the accident, and she seemed to be having difficulty in organizing her papers and also in getting started on them soon enough to get them turned in on time. Although her writing was extremely good, the material pertaining to each point that she sought to cover tended to be scattered throughout her paper, rather than being all together in the same place. Sharon was afraid that her organizational skills and her initiation ability had been impaired by her injury.

"I hate English now," she complained to me one day. "It's too hard. I don't think I want to be an English teacher anymore, and besides I don't see how I'd ever be able to teach anyway, because I wouldn't be able to talk loud enough for my students to hear me. I think that I should change my major to something else, but I don't have any idea what I want to do now."

This realization was completely devastating to me, as I had never considered pursuing any other career path. I felt like an utter failure when I acknowledged that being an English teacher might not be in the cards for me after all.

162

When Sharon shared her concerns with Dr. Ed, he agreed that a change in her major was probably a wise decision. However, he disagreed with her belief that the problems she was facing were a result of her injury. "You're doing very well in recovering from your brain injury." he encouraged her. "I think that your uncertainty about what career to pursue shows that you're just a normal twenty-one-year-old who isn't sure yet what she wants to do with her life. And although your testing did show that your organizational skills had been slightly affected by your injury, it isn't severe enough to cause the problems that you're describing to me. I think that you're having difficulty because you haven't been in school for a while, and that things will get easier for you as you get used to being back in college again.

After talking to Dr. Ed, Sharon began analyzing the method that she was using to write her papers, and comparing it to how she used to do it before her accident. As she considered this, it suddenly dawned on her that her organizational problems were occurring because she was trying to do something now that she had never been able to do successfully before her injury. She was trying to compose her papers as she typed on the computer, rather than writing them out in longhand first and then typing them, as she had always done before. When she returned to her previous method of writing papers, her organizational problems disappeared.

What a relief to discover that I was simply trying to compose papers in a way I had not done prior to my injury! Realizing that this was causing my supposed "organizational problems" too was outstanding – whew!

As the semester drew to a close, Sharon began considering the possibility of going into the field of occupational therapy or recreational therapy, so that she could be a help to others who had sustained injuries similar to hers. "The thing that I longed for the most when I was in the hospital was for someone to honestly be able to say to me 'I understand what you're going through', but there was no one there who could do that for me," she remarked one day. "If I become a therapist and work with people who have had brain injuries or strokes, I'll be able to tell them, 'I know what it's like to be paralyzed on one side, and to not be able to eat or drink or make a sound.' I could truthfully say, 'I understand what it feels like to be where you are, because I've been there.' And I can give them hope that they can get better too—when they see how well I've recovered."

One day, shortly after school was out, Sharon called St. Joseph's Rehabilitation Hospital to talk to Debbie, her former occupational therapist, in order to find out what would be involved in preparing for a career in that field. However, Debbie was not available, and instead she ended up talking to Rebecca, who had been her recreation therapist when she was in the hospital.

After talking to Rebecca, Sharon realized that therapeutic recreation would probably be a better fit for her interests and abilities than occupational therapy would. One advantage of a major in therapeutic recreation was that it required only a bachelor's degree, rather than the master's degree that must be earned to become an occupational therapist. Since Sharon had already been in school for three years by this time, and she was now only able to attend college part-time due to her injury, she felt that it would take her far too long to earn a master's degree. Another advantage was that there were not nearly as many science courses required for a recreation therapy degree as there were for a degree in occupational therapy. This was very important to Sharon, since she didn't like science very much and was concerned that she might not do very well in it. In fact, one of the main reasons she had hesitated to even consider becoming a therapist was because so many science classes were required for it. In addition to these considerations, Sharon's creative abilities would be invaluable if she were to become a therapeutic recreation specialist.

I had never considered another career path besides English Education, so I was in uncharted territory now that I was considering becoming a therapist. I truly felt that I would be able to offer a valuable and unique perspective to my clients in this new arena. I also felt the impact I could have would be more far reaching than I would have had as an English teacher, and thus my decision was made.

After considering the possibility of this totally new direction in her life, Sharon finally decided that this is what she wanted to do. We learned that the University of Northern Colorado in Greeley was one of two schools in the state that offered a major in therapeutic recreation. We live in the southwestern corner of Colorado, and Greeley is located in the northeastern corner of the state—a nine-hour drive from our home. Since Sharon didn't feel that she was ready to move that far away from us yet, she decided that she would remain at Fort Lewis for one more year and take some courses there that would apply toward the requirements for her new major. Then she would transfer to the University of Northern Colorado in the fall of 2000.

Chapter 11

Throughout the winter and spring of 1999, Sharon's voice and her walking improved very slowly, although she still continued to walk with a limp and speak in a very low, soft, and husky voice. She had been discharged from physical therapy shortly before Thanksgiving, and from speech therapy in the middle of January— not because she was totally healed and back to normal, but because the therapists felt that they had done all that they could do to help her at that time. However, this was not the end of Sharon's efforts to improve her physical abilities. She began working out once or twice a week at a local gym—spending twenty minutes each on the stair stepper, the stationary bike, and the treadmill, on which she was now able to walk at a pace of two miles per hour. She also began going to a massage therapist who was able to help loosen up her tight muscles, especially those in her shoulders and neck. And she began learning therapeutic yoga stretching exercises—in order to stretch the muscles that were still in spasm in her left leg, foot, and toes.

In addition to this, she attended her swimming class twice a week. At first, this class was a discouraging challenge for Sharon. She did well with floating on her back and on her face, and she was able to hold onto a floater board and kick. However, she found it hard to keep the two sides of her body moving in the rhythm required for successful swimming. It was also difficult for her to make her left leg kick, and to coordinate her breathing with her swimming, which sometimes caused her to breathe in some water.

Her swimming teacher was Jason, a college student who was majoring in exercise science, and who was acting as her personal trainer in order to fulfill one of the requirements for his own major. However, Jason was totally uninformed about the difficulties and special needs of someone who had suffered a brain injury. He often added to Sharon's discouragement by acting like a coach and telling her what to do and what not to do. He didn't seem to grasp the fact that she was doing the very best that she could do, and that there were some things that she absolutely could not do because of her injury. In fact, on one occasion he actually could have put her in serious danger of further severe brain injury, or possibly even death, by telling her to dive from the diving boards—including the high dive.

The thought of diving off the low dive—let alone the high diving board—absolutely terrified me, and I had also been told by my medical providers that it would be extremely dangerous if my head were to hit the water first before my hands! I strongly felt that some "disability awareness" needed to be included for these students who were acting as fitness partners for those of us with disabilities taking this course. Also, because I had been athletic prior to my brain injury, I was further humiliated by Jason's drill sergeant-like method of "motivating" me. I already knew I was not doing as well as I would have liked to have done and him yelling at me to try harder, do better, swim faster did nothing but discourage me and cause me to have an aversion to swimming for years to come.

However, in spite of these problems, Sharon's swimming ability improved significantly. By the middle of March, she was able to swim twenty feet, with her legs working together in unison, and was able to successfully coordinate her breathing with her swimming. And in early May, when she and I went swimming together one day, she could swim faster than I could, and she won every time that we raced each other.

In January 1999 we sought the help of Dr. Sloan to find out if he had any suggestions on how the spasms in Sharon's toes could be relaxed so that she could walk better. Dr. Sloan was a physiatrist who worked at St. Joseph's Rehab Hospital in Albuquerque, New Mexico, but who also made regular trips to Farmington to see patients there. He had first seen Sharon when he had visited her when she was a patient at Presbyterian Hospital in Albuquerque, in order to determine whether she met the criteria to be admitted to St. Joe's for rehab. He had not seen her since she had been released from the hospital in October of 1997. When Sharon walked into his Farmington office, he didn't even recognize her because she had changed so dramatically. He was amazed at the wonderful progress that she had made and thrilled to hear that she was living independently, driving again, back in college, and making good grades. "Sharon, your coming in here has 'made my day'!" he exclaimed enthusiastically, "Did you just come in here so I could praise you, or can I help you in some way?"

After examining her, he recommended that she should continue her exercise program until March and then return to see him again. He said that if she hadn't improved by that time, he would recommend Botox injections again to relax her leg and toe muscles that were in spasm. Unfortunately, Sharon did not make substantial progress in the next two months, so in early April, Dr. Sloan referred her to Dr. Esparza to get Botox shots. Dr. Esparza took a long needle and gave her three shots in her left calf—one on each side of her leg and one in the middle, and then two shots in the sole of her left foot.

The shots were extremely painful, but the results were immediate and dramatic. As soon as she received them, her muscles relaxed and she was able to walk much more rapidly and normally. She said that she didn't even have to think about walking, her toes were relaxed, her foot was able to come down flat on the floor without turning in or out, and her limp was almost gone. Best of all, Dr. Esparza said that the full effect of the shot would not even be felt for two weeks, and that it would continue to work for three to six months. During that time, Sharon would be doing exercises to stretch her muscles and keep them from tightening up again. How we rejoiced to see her ability to walk improve remarkably!

However, our joy proved to be extremely short-lived. Within only three days, the effect of the shots seemed to have worn off, and the muscle spasms returned, and she once again had as much difficulty in walking as she had experienced before she had the injections. Several weeks later, when she went back to Dr. Esparza, he regretfully informed her, "Ten percent of the people who receive Botox injections develop an immunity to them, so that the shots are no longer able to help them. Unfortunately, Sharon, you seem to be one of those who have become immune to its effects. There is no point in giving you any more Botox shots, unless a new strain of Botox is developed. This is the only type that is available right now."

When I walked almost normally out of Dr. Esparza's office that day, I feared the almost instantaneous results were too good to be true, so I was crestfallen a couple of days later when the effect seemed to have worn off.

When he heard what had happened, Dr. Sloan suggested surgery as a last resort in solving Sharon's problem with muscle spasms. However, we weren't willing to agree to that yet, and decided instead to take her to a myotherapist for treatment. A myotherapist uses pressure on trigger points to release muscles that are in spasm, and after they are released, uses stretching exercises to keep them relaxed. Unlike a chiropractor who requires many return visits to his office, the goal of a myotherapist is to teach the patient the techniques of putting pressure on the trigger points and doing the stretching exercises so that she can do them herself at home. Since the closest myotherapist was a five-hour drive from where Sharon lived, we planned to make a trip there during the summer and stay for the week that would be required for the treatment. We also felt that it would be valuable for Sharon to return to Rosie, her former physical therapist in Cortez, for therapy several times a week during the summer months, so that she could take advantage of Rosie's expertise.

Another discouragement during that winter and spring involved the frustrating mystery that surrounded Sharon's voice problems. Everyone who examined her was baffled because there seemed to be no physical explanation for her difficulties. Although Dr. Wylie, the ear, nose, and throat specialist, Phyllis, the voice specialist, and Joyce, Sharon's former speech therapist, scoped Sharon's vocal cords in February, and then again in April, they could see no abnormality that would explain her inability to speak in a normal voice. They could only speculate that perhaps the difficulty was being caused by a lack of coordination between her two vocal cords. They theorized that her left cord was probably moving more slowly than her right one, and that by the time it reached the middle of her larynx, her right cord was already beginning to move away from that point and back in the other direction. In addition to this, they felt that there might be a slight gap between the two cords at the back of Sharon's larynx, which allowed air to escape, thus causing her breathy voice. They also felt that she was having trouble in coordinating her breathing with her speaking, and that she had lost the ability to gauge and control the volume of her voice.

Based on these theories, they tried various therapeutic techniques—"shouting therapy," in which Sharon tried to yell as loud as she could, and "breathing therapy," in which the therapist wrapped rubber Thera-Band tightly around her stomach over her diaphragm and had her breathe in and out against this resistance. However, no matter what they tried, nothing was effective. Although Sharon's voice continued to improve very slowly and gradually, the improvement seemed totally unrelated to anything that the therapists tried. Though they suggested several types of experimental surgery, Sharon didn't feel comfortable with having any of these operations, because no one could guarantee that her voice would improve as a result of them, so she felt that the possible complications outweighed any benefit that she might receive from them. At last, it was decided that she should see one of the top laryngologists in the country in Salt Lake City, Utah during the summer to see if he had any further suggestions for helping her voice.

*Regarding the surgeries proposed to help improve my voice, Dr. Wiley said something like, "Well, the surgery to cut a hole in your throat and place a piece of plastic against one of your vocal cords moving it to midline permanently **might** help." I'm sorry, but if you are proposing cutting a hole in my throat to permanently place a piece of plastic against one of my vocal cords, thereby cutting my airway in half, you are going to have to give me more reassurance than "it **might** help!" The way I looked at it was that I could talk right now, albeit softly, but none of the procedures could even offer me any hope that they would improve my voice at all! I felt that we should just leave well enough alone.*

There was one bright spot during this time of agonizingly slow recovery, however. In January, six months after her eye surgery, the ophthalmologist announced that her eye had healed well, and that the surgery to correct her double vision was a complete success. Sharon was elated at this news, because it meant that she could now begin wearing contacts to correct her near-sightedness, rather than having to wear glasses all the time.

Being able to wear contacts rather than having to wear glasses was so liberating! The acuity of my vision was much sharper as the correction is placed directly on the eyeball without the distance between the eye and the glasses. Wearing contacts opened up a whole new world for me, literally!

The 1998-99 school year was a lonely one for Sharon. Although she attended classes at Ft. Lewis, she really didn't make any friends there. During this whole year, she continued to experience deep depression, anger at God, and questions about why He had allowed her accident to happen. Unfortunately, when she honestly expressed these emotions to some people she had met at a Bible study, they acted shocked at her feelings and were at a loss to know how to respond to her. Because of their reaction to her, she finally stopped going to the Bible study.

*Ironically, what it took to pull me out of this deep dark depression was **another** car accident! On March 8, 1999 I rolled my car and totaled it, but amazingly I walked away with only cuts on my hands and a stiff neck and shoulders. Most importantly however, I was given the gift of a perspective shift. I could now say, "Oh! I've been so focused on what I **lost**, I forgot to notice what I still **had**. I can't run, but I **can** walk. I can't sing, but I **can** talk."*

A man who had been driving behind me saw me go off the road and came to my aid. He called 911 and waited with me until the ambulance arrived. After they broke the windshield and I crawled out of the car, the EMTs told me that I was very fortunate that someone had seen me go off the road, because otherwise my car would not have been visible from the road. They also told me that if my car had gone just fifteen feet further, it would have plunged into a deep ravine!

We didn't hear of the accident until later that evening when Sharon called us, and she didn't even tell me about it right away. Since I knew that she had gone to Farmington that day to see Phyllis for a voice evaluation, I asked how it had gone.

"Fine," she replied, "but I have a problem, Mom. I'm supposed to go see Phyllis again on Thursday, but I don't have any transportation to get there."

"What happened?" I asked. "Are you having car trouble?"

"No," she replied, "I wrecked my car."

"You had an accident? Are you all right?" I asked anxiously, thinking that it must have been a minor "fender-bender", since we were talking on the phone and Sharon seemed fine.

"Yes, I'm fine, but my car is totaled. I rolled it," she answered miserably.

"You <u>WHAT</u>?" I cried in panic, "Why aren't you in the hospital then? What are you doing at home? Are you <u>sure</u> that you're all right?"

"I'm fine, Mom," she reassured me. "The EMT's checked me out, and since I wasn't hurt, I just told them to take me home. I didn't want to go to the hospital. I've been in the hospital enough."

Joe and I were appalled, however, that any medical professional would allow a patient who had a history of such severe trauma as Sharon had suffered to go home after such a serious accident, without at least being examined in the emergency room. So the next day, we drove to Durango and insisted that Sharon go to the urgent care center at the hospital for a more thorough examination, which confirmed that indeed she did not have any serious injuries from the accident. How we thanked the Lord for His miraculous protecting power in sparing Sharon from death, paralysis, or another serious brain injury from which she would never have been able to recover. And when we drove to the junkyard later and saw the terrible damage to the roof of Sharon's car, especially on the driver's side, I was convinced that God had sent a guardian angel to cushion Sharon's head and spare her from injury!

When I was examined by the doctor at the Urgent Care, he asked me why I was there. I simply replied that my parents made me come. I told him I had been in a car accident the day before, but that I was uninjured. After checking me out, he confirmed that what I had told him was true. Aside from superficial cuts on my hands, there was nothing else wrong with me.

After this second accident, Sharon's extreme struggle with depression left her. Although she still had times when she felt very sad, she had learned that her happiness depended on her attitude, and that she could choose whether she was going to focus on what she had lost or on what she had left. If she felt herself beginning to slide back toward depression, she would say to herself, "No, I'm not going to go there! I've been there already, and I don't want to go back!" And she would focus her thoughts on what she had to be thankful for, rather than her difficulties. And in early June she was able to discontinue taking Wellbutrin, because she no longer needed it. How I rejoiced that God had answered my prayer, and that Sharon was now totally medication-free.

When Sharon told Dr. Ed about what had happened to her, he was both flabbergasted and thrilled at the dramatic change in her attitude and her outlook on life. Just the previous week, when Sharon had met with him, he had done some role-playing with her, in which each of them had pretended to be the other one. As "Sharon", he had mournfully sighed, "My life stinks! I just feel like giving up on everything! I can't find anything to be thankful for!"

Sharon, as "Dr. Ed", had responded, "Can't you think of anything good in your life to be thankful for?"

And he had replied, "Well, I suppose there's something, but I can't think of it right now."

When he saw that Sharon was now thankful to be alive and that she was focusing on the things that she could do, rather than on what she couldn't do, he remarked, "Well, Sharon, it looks like you've made it through your first emotional and spiritual crisis. Based on the way that you felt last week, I would have thought that you would have been very glad if you had died in this second accident. But instead, you've finally begun to be thankful to God for giving you such an amazing recovery, instead of being angry at Him for allowing your injury."

"And so it took my having another accident for me to come to that point?" Sharon questioned him.

"Yes," he responded, "for you that's what it took. Anyway, I'm really glad that God intervened directly in your life to show you what I've been trying to tell you for months—that God wants you to live, and that He has a wonderful plan for your life. In fact, you must be a mighty special person, because God has given you not just one, but <u>two</u>, invitations to live!"

I still had some hard days, but my lows were not nearly as low now that I had shifted my perspective and realized that what I focused on would determine how I felt. I also knew the incredible struggle I would have to face if I gave into the depression again, so I was very cautious to avoid sliding back down into that slimy pit – the pit of despair!

Since Sharon's car was a total wreck, we immediately began looking for another vehicle for her, and about ten days after the accident, we found one—a white 1992 Nissan Sentra sedan that was in wonderful condition and had fairly low mileage. Best of all, its total price was covered by the insurance settlement that Sharon had received for her old car. As I watched Sharon drive her new car out of the car dealer's parking lot and onto the highway, I once again committed her to her Heavenly Father's protection. Once again, I realized that, as much as I longed to protect her from danger, it was beyond my ability to do so, and I had to leave her in God's Hands.

*I was so thankful to find such a nice new car so quickly! I finally recognized that I **was** truly blessed. It was unreal to see God's direct provision in such a tangible way!*

Following the second accident, Sharon decided to make a scrapbook, in which she placed newspaper clippings, pictures of the wrecked vehicles from both accidents, some of the funny and touching cards that she had received while she was in the hospital, and some other memorabilia of her experiences during her recovery. Making the scrapbook proved to be a wonderfully therapeutic activity for Sharon, because it became a visual record of what miraculous progress she had made, and of how much she had to be thankful for. It also became a useful tool for Sharon to use when she wanted to share her story with someone who was not familiar with her history.

Sharon also continued to regularly attend the brain injury support group, where she was such an encouragement to others that one day Sunny, the leader of the group, remarked, "Sharon, you're like a bright shining star! You're an inspiration to everyone, and especially to other people who have suffered brain injuries."

I was encouraged by Sunny's kind words and also received practical help from attending the brain injury support groups, as people who were further out from their injuries would share their words of wisdom regarding how they had dealt with situations they had encountered following brain injury. I received much guidance and direction from their stories, as I was much closer to my injury and so was experiencing for the first time many of the issues they talked about. I began to truly appreciate the power of support groups, especially for traumatic brain injury (TBI) survivors, because our concerns were so unique and individual, although we shared many similar effects and challenges.

After school was out for the summer, Sharon finally had time for some fun activities. At the end of May, she traveled to Utah with Carol and some friends, and went camping and rock climbing, and she was actually able to climb ten feet up the side of a vertical rock wall! In late June, she attended a folk music festival and went camping again with her friend Tina. On July 12th, 1999, the second anniversary of the accident, our whole family got together and took Sharon out to dinner and then went bowling. Although she was discouraged by the fact that she only scored forty-eight, she did get one spare, and I couldn't help but marvel at the fact that she was even able to bowl at all.

What fun to go camping again and to try my hand at rock climbing too! I had to learn a new way to bowl—given my physical disabilities—and over time, my persistence paid off! I now throw a mean curveball when I bowl! ☺

In mid-July, Sharon and Carol traveled to Oklahoma to attend a reunion at the high school that they had both graduated from. It was a joy to Sharon to see many of her old friends there, although the joy was mixed with sadness when she visited Ernie's family and met Ernie's new girlfriend Samantha, who was also visiting them. But the most exciting social event of Sharon's summer occurred in mid-August, when she had the first date that she had had since breaking up with Ernie. Steve, the young man that she went out with, took her to the fair and then out to dinner, and he repeatedly told her how beautiful she was, which was a tremendous source of encouragement to her. Unfortunately, he was only visiting briefly in Durango on vacation, so he soon returned home to Virginia, but they continued their friendship via e-mails and phone calls.

I cannot emphasize enough the importance of my date with Steve! This was the first guy who had taken an interest in me since Ernie left me, so of course I was thrilled to be the object of his admiration! He was such a kind and thoughtful man that I was deeply saddened to have to say goodbye so soon. However the positive effects which his admiration had on my self-esteem stayed with me long after he left!

Chapter 12

The most exciting event of that summer of 1999 was a twenty-one-hundred mile trip that Sharon and I made to seek help for her walking and for her voice, and also to find out more about the University of Northern Colorado (UNC) and about the field of therapeutic recreation. Our first stop was in Walsenburg, Colorado, where we visited a myotherapist, Judy, hoping she would be able to release the spasms in Sharon's left leg, foot, and toes. When Judy examined Sharon, she discovered that Sharon had tight muscles all over her body—not just in her leg and foot. For five days in a row, Judy spent more than an hour each day pushing on trigger points on various parts of Sharon's body to release the spasms, stretching and massaging her muscles, and then teaching these techniques to Sharon. And by the end of the week, her muscles were much more relaxed, and her walking had improved noticeably.

Another wonderful event also occurred that same week. During the time that Sharon was receiving her myotherapy, we stayed with some dear friends who live in Pueblo, our former pastor, Dan Searcy, his wife Esther, and their family. Sharon had known them ever since she was a small child, and so it was a joy to her to see them again. Naomi, one of their daughters, worked at a store that sold orthopedic shoes. Since Sharon still had to wear an oversized shoe on her left foot, in order to accommodate her brace, we decided to buy some special shoes for her, hoping to find something more attractive than the old tennis shoes she had been wearing for so long. To our great amazement and joy, rather than trying to help us find shoes, the orthopedic shoe specialist told us that Sharon no longer needed to wear the brace anymore at all. She said that it was actually hindering her recovery and impeding her walking, because it was keeping her ankle and foot immobile and contributing to her limping and her toe spasms. Judy, the myotherapist, also agreed with this evaluation, so on June 17, 1999, almost two years after the accident, Sharon finally quit wearing her brace, and she was free of all adaptive equipment at last! We were overjoyed to see that, without the brace, she didn't limp as much, she was able to hold her foot straight, her toes were more relaxed, and she could walk faster and more evenly. And Sharon was thrilled that she could once again wear a pair of shoes that were both the same size. To celebrate, we promptly went out and bought her two new pairs of shoes.

*Imagine how wonderful it was to finally be free of the cumbersome brace and oversized shoe! It was a relief—to say the least—to be moving forward in this respect and to discover that not only was the brace **not** helping me anymore, but it was actually **hindering** my recovery!*

Our next stop was Denver, where we visited Sharon's friends Tim and Ruth, who had been her coach and her English teacher during her high school years. They were amazed at the progress that Sharon had made since they had last seen her, and fellowshipping with them was a great encouragement to her. While we were there, they invited a group of Sharon's friends who lived in the area to come to a cookout in her honor. On the day of the party, a nearby airport was presenting an air show, which was easily visible from their back yard. However, some of their guests wanted a better view of it, so they climbed up onto the roof of the house, and to my amazement and trepidation, they helped Sharon climb up two ladders to join them on the roof.

It was so much fun to hang out with Tim and Ruth again, along with other friends from high school! And although it was anxiety-producing to my mom, it was such fun to be included with the group to watch the air show from their roof!

While we were in the Denver area, we drove to Greeley and visited the campus of the University of Northern Colorado, the school to which Sharon was planning to transfer in the fall of 2000. After talking to an advisor, she was greatly relieved to find out that all of the courses that she had previously taken would be accepted by UNC. While she was there, she also learned what courses to take during her final year at Fort Lewis College to help prepare her for a major in therapeutic recreation.

But the real highlight of the trip to Denver occurred when we visited a recreation therapist named Sherry, who worked at the University Hospital there. The story of her life was amazingly similar to Sharon's experiences. Sherry herself had suffered a severe traumatic brain injury in a car accident when she was eighteen years old. Like Sharon, she had been in a coma, had experienced left-side weakness, and had limped for a while. She had also found college to be much more challenging following her injury, and so she had changed her major to recreation therapy, just as Sharon was planning to do. Now in her forties, Sherry was married, had a daughter, and was busy with a fulfilling career in therapeutic recreation. What a wonderful role model she was for Sharon—as a living demonstration of what would be possible for Sharon to accomplish with her own life. And what an encouragement it was for Sharon to talk with someone who could not only give her information about the field that she was considering for her lifework, but who understood what she had been through, because she herself had "been there." In addition to talking with Sherry, we were privileged to see her in action, as we observed her working with a small group of stroke victims and using pictures of various events that had happened when they were young people to try to improve their memory and speech skills. Sherry even let Sharon assist her as she worked with the group. After visiting Sherry, Sharon felt confident that she was making the right choice in changing her major to therapeutic recreation.

It was tremendously encouraging to meet Sherry and to observe her in action using therapeutic recreation with her patients! It gave me assurance concerning my own career choice as well as hope for future plans! This experience made the prospect of majoring in therapeutic recreation more real and I could easily picture myself in this field using my own experiences to draw from as I worked to help my clients improve their functioning.

Our last stop on our trip was Salt Lake City, Utah, where we went to the University of Utah Hospital and Sharon was evaluated by a laryngologist, Dr. Smith, who is one of the best voice specialists in the nation. After examining Sharon's vocal cords, he announced that he had not found any paralysis or weakness in them. He also told us that, although Sharon's right vocal cord had been damaged a tiny bit by the breathing tube that had been in her throat, it was not bad enough to explain her voice problems. He then made his recommendations. "Sharon," he said, "I think that tight muscles are the major cause of your voice problems. When you were trying to start talking again, you tried so hard that you overcompensated. So now your throat muscles and the muscles around your larynx are so tight that they have caused your voice box to move up too high in your throat—into an unnatural position which makes it impossible for you to talk in a normal voice. There's a treatment that can alleviate this problem, though. It's called circumlaryngeal massage, in which the muscles around the larynx are massaged so that the tension can be released and the voice box can return to its normal position. It often has dramatic results. In fact, many times it only takes one treatment to solve the problem and restore a person's voice to normal." With that, he briefly massaged and pressed on Sharon's throat, as a test to see whether or not this therapy would be effective, and her voice immediately became noticeably louder. How exciting it was to think that we had at last found the answer to Sharon's voice problem, and how amazing it was that it appeared to be so simple.

"I'll send some information about this technique to your speech therapist, Sharon. Perhaps she will be able to do it for you, but if not, you should come back here this fall. Dr. Roy, the man who developed circumlaryngeal massage, is joining our staff this year, so if you can't find anyone to help you in your area, you should come and see him. I'm sure that he'll be able to help you," Dr. Smith continued. "However, in addition to your tight muscles, you do have some other problems that are contributing to your difficulties. Your breath support and coordination need improvement, so I would recommend that you take singing lessons to help with that. And I'm afraid that you probably have acid reflux, which can irritate your vocal cords, so I'm going to prescribe Prilosec to help remedy that problem. You could also benefit from resonance therapy, which will teach you to how to make your voice resonate in your mouth cavity and cheekbones, so that your voice will be originating in your mouth, rather than from way down deep in your throat, as it does now. There is also one more thing that is contributing to your problems. Your soft palate is not closing completely, because it is still a bit weak, but that is just a minor factor in the whole equation."

To receive good news about how to potentially improve my voice was terrific, but I was still skeptical at best, after pursuing so many other therapies to improve my voice with minimal results.

What a relief it was to finally receive some answers about the cause of Sharon's voice problem, and most of all, to find someone who could recommend some solutions for it. To celebrate this joyful news, we treated ourselves to a special dinner and a musical play that night, and the following day, we returned home—praising God for all the marvelous things that had happened on our trip.

When Sharon got back to Durango, her speech therapist, Joyce, began trying to implement Dr. Smith's suggestions, but met with little success, especially with the circumlaryngeal massage. Since Joyce seemed unable to do it, Sharon then turned to her massage therapist, Jessi, and had her try doing it. Although there was marked improvement in the loudness and quality of her voice the very first time that Jessi massaged Sharon's throat, her voice was still far from normal, and additional treatments didn't seem to make much difference. In mid-August, we once again visited Judy, the myotherapist, for several days, to see if she would be able to figure out how to use this technique to help Sharon, but once again, it didn't seem to help her voice very much.

Because Sharon had not found the help that she had hoped for, we finally decided to go back to Salt Lake City at the end of September, to see Dr. Roy, the specialist in circumlaryngeal massage who had been recommended to us by Dr. Smith, the laryngologist. By this time, I was facing an unexpected challenge in my own life. In August, I had been diagnosed with breast cancer. I'd had one operation in late August and another in early September, and I was due to begin six weeks of daily radiation therapy in October. Fortunately, Sharon's appointment with Dr. Roy was scheduled for the time between my surgeries and the beginning of my radiation therapy, so I was able to take her to Salt Lake City, for which I was very thankful.

However, contrary to our high expectations for it, Sharon's visit with Dr. Roy proved to be one of the most discouraging experiences of this period of her recovery. For an hour and a half, Dr. Roy massaged and manipulated the muscles in Sharon's neck, instructing her to talk and to make various sounds as he did so. During this entire time, he praised Sharon lavishly—telling her how well she was doing, how quickly she was learning, and how good her voice sounded. And her voice did sound wonderful—for as long as he was pressing on her neck and telling her what to do-- but when he stopped his massaging, her voice reverted right back to the way it had been before.

When it finally became apparent that, despite Dr. Roy's best efforts, Sharon was not going to be able to produce that same voice by herself, Dr. Roy turned to her and abruptly announced, "I'm sorry, but I'm not going to be able to help you with circumlaryngeal massage. Unfortunately, your main problem is still neurological, due to your brain stem injury. Although the spasticity of your muscles is definitely part of the problem, there are several other contributing factors. Even though your vocal cords appear to be working normally, the right signals aren't getting through from your brain to your larynx, so your vocal cords aren't coming together properly at the top and your soft palate isn't closing completely. Air is escaping from both of those places, creating your soft, breathy voice. I would recommend trying an injection of Gel-Foam to puff up your vocal cords which would make them meet better. That would only be a temporary solution, but if it works, we could correct the problem permanently by removing a small amount of fat from another part of your body and injecting it into your vocal cords to make them fatter. We could also solve the problem with your soft palate by making an appliance that you could wear to keep it closed. However, I think that we should wait a while before we do anything, to see whether or not your voice will continue to get better on its own. Come back to me again in six months, and we'll see how you're doing then." After all of Dr. Roy's initial encouragement, the effect of his unexpected announcement of failure was utterly devastating.

The best way to describe the sudden let down from this experience with Dr. Roy is to picture a balloon being inflated and with each additional breath, the balloon gets larger and larger. But then suddenly, without warning the balloon is released and it flies around the room as the air escapes—finally coming to rest on the floor deflated and defeated.

Once again, the process of Sharon's recovery felt like an emotional roller-coaster, in which our spirits were raised because of the prospect of finding a solution to one of her problems at last, only to have our hopes suddenly dashed. Another discouraging development of that summer and fall of 1999 occurred when it became apparent that, in spite of the myotherapy that Sharon had received, and her hard work in physical therapy with Rosie, her basic problem with spasticity in the muscles of her left leg, foot, and toes had not been corrected. Although her balance and her speed in walking improved, she still limped, because the muscles that were in spasm caused the little toes of her left foot to bend down and under in a hammer-toe position. Finally, Sharon reluctantly decided that she wanted to return to Dr. Sloan, her physiatrist, and ask him to refer her to an orthopedic surgeon to find out what surgical options were available to correct her problem. She hoped to have the surgery done during her Christmas break from college that year, so that she would have time to heal before beginning her second semester of classes.

One bright spot of that summer was the results of the neuropsychological tests that Dr. Ed gave to Sharon in August. Once again, the testing showed that Sharon had excellent verbal skills, and it also showed that her visual memory skills had improved during the previous year—moving from the impaired range to the low normal range. Or as Dr. Ed put it, "Sharon, you have now moved from the 'bottom of the barrel' to the 'middle of the barrel!'" Even though her abilities in that area were still far from what they had been before the accident, we were thankful for each improvement. However, at this stage of her recovery, her progress seemed to move forward at a snail's pace, and could only be measured in tiny, almost imperceptible baby steps. We were encouraged, however, by the knowledge that people who have suffered brain trauma continue to improve, very slowly and gradually, for many years following their injuries.

I was greatly encouraged by the news from Dr. Ed that my visual memory skills had improved, as well as hopeful to learn that my progress would gradually continue for years to come! The gradual nature of my recovery at this point, however was discouraging because I had been used to being able to just "try harder" before my accident and notice results immediately. Although my hard work was ultimately paying off, the improvements were excruciatingly slow and almost imperceptible!

At the end of August, Sharon began her second year at Fort Lewis College—attending class daily and taking two courses, Life Span Human Development, and Intermediate Algebra, which together totaled seven credit hours. In contrast with the English courses that Sharon had taken the previous year, she found that she enjoyed these subjects and did very well in them. She ended the semester with A's in both of her courses, an academic achievement award, and a grade point average of 4.0, for the first time since her accident! Although algebra was a real challenge to her at first, she soon found that she was able to understand it well, with the help of an outstanding teacher, Cathy, and an excellent tutor, a girl named Ellen. To her amazement, she found that she actually liked mathematics courses much better now than she had before her accident—perhaps because of the fact that math is very concrete and its problems have only one right answer. And Sharon also received a completely unexpected benefit as a result of the time that she spent with Cathy and Ellen, because she soon developed close friendships with each of them.

I found that I actually liked mathematics now because the material was not abstract like the English courses I had tried to take and that once I learned the equations, all I had to do was plug the numbers in to get the correct answer!

Another friend who was a real encouragement to Sharon during this time was Joel, a young man who attended our church, and whom Sharon had known since they were both about ten years old. He was the only one of her Christian friends who made an effort to understand her feelings, including her anger at God for allowing the accident to happen. "Sharon," he said one day, "I've thought a lot about how I would feel if I were in your situation, and I have no idea how I would react. I think that I would be mad at God too! In fact, I think that you're doing pretty well that you've been able to work through your anger at God and get over it as soon as you have. If it were me, I'd probably still be mad at Him!" Joel's understanding, caring, non-judgmental attitude was like a healing balm to Sharon's wounded spirit, as she contrasted his reaction to that of her other Christian "friends" who had preached at her and judged her.

Having Joel take a special interest in encouraging me during this time was especially significant because I had lost so many of my other "Christian" friends because they did not or could not understand my anger at God. It was so meaningful for him to try to put himself in my shoes and to try to consider how he would feel if the same events had happened to him. He reassured me that it was actually normal for me to feel the way I had been feeling and that God did not judge me for my feelings even though many of His followers did.

That September Sharon and I attended a very special event—the wedding of Debbie, who had been her occupational therapist at St. Joe's. Like many of the other medical professionals who had worked with her, Debbie had become not just her therapist, but a good friend as well, so Sharon was delighted to be invited to her wedding. At Debbie's wedding, Sharon also had the joy of seeing Dr. Spaulding, who had been her physiatrist and her husband Tim, who had been Sharon's physical therapist. They were thrilled to see the wonderful progress that she had made, and once again proclaimed her to be "a walking miracle." And her former recreation therapist, Rebecca, didn't even recognize her because she had changed so much. When Rebecca heard that Sharon was planning to become a therapeutic recreation specialist, she exclaimed enthusiastically, "Sharon, when you get ready to do your internship, you should come and do it at St. Joe's. I'd love to have you." When I heard Rebecca's suggestion, I thought how amazing it would be if Sharon should end up doing her internship at the very same hospital where she had been a patient.

I felt honored to be invited to Debbie's wedding and was greatly encouraged to see doctors and therapists who had worked with me during the time I was hospitalized at St. Joe's. I was given the gift of perspective when I talked with them and they were able to contrast the incredible progress I had made in a relatively short amount of time with the condition I had been in upon discharge from the hospital. I had learned since my injury that I needed to adjust my timetable regarding my recovery. Rather than thinking of improvement in days or weeks, I now had to consider improvement in months or years, now that it had been a little over two years since my accident.

That night as we drove home from Santa Fe, New Mexico, where the wedding had taken place, the last part of our trip retraced the route that Sharon and Shoni had taken the night of the accident, when they were returning from Lake Abiquiu. This was the first time that Sharon had traveled that way since then, and as she drove the last leg of the journey, from Pagosa Springs to Durango, and passed the site of the accident, any fear that she had still harbored about driving that way again disappeared. As we passed the place where her injury had taken place, I joyfully praised the Lord that we still had our precious Sharon.

Later, I wrote in my journal some reflections about how, even though Sharon had been changed in many ways by her injury, she was still the same sweet, wonderful young woman that she had always been. "There is a sense," I wrote, "in which, as Sharon often declares, the 'old Sharon' did 'die' in the accident, because she has lost so many of her physical abilities, and the 'Sharon' that we now have is the 'new Sharon'. Sharon says that, as time passes, she thinks less and less about herself as she was before the accident, and more and more about herself as she is now. In fact, she says that her life before her injury often seems almost like a dream. And strangely enough, when I think of Sharon, I also find myself doing the same thing—just seeing her as she is now, and having difficulty even picturing her as she was before her accident. Of course she has been changed by the experiences that she has been through, as anyone would be. Yet in every way that is important, Sharon is still the same person that she always was, and I'm so thankful for that! Unlike many people with traumatic brain injuries, whose personalities have changed, or who have lost their memories or their intelligence or have been physically disfigured, she still has the same delightful personality and radiant beauty that she had before, and her intellect and her memory are intact too! Thank You, Father, for preserving all those special things about Sharon that make her uniquely herself!"

As time passed and I learned more about brain injury, I gained a new appreciation for the fact that I had been spared the effects of having a personality change as well as being allowed to retain my memories along with my intellect. Blessings indeed!

In early November, as she had planned, Sharon went back to Dr. Sloan, her physiatrist, and he referred her to Dr. Mitchell, an orthopedic surgeon whose office is located in Albuquerque, New Mexico. Shortly before Thanksgiving, she had an appointment with Dr. Mitchell. After she had examined Sharon's foot and taken X-rays, Dr. Mitchell, who is a specialist in foot and ankle surgery, announced, "Because of your spasticity, you have a condition that is called hammer-toe, which causes all four little toes on your left foot to curl under. Fortunately, there is a fairly simple surgical procedure that can be done to correct this problem. It will be outpatient surgery, done under local anesthetic. In this operation, I will remove a small amount of bone from each of your little toes, and then insert a metal rod in each toe. The pins will stay in your toes for about a month, while your toes are healing, and then I will remove the pins. The result of the surgery will be to slightly shorten your toes, effectively making your tendons seem longer and allowing your toes to relax and be straight again. After you heal from your surgery and do some physical therapy, you should be able to walk much better and faster." What a relief it was to hear that there was a fairly simple procedure that could correct Sharon's problem, rather than the extensive leg surgery which we had been led to believe would be necessary.

On December 17, 1999, Sharon had her toe surgery. During the operation, which took just half an hour, she was awake and talked and joked with Dr. Mitchell and the other medical personnel. How happy we were when Dr. Mitchell informed us that the surgery had gone well and been completely successful. It did seem strange, though, to see something that looked like a silver fishhook protruding from the end of each of the four little toes on Sharon's left foot.

However, although the operation was classified as a minor one, Sharon suffered through an extremely long and painful recovery, because of the fact that a piece of bone had been removed from four of her toes. For the first five days, in addition to taking strong pain medication and elevating her foot, it was necessary to keep an ice pack wrapped around her foot continually. Four days after the surgery, we had to make the long trip to Albuquerque again to have her dressing changed, and nine days later, we had to return there again to have her stitches taken out. After Dr. Mitchell had taken out the stitches, Sharon mentioned that her "pinky toe" was not even with the other three toes, and that it hurt worse than the others did. Dr. Mitchell immediately took an X-ray of it and discovered that the pin had been inserted too far into that toe. To our amazement, and Sharon's great discomfort, Dr. Mitchell quickly took a pair of pliers, grasped the end of the pin in Sharon's "pinky toe" and pulled it further out. She then cut off the extra metal with a wire cutter and tried to bend the end of the pin back into a fishhook shape. Although this procedure, which was done without benefit of anesthesia, was very painful to Sharon, she soon noticed that the pain she had experienced in that toe had markedly decreased.

Although classified as a "minor surgery," the recovery from the surgery was anything but! I was taking Intro to Economics at Fort Lewis College this semester and I vividly remember thinking as my professor droned on and on about Supply & Demand that I was in severe pain! Needless to say, I had a difficult time concentrating on the subject matter presented. I was on crutches for the majority of this semester as well and was taking tutoring to help me understand the abstract concepts in my Economics class. So between Economics, tutoring, physical therapy, and recovering from "minor" surgery my plate was quite full.

A month after the surgery, Dr. Mitchell removed the pins from Sharon's toes. Surprisingly, removing the pins was not very painful, although her toes did bleed quite a bit during the process. However, as soon as the pins were out, her toes became excruciatingly painful! In fact, her pain was just as bad as it had been immediately following the operation. This was a totally unexpected development, because Sharon had not been informed of this possibility at all. She had been expecting to be able to begin physical therapy as soon as the pins were taken out. Instead, she was still walking on crutches and wearing the same unwieldy support shoe that she had worn strapped around her foot since her operation, and she was not able to put any weight on her left foot at all. When Sharon's pain had still not lessened after almost two weeks, we once again returned to Albuquerque, and Dr. Mitchell wrapped each of Sharon's toes with Coban wrap, a soft, blue stretchy tape that adheres to itself. This tape gave support to Sharon's toes, and amazingly enough, within several hours, her pain was greatly alleviated. Dr. Mitchell also prescribed a muscle relaxant for Sharon to take, since some of the pain was the result of muscle spasms.

During this time while I was experiencing a significant amount of pain, I would call the doctor's office to inquire whether or not this was normal and each time the nurse would simply respond that each person's pain tolerance was different, giving me the impression that they thought I was a wimp!

A month later, in early March, Sharon again returned to Dr. Mitchell for a check-up, and after X-raying her toes, Dr. Mitchell announced that the operation had been a success, and that Sharon could now begin physical therapy. So, several weeks later, Sharon began therapy with Dave, who was a physical therapist who specialized in working with foot and ankle problems. However, Sharon's pain persisted, and in May, during her last visit to Dr. Mitchell, she gave Sharon the unwelcome news that, although the operation had been successful, her pain would probably continue for a full year after the surgery, since that is how long it takes for bone to heal. She also prescribed two orthotics to take the pressure off of Sharon's toes—a special insole with a bubble in it to give support just behind the ball of Sharon's left foot, and a metatarsal bar to be fastened across the sole of Sharon's left shoe, building it up slightly. Both of these aids proved to be quite helpful, and in spite of the ongoing discomfort that she experienced, Sharon's walking did improve as her toes gradually healed, and as she did her physical therapy. Although she still had a slight limp, she was able to walk much faster and better than she had before the surgery.

During one of our many trips to Albuquerque, we decided to schedule an appointment for Sharon with Dr. Spafford, a laryngologist who practices at the University of New Mexico Hospital. We hoped that he would be able to do the injection of Gel-Foam that Dr. Roy had recommended to puff up Sharon's vocal cords, so that they would meet better and her voice could improve. However, after thoroughly examining Sharon, he informed us that there was nothing physically wrong with her vocal cords and that they appeared to be working normally, and that therefore, injecting Gel-Foam or doing any kind of surgery on them would not be an option. Shaking his head, he remarked in frustration, "Sharon's vocal cords look fine. I'm not sure why she doesn't have a normal voice. However, it may be a combination of tight muscles and poor breath support. I'll have the speech therapist try some electrical stimulation on her throat and neck to try to get her muscles to relax." However, when Carol, the speech therapist, applied the electrical stimulation to Sharon's throat and neck muscles, nothing changed. Once again, Sharon's voice problem had mystified the experts, and no solution for it had been found.

Since Sharon had tried everything else in a fruitless effort to improve her voice, she finally decided to take singing lessons to see if they might help her. And the Lord led her to a very special and unique voice teacher, Jill, who was a professional singer. Jill had lost her own voice as the result of a car accident, and after her doctors had been unable to help her, she had regained her voice by using exercises that she had designed herself, and she was now singing professionally again. She began teaching these same exercises to Sharon with wonderful results. She had Sharon do various stretching, diaphragmatic breathing, and humming exercises—sometimes humming a note along with the piano, and sometimes humming and playing the flute at the same time. As the spring and summer months of 2000 passed, the quality, volume and range of Sharon's voice improved greatly. Although her voice was still soft, low, and rather husky, causing people who didn't know her to think that she was getting laryngitis, it was a very pleasant and understandable voice. And at last she was able to sing some simple songs, since her vocal range had now expanded to about an octave. How encouraging it was to Sharon to finally see some improvement in her voice.

How exciting to finally find someone who could actually help **improve** *my voice! I had more improvement from a few months of singing lessons with Jill than from years of speech therapy. It was so encouraging to actually hear results for the first time since my injury!*

During the spring semester of 2000, Sharon took only one three-hour course, Intro to Economics, because there were no other courses that Fort Lewis College offered which would count toward her major in therapeutic recreation. However, it was extremely fortunate that she had such a light load that semester, since she had to spend several months on crutches, due to her lengthy recovery from her toe surgery, and since she was also very busy during that time with physical therapy and singing lessons. Also, economics proved to be quite a demanding and abstract course, so she was thankful that she wasn't taking anything else, and she was very grateful when she ended the semester with a B+.

That spring, Sharon had applied to the University of Northern Colorado in Greeley and had been accepted as a student for the fall of 2000, so during the summer she had to make two trips to Greeley to register for her classes and to find housing there. Since all three girls who had been Sharon's roommates during her time in Durango had proved to be financially irresponsible, not paying their share of the living expenses, she decided that when she moved to Greeley, she would live alone, with only her cat for company. She hoped to find a two-bedroom apartment and use one of the bedrooms for a home office.

Originally she had asked me to go with her on those trips to Greeley, but then she realized that if she were going to attend a college that was located four hundred forty miles away from home, she would have to be able to travel back and forth by herself. So on June 7th, she left Durango for the eight-hour drive to Greeley—the first long trip that she had taken by herself since the accident.

Although it was hard for me to see her go, I knew that this was something that she needed to do, and I was so thankful that she was able to do this on her own. Once again, I entrusted Sharon into the Lord's Hands, knowing that He could protect her far better than I could.

When she returned safely, after two successful trips, on which she had registered at the college and found a nice two-bedroom apartment in which to live, I rejoiced with her that she had been able to take this next step toward independence. So with great joy in her accomplishments, mingled with sorrow that she would now be living so far from us, Joe and I helped Sharon move her belongings to her new home in Greeley on August 2, 2000, just a little more than three years after the accident!

I was thrilled to embark on this new adventure and to begin this new chapter of my life! I would now be living in the opposite corner of Colorado from where I had grown up –in completely different surroundings with opportunities for new beginnings.

Chapter 13

On August 28th, Sharon began her first year at the University of Northern Colorado (UNC), taking three very challenging courses, which totaled nine credit hours--Introduction to Recreation, Abnormal Psychology, and Introduction to Statistics. She did very well in school during the fall semester of 2000, making the highest score in the class on several of her tests, and receiving A's in all three of her courses, giving her a 4.0 grade point average for that semester. She found that it was easier to concentrate and to keep up with her daily assignments than it had been the previous spring, and that she was also able to study for longer periods of time and to retain more of what she was learning. How we rejoiced at this evidence that her brain was continuing to heal—even though it was now more than three years after her injury. "You know," Sharon said to me one day, "now I'm studying the way that I should have studied before my accident. Before I had a brain injury, I always used to wait until the last minute and then "cram" for my tests, and even though I always made good grades, I really didn't retain what I had learned. Now, though, I take things slower and study on a regular basis over a longer period of time, and I'm remembering more of what I've learned."

However, although Sharon's grades were excellent, that fall was an extremely lonely time for her. She deeply missed the friends that she had left behind in Durango, and she was having difficulty making new friends in Greeley. Since she lived alone in an apartment, rather than in a dormitory, the only time that she saw the other students was during her classes, and no one seemed interested in taking the time to get to know her. "Mom," she told me sadly, "I don't know what's the matter with me. People always used to like me, but now they don't seem to want to talk to me or spend time with me. I think that maybe they 'shy' away from me because I limp and because my voice sounds different." Since Sharon has always been out-going, friendly, caring, and well-liked by others, this experience of being rejected by her peers was especially painful to her. During this difficult time, two conflicting emotions filled my heart—sadness for Sharon because of the emotional pain that she was enduring, and anger at the people who were judging her by such superficial standards, never realizing what they were missing by not becoming better acquainted with her.

Since Sharon was experiencing such an emotional struggle at this time, it was only natural that she should look back with longing at the way things were before her injury, and contrast the way her life had been at that time with the way it was now. She often remarked that because of her accident, she had a totally different life than she would have had if it had never happened. "If I hadn't been in that wreck," she would often say, "I'd be married to Ernie, living in Oklahoma, and teaching high school English right now." And when she heard that Ernie and Samantha, his new girlfriend, were planning to get married, and then later heard that their wedding had indeed taken place, it was yet another painful reminder of how much her life had changed. Her feelings of grief for all that she had lost are best expressed in a poem that she had written the previous spring:

GLIMPSES

Glimpses, glimmers of remembrance,
As if viewed in a mirror, thru smoke
Shadows are all that remain
Fragments of an obliterated life
Pieces of shattered dreams
With no way to piece them back together
To form the life which once existed
Even if it were possible to glue the pieces back together,
The cracks would still show

However, Ernie's marriage did serve to bring a very definite ending to that chapter of her life, and as time passed, Sharon very gradually began to be thankful that she had not married him, and also to look forward with anticipation to her new career. Sharon did really miss having the companionship of a boyfriend, though. During her last few months in Durango, she had been involved in two brief relationships, but in each case, she had soon learned, to her disappointment, that the young man whom she was dating was not a person of good character, and she had quickly broken up with him. I firmly believed that God was going to bring a very special man into Sharon's life to be her husband, and I often tried to encourage her by telling her that, but at this point in her life it was very hard for her to believe it.

Moving so far away from family and friends was challenging. It was very difficult for me to go to classes with people who had no interest in getting to know me or spend time with me. Even though I knew it was largely because they were much younger than me and also because I'd had life experiences that made me older than my years, the pain was still fresh each time I failed to make a connection with my classmates. We as a society and culture do not embrace disability or anything different than the 'norm,' so when I encountered this attitude at college, I began to realize this was representative of a much larger population. It was particularly painful during this stage of my life though, when I was in the process of formulating an identity and choosing a career path that I would pursue for the rest of my life.

Toward the end of the semester, Sharon began to find some new friends at last. Tiffany, a girl who was in one of her classes, invited Sharon to go out to dinner and to a Christian coffee house with a group of her friends, and from that time on, they included Sharon in their activities. One night, they decided to go bowling together. Although Sharon was hesitant at first about going with them, because she had not been able to bowl well since her injury, she finally agreed to do so. And to her astonishment, she found that her bowling skills had improved dramatically since the last time she had gone. She got one or two strikes, plus some spares, in each of the first three games they played, and in the fourth game, she got a "turkey"—three strikes in a row, and she won the game with a very respectable score of one hundred twenty seven! How thrilled Sharon was at this accomplishment.

Another encouraging development of that late fall was Sharon's joyful discovery that she could finally sing again. Although she had been trying for a long time to sing, it had been very difficult for her to stay on pitch, and her singing had often sounded more like talking than singing. One day, as she tried to sing along with a song on her radio, she suddenly noticed that her voice sounded different, and she could feel the change in her throat. Excitedly, she called me and sang to me over the phone. Tears of joy streamed down my face as I heard Sharon sing several songs of praise to God. Although her voice was still soft and husky, she hit the right pitch on every note, and she was actually singing—not just talking on different pitches. It was truly the sweetest music that I had ever heard.

While Sharon was home from college for her Christmas break, she experienced yet another exciting milestone in her recovery. For the first time since her accident, she was able to go skiing again! She enrolled in an adaptive ski program, one specially designed for skiers with disabilities, at the Telluride Ski Area, seventy-five miles from where we live. I was deeply concerned that she might fall and re-injure herself. But once again, I had to remind myself that it was beyond my power to protect Sharon from danger, and that I must let her go and trust the Lord to protect her. (However, I was still very thankful to learn that she would be wearing a safety helmet, and that two people, a ski instructor and a "ski buddy", would be with her at all times.)

Before the accident, Sharon had been a very competent intermediate level skier. Though she was eager to get back on the ski slopes again, she was also afraid that she might be very disappointed and discouraged by her performance when she tried skiing again. On the first day of skiing, her ski instructor fastened a device called a "ski bra" to the tips of her skis to hold them together in a wedge position to keep her from going too fast. The instructor also gave Sharon a pole to hold onto to keep her balance, and they went very slowly down the "bunny hill", the ski run for beginning skiers. Although she did fall once during the day, she merely landed in a sitting position and wasn't injured at all, for which we were all very thankful.

However, the second time that she went skiing, Sharon found that she didn't need any adaptive equipment at all. And on the third day that she went, she suddenly found, to her amazement, that all of her previous skills had returned to her and she was able to ski down the same slopes that she had skied on prior to her injury. She was once again skiing on an intermediate level, and for the first time since the accident she felt "normal" again. "All the movements that my body needs to make when I'm skiing came back to me and I remembered how to do it!" she cried excitedly. "On the ski slopes, I don't feel disabled, because I can ski as well as anyone else."

I was reluctant at first at the thought of going skiing again because I feared I would find yet another thing I could no longer do, but imagine my delight to discover that my muscles remembered how to ski even though I had been injured! On the ski slopes, the playing field was leveled. I even saw someone who was a

paraplegic skiing on a Monoski and other skiers who were blind!
*No one was "disabled" and we **all** walk funny in ski boots!* ☺

What a joy it was for us to see Sharon so happy again, as she did
something that she so thoroughly enjoyed! And how wonderful it
was to know that her strength, balance, and coordination were now
good enough for her to be able to participate safely and
successfully in such a vigorous athletic activity. Skiing also
helped to increase Sharon's endurance and to strengthen her left
leg increasing her confidence about putting her weight on it, which
helped her walking to improve. When she first began skiing again,
the muscles of her left leg had quivered a lot, but by the last time
that she went, they hardly shook at all. And after she had gone
skiing several times, she began leading with her left foot and
putting it forward first as she walked downhill, without even
thinking about it—something that she had never been able to do
since the accident. When Sharon left to go back to school for her
second semester, she could hardly wait until spring break when she
would be able to go skiing again!

Sharon also had many enjoyable visits with her friends in Durango
and Cortez during that Christmas vacation. But none was more
special than the time that she spent with Matthew and Paula, a
young couple from our church whose lives were forever altered by
a deep tragedy that occurred shortly after Christmas that year.
Just before Christmas, Sharon had spent a joyful day at their house
making cookies with Paula, who was eagerly anticipating the
arrival of their first child. However, after the baby was born, she
had lived for only a few seconds before suddenly and unexpectedly
dying of unknown causes. As Sharon grieved with Paula and
Matthew, she was amazed to discover that although their sorrow
originated from a totally different cause than hers, yet she could
still identify with their deep feelings of loss, and they with hers,
and so they were able to be a comfort to each other.

One night while Sharon was home, she decided to call Theresa, the
mother of Robert, the young man who had been in the room next to
Sharon's when she had been at St. Joe's Rehab Hospital. She was
saddened to hear that Robert's recovery was much slower than hers

had been. During her conversation with Theresa, Sharon sought to explain, from her own experience, how Robert must be feeling and how Theresa could best help him, and then asked, with great concern, how Theresa herself was coping with the situation she was in. As I observed how effective she was in counseling Theresa, I could see what a great help Sharon would be, as a Therapeutic Recreation Specialist, not only to her patients themselves, but also to their families, as she helped them understand what their loved ones were going through. After Sharon hung up the phone, we prayed together for Robert and Theresa, and I rejoiced to hear Sharon say something that she had never said before. "Lord Jesus," she prayed, "Thank You for the good recovery that You have given me." How thankful I was that, instead of continuing to concentrate on all that she had lost, Sharon was finally beginning to focus on the many things for which she could be thankful, and that she was grateful to God for the miraculous healing that He had given her.

I was always hesitant to talk to Theresa because I feared I might be a reminder that Robert was not doing as well as I was. However, she always seemed to be encouraged by talking with me, because I gave her hope for the type of recovery her son could make. Each time I talked with her, I was also reminded anew of how much I had to be grateful for!

When Sharon returned to college after Christmas, she was only able to enroll in two classes—Introduction to Therapeutic Recreation and Introduction to Human Rehabilitative Services, which together totaled six credit hours. Since she had already completed all of the general education requirements for her degree, the only courses that she still had to take were those that related specifically to her therapeutic recreation major. Unfortunately, however, each of the courses that she needed was offered only on alternate semesters, so it would still take her three more years to fulfill all of the requirements for her major, and she would not be able to graduate until the spring of 2004.

Once again Sharon did well in her classes, even though one of the courses was made very difficult because her teacher's lectures were extremely unorganized and hard to follow. In addition to this, the textbook, which was co-authored by the professor, was very boring, redundant, disorganized, and difficult to read. However, in spite of these challenges, Sharon finished the year with A's in both courses, and she was able to maintain her 4.0 grade point average!

Sharon's courses did include some very interesting work to be done outside the classroom, though. Ironically, some of these assignments were designed to help the students experience vicariously, by using their imaginations, the very things that Sharon had been forced to live through in heartbreaking reality. As part of the Disability Awareness activity for one class, each student had to spend some time in a wheelchair, testing the handicapped accessibility of various buildings on the campus, and noticing how differently people reacted to them when they appeared to be disabled—something Sharon knew about from painful personal experience. And for the other course, everyone in the class was required to interview a person who had a disability and write a paper about him. Since Sharon had first-hand knowledge of this subject also, she asked for, and received, permission to write a paper about her own experiences.

*During the Disability Awareness activity, my non-disabled classmates were instructed to simulate a disability by spending some time in a wheelchair. I was indignant at the actions of my classmates, who when faced with an inaccessible situation, would simply jump up out of the wheelchair and **walk** up the stairs! I insisted that if they were actually disabled, they would not have the luxury of giving up their disabilities when faced with a challenge, and I encouraged them to try to find alternate solutions.*

Another requirement of these courses was that each student should serve as a volunteer helping people with disabilities. Sharon thoroughly enjoyed this responsibility, and spent time helping at a weekly support group for people who had multiple sclerosis. She also served as a volunteer at a Special Olympics basketball tournament. Sharon's delight in working with these athletes who had disabilities was marred, however, and she was deeply hurt, when an insensitive co-worker assumed that she was one of the participants, rather than a volunteer. In spite of this unfortunate incident, though, Sharon was glad to have the opportunity to reach out in understanding to others who were struggling with disabilities.

I cannot adequately describe to you how insulted I was by the other volunteer's assumption that I was an athlete rather than a volunteer. I felt humiliated by the ignorant volunteer's condescending attitude and in that moment all the gains I had made in my recovery were minimized.

That semester, Sharon also determined to become involved in some campus organizations, so that she would have a chance to meet more people and find some new friends. She joined the Human Services Club, which had been organized for students majoring in the various "helping" professions, and was chosen to be on the social committee. She also began attending a support group for students with hidden disabilities. However, she soon found that the "hidden disability" support group, which included people with learning disabilities and psychiatric problems, as well as those with brain injuries, covered too broad a spectrum of disabilities to meet her specific needs. Since there were three others in the group who had also suffered brain injuries, Sharon suggested to them that they form their own support group, so Sharon, Joey, Jen, and Cindy, (or the "coma group", as they jokingly called themselves), started their own brain injury support group. Their meetings were a source of great encouragement to Sharon and to everyone else in the group, and they all quickly became good friends, since they shared a special bond that came from truly understanding what each other had experienced.

The brain injury support group met our specific needs for support and encouragement in the academic realm, as we were all learning new ways to study and adapt to our different learning styles. The hidden disability support group attempted to include everyone with disabilities and while it was entertaining to attend, as fellow group members compared and contrasted psychiatric medications they were taking, we found it difficult to gain any benefit from the group itself.

Although Sharon had enjoyed participating in the group that she had helped to start in Durango and she had made some dear friends there, it was refreshing to her to be with others who were closer to her age and were also attending college, just as she was. However, just as had been the case in Durango, Sharon was the only one in the group that was still struggling with physical aftereffects from her injury, although all of those who attended suffered cognitive problems that had been caused by their injuries. In contrast to Sharon, though, the others in the group had much more severe cognitive difficulties, such as memory and concentration problems, as a result of their accidents. As we had noticed since the time of Sharon's accident, it often seemed that the more a person with a brain injury was affected physically, the less he was affected in the areas of cognition, and vice versa. And as always, I came to the conclusion that, although both effects are heartbreaking, the cognitive effects were worse, because they destroyed that part of a person that had made her uniquely herself. Once again, I thanked God that Sharon had not been substantially affected in that way by her injury, and that she was still herself.

Although I was thankful that I did not have significant cognitive impairments as a result of my TBI, it was still extremely difficult for me to attempt to overcome the social stigma associated with physical disability. It was a fairly common occurrence for a complete stranger to approach me and ask "What's wrong with you?" or "Why are you walking like that?" Each time I encountered a situation like this, I was always very accommodating and answered their questions, but upon reflection, after the fact, I was angered at their insensitivity and the intrusive nature of their questions.

Since Sharon had a fairly light load of classes that semester, and since her toes had finally healed, she decided to seek some more physical therapy in order to improve her walking. She went to a foot and ankle specialist in order to get a prescription for the therapy, but the doctor refused at first to give her one. "It's been three and a half years since your injury, and a year since your toe surgery, Sharon," Dr. Weber said. "I believe that your problem is caused by spasticity in the muscles of your leg and foot, and I don't think that physical therapy is going to help you at this point. I want you to go to a neurologist for a nerve conduction test, in order to find out if there has been any nerve damage. Then, I want you to go to the Spasticity Clinic at the Swedish Medical Center in Denver so that they can evaluate you and make some suggestions about how to relax your muscle spasms." Although Sharon was willing to follow the doctor's recommendations, she heartily disagreed with her conclusion that further physical therapy would not be helpful. On the contrary, she believed that, now that her pain was gone, she could benefit greatly from additional therapy, so she continued to ask the doctor for a prescription, until at last the doctor finally agreed to give her one.

And once again, the Lord led Sharon to a very special physical therapist—Susie, who had decided to enter that field because she herself had been in a car accident when she was nineteen years old, and had suffered a mild traumatic brain injury and numerous broken bones. Since Susie had had to relearn how to walk after her injury, she was an expert in analyzing each tiny component that is an integral part of walking, and she was able to pinpoint exactly what changes Sharon needed to make in order to walk better. Though Sharon needed to relearn each little detail of walking properly—all the things that we do so automatically--yet when she was told exactly what she needed to do to improve her walking, she was able to do it. As it had been throughout her entire recovery, it seemed that the knowledge of how to do various things was lying "asleep" or "dormant" within her brain until someone instructed her how to do it. Then, when she was reminded of how to do something, it was as if her brain suddenly "woke up" and "remembered" how to do it, and said, "Oh, yes! I knew that!"

I was immensely grateful for Susie's expertise as she watched me carefully and analyzed each motion I made in an effort to walk properly. She had the ability to break down the activity of walking into tiny steps, no pun intended, and then to bring it all together to assist me with gradually improving my walking ability.

Within just a few weeks, Sharon's walking had improved significantly. Her strength and range of motion in her left leg, foot, and toes increased until they were almost normal again! Her limp was so slight that it was hardly noticeable, and she was walking so much faster that she could now walk the block and a half from her house to her favorite coffee shop in five minutes, rather than fifteen. When Sharon came home for spring break, we were thrilled and amazed to see how much progress she had made since we had last seen her, just two months before. And when she went skiing that week, she was able to ski down a trail that was five miles long—from the very top of the mountain to the bottom.

In addition to helping Sharon to improve her walking, Susie proved to be someone with whom Sharon could share her emotional struggles, knowing that Susie understood what she was going through, since she had experienced similar difficulties herself. One day Sharon told Susie, "I just wish that I could be back to normal again. I know that my situation could be a lot worse, and I'm really thankful that it's not, but I can't help wishing that I would get better and be able to do all of the things I used to be able to do. Sometimes I feel guilty for feeling that way, because I think I should be more grateful for what I do have."

Susie reassured her that her feelings were normal, and that she herself had often felt the same way. "From such a massive injury as you suffered, Sharon," she said, "you'll probably always have some residual effects, just like I still have to live with some problems that were caused by my accident. I believe that you will eventually play volleyball again, although you may find that you can't move as quickly as you used to. And I think that you will be able to go hiking too, even though it may be too difficult now for you to walk up hills that are as steep as those that you used to climb. But don't ever let your mind limit your abilities by allowing yourself to think that you can't do something when you really are able to do it, or by keeping you from even trying it, or by giving up too soon."

*What amazing words of encouragement I received from Suzie!
They were so much more meaningful because I knew she truly
understood what I was going through and the challenges I faced
on a daily basis. There really is no substitute for the gift of
understanding dearly bought by personal experience – this was my
hope for the service I would be able to provide through my new
career as a Therapeutic Recreation Specialist!*

As her doctor had suggested, Sharon did go to a neurologist for a
nerve conduction test. In order to find out how well her muscles
were working and whether she had any nerve damage or any
spasticity in her leg or foot, long needles were stuck into Sharon's
leg to measure her muscle contractions and nerve impulses.
Fortunately, the nerve damage proved to be very minimal, but the
examination did show that the muscles in her calf were in a
continual state of contraction because of her brain injury. Because
of their spasticity, these muscles were hindering Sharon's ability to
walk properly, since they were pulling on her toes and causing
them to curl under, in spite of the surgery that she had had to try to
correct this problem.

Later that spring, Sharon traveled to Denver to be evaluated by a
team of specialists at the Spasticity Clinic at the Swedish Medical
Center there. She was examined by a neurologist, a physiatrist, a
physical therapist, and an occupational therapist. They all agreed
that although Sharon's strength was good and the spasticity in her
leg wasn't evident when she was in a reclining or sitting position,
it was definitely causing difficulties with her walking, and might
even undo the effects of her surgery if it was not alleviated. When
they recommended Botox shots to relax the muscle spasms, we
immediately informed them that Dr. Esparza had told us that
Sharon had built up a resistance to Botox, and he had said it would
no longer be helpful to her. However, to our amazement, they
assured us that Sharon was indeed a good candidate for Botox
injections, and that she had probably not developed an immunity to
them after all.

"I believe that Sharon's doctor probably missed the muscle entirely
when he gave her those shots," Dr. Seeberger informed us. "The

fact that she had such immediate results from the treatment proves that this is probably what happened. You see, normally, it takes a week for the effects of a Botox shot to be seen. The dramatic change that you saw probably came from what we call an 'acupuncture effect', in which the insertion of the needles to give the shots caused Sharon's muscles to relax temporarily. I would like to refer Sharon to Children's Hospital here in Denver for a gait analysis test, so that we can determine how well each of her muscles is working and pinpoint which ones are causing the problem. Then we will be able to tell exactly where to inject the Botox for the maximum benefit. In order to do this test, they will do a nerve conduction test while Sharon is actually walking and they will videotape her walking and analyze how her muscles are working. I want Sharon to have this examination conducted as soon as possible, and then, after we receive the results, we will do the Botox shots. The effects of the injections will last for three to six months, and some people need only one or two treatments to relax their muscles. On the other hand, there are others who have been returning to us regularly for injections for twenty years."

I was greatly encouraged by the prospect of possibly reducing the spasticity in my left leg! Could it be that Dr. Esparza had missed my muscle completely and there was still hope that I could find some relief?!? It seemed too good to be true!

How wonderful it was to hear that there was still something else that could be done to relax the muscle spasms in Sharon's leg, and how I hoped that she would be one of those fortunate individuals who could be helped quickly and permanently by Botox. However, to our great disappointment, although Sharon's walking was analyzed that August at the Children's Hospital, and she received the Botox injections at the Spasticity Clinic during September, this treatment had absolutely no effect! When the shots failed to produce any results, Dr. Seeberger then recommended that Sharon should return to the clinic later so that they could try a stronger dose of Botox and inject it in more places, or use a different strain of it, to see if that would be effective.

While we were talking with Dr. Seeberger, though, we received the answer, at last, to the mystery of Sharon's voice problems. When we mentioned that no one seemed to understand why she continued to have this difficulty, the doctor commented matter-of-factly, "Why, that's a 'brain-stem injury' voice. Stroke patients who have suffered damage to their brain stems are often left with a voice like Sharon's. The low, husky quality of her voice is typical of that condition, but Sharon's speech is much more fluent than most patients who have that problem." Although she gave us no suggestions for any treatment that might help Sharon's voice, or any hope that it would ever improve, yet it was a relief to finally know the reason for her difficulties. And since we had seen a very slow, but steady, improvement in Sharon's voice quality, volume, and pitch during the almost four years that had elapsed since the accident, we still had hope, that with the Lord's healing, it would continue to get better.

Chapter 14

The spring and summer of 2001 proved to be a time of unusual honors and unique opportunities for Sharon. After being nominated by Dr. Carter, the chairman of the recreation department of the University of Northern Colorado (UNC), she received one of the academic achievement awards that are given yearly to outstanding students by the college's Disability Access Center, and was honored at a special reception.

She was also was invited to join the Mortarboard Honor Society, a national honor society for college seniors, which selects its members on the basis of their excellence in scholarship, leadership, and community service. Out of the seven hundred students at UNC who received invitations to join Mortarboard, only one hundred twenty applied for membership, and of these, only forty, of whom Sharon was one, were actually chosen to become a part of the society. She was "tapped", or notified, of her selection when a representative of Mortarboard visited one of her classes, presented her with a bouquet of flowers and publicly announced that she had been selected to become part of this prestigious group. Then, on April 29th, she was formally inducted into the Mortarboard Honor Society, an event which I had the privilege of attending. The induction ceremony was much like a graduation, featuring several special speakers, with the members of Mortarboard attired in caps and gowns. As each inductee's name was called, a representative of Mortarboard read a list of all the scholastic achievements and honors that the new member had received and the activities that she had been involved in during her college career. The new member then signed the society's official roster and was presented with a long-stemmed red rose and a pin with the Mortarboard insignia on it. As I watched Sharon accept her award, I silently thanked God for His miraculous healing that had made it possible for Sharon to still be capable of earning such an honor.

What a privilege and honor to be selected for induction into this elite honor society. It was such a special privilege to be chosen for inclusion in this prestigious group, and I was overcome by being able to participate in the induction ceremony!

A few days later, Sharon received the most unexpected and astounding honor of all. She received a call from the office of the Governor of Colorado, Bill Owens, informing her that he had appointed her to his Statewide Independent Living Council (SILC), an advisory board that makes recommendations to him regarding state policy that affects people with disabilities. (She later learned that, at age 24, she was the youngest member of the council, and that she was the only one who had suffered a brain injury.) Sharon had applied for this position the previous year, but she had almost forgotten about it, so she was astonished to learn that she had actually received this appointment.

Several weeks later, she attended her first SILC meeting in the Capitol Building in Denver, but due to her brain injury, she found it to be extremely challenging and discouraging. The meeting lasted for six hours, including a "working lunch", without any breaks, so by the time lunch was over, her brain had become so fatigued and overloaded that she could no longer follow and comprehend the discussion. "It was like my brain just 'shut down', Mom," she said in frustration. "I could see people's lips moving and I could hear words, but I couldn't make any sense out of what they were saying. It's been almost four years now since the accident, and I thought I was further along in my recovery than that! I don't know if I'll be able to do this job or not." When I heard Sharon say that, I was reminded that Dr. Ed had told her that mental fatigue was the most long-lasting effect of a brain injury, persisting for years afterwards.

I vividly recall the extreme fatigue my brain experienced during this lengthy meeting. Everyone on the SILC knew what they were talking about, so they commonly used acronyms galore! At the beginning of the day, they defined some of the acronyms so I was futilely trying to define them internally while attempting to keep up with the flow of the meeting, but by the time the "working lunch" rolled around, my brain was no longer able to follow even the simplest of conversations.

After the session was over, Sharon had shared her difficulties with the chairperson, who had immediately suggested that Sharon needed a "cognitive interpreter", someone who would take notes for her during the meeting and then discuss them with her at the end of the day. This would set Sharon free to concentrate on what was taking place at the moment, and relieve her from having to remember all that was discussed and having to identify what was most important. Hearing that this type of help was available was an encouragement to Sharon, and she hoped that with this "accommodation", she would be able to fulfill her responsibility as a member of the council. As time went on, though, Sharon found that as she became more familiar with the material that was discussed at these meetings, she was able to concentrate and understand better, and she no longer became so exhausted, so she was able to participate without the help of a cognitive interpreter.

However, the most unique and rewarding opportunity that came to Sharon that spring and summer occurred when she began working at the first job that she had held since her accident—that of a counselor at the Rocky Mountain Village Easter Seals Camp, in Empire, Colorado, just west of Denver. It is a facility especially designed to provide a camping experience for children and adults who have disabilities. There, Sharon joined an international staff who had come from places as diverse as Scotland, Uganda, the Ukraine, Australia, Wales, and South America, as well as from various parts of the United States, in working with campers who had a wide variety of disabilities. Each week was reserved for campers with a different type of disability, such as traumatic brain injury, Cerebral Palsy, paralysis, Down Syndrome, or Muscular Dystrophy, as well as many other conditions.

What an amazing opportunity! I first learned of this potential employment through the Camp Day at UNC. It was such a relief to find the Rocky Mountain Village booth after visiting numerous other booths that proclaimed, "Any type of outdoor activity! Hiking, biking, camping, rafting!" Considering my limited physical abilities and soft voice, I felt anything but capable of doing a job at any of these other camps. To actually be welcomed and encouraged to apply for employment at this camp that specifically served people with disabilities – how exciting, not to mention providing a much needed boost to my self-confidence, as this would be my first employment since sustaining my TBI four years earlier!

Sharon worked with one to three campers each week, and was responsible for their safety, for helping them with any aspects of their personal care that they needed assistance with, and for supervising their activities, their interactions with others, and their behavior. It was a great joy to her to finally be in the role of a "care-giver", rather than a "patient", and it provided excellent, practical training for her future career. She proved to be a wonderfully effective counselor, the campers loved her, and she found the work to be extremely satisfying and rewarding. And best of all, Sharon could give the campers something that few of the other counselors could give—a genuine understanding of, and empathy with, their struggles. At last, she felt that the terrible suffering that she had endured had not been useless after all, because she was now uniquely qualified to identify with, and help, others who were experiencing similar trials.

To finally receive validation that all I had endured had not been in vain! I cannot even begin to convey how fulfilling it was to be able to provide the very thing I had longed for ever since my injury – the gift of understanding!

The previous semester, in a paper that Sharon had written describing her accident and her recovery, she had stated, "The main thing that I feel I can bring to the field of therapeutic recreation is my experience and understanding. When I was going through everything, the one thing that I wanted more than anything was for someone to be able to honestly say, 'I understand.' Everyone was telling me, 'I'm so sorry this happened! I wish there was something I could do! This is so terrible!' But there was no one that could say, 'I understand.' I want to be that person for someone! I want to encourage them that they can keep going. I want to stand in front of them and say, 'I know what you are going through. I have been there. Look where I am now. You can do it. Don't give up!'" And that is <u>exactly</u> what she did that summer at camp. She spent the summer "being that person" for the campers with whom she worked!

Sharon's summer at camp also had several unexpected, but welcome, effects on her continued recovery. Her limp decreased significantly, and she was able to walk much faster, enabling her to travel one city block in only three minutes, in contrast to the fifteen minutes that it had taken her to cover the same distance just one year before. The volume of her voice also increased, making it easier for others to hear her, even in situations where there was a fair amount of background noise. The fact that she had been forced to walk substantial distances each day while she was at camp and that she had to move rapidly enough to keep up with her campers had helped her walking to improve. And since it had been necessary for her to speak loudly enough to make herself heard by others in a noisy environment, her voice had become louder. Her summer's activities had been unintentional therapy for her, which had borne great dividends. Another wonderful result of her summer's work was a marked increase in her self-confidence and feelings of competence, due to her success at counseling at the camp, especially since her supervisor's evaluation of her performance stated that she had done an outstanding job.

*To receive feedback from my supervisor that I was "an exceptional counselor working with all individuals at camp" was a tremendous boost to my self-confidence, and the realization that I could not only do a good job in my future career, but do it **well**, exceeded my expectations!*

The fall semester of 2001 proved to be a challenging one for Sharon. She took ten hours of classes, which was the heaviest course load that she had taken since the accident. In addition to two recreation courses, Leadership in Recreation and Programs in Recreation, she also took Anatomy and Physiology, which was an extremely difficult class that required three hours of lecture and three hours of laboratory work and involved the memorization of a multitude of facts, terms, and definitions. In order to absorb all the material that she needed to learn, Sharon decided to go to the lab portion of the class twice during the week, thus adding another three hours of class to her schedule. The recreation courses involved a lot of out-of-class work also, including observing and reporting on recreation programs, creating several original recreation programs of her own, and writing a paper that described her personal philosophy of recreation leadership.

This semester proved to be incredibly challenging for me as I attended two Anatomy & Physiology (A & P) labs, the lecture for A & P, two recreation courses AND went to tutoring as well! As an academic accommodation, I tape recorded class lectures and listened to my textbooks on tape. So essentially I was going to each class twice, listening to the books on tape, while going to tutoring, not to mention completing the requisite coursework! What a load – whew!

With all of these responsibilities, Sharon felt overwhelmed and depressed. She was especially afraid that she would fail Anatomy and Physiology, and she believed that the only way that she could pass this course was if she had a private tutor to personally teach her the material. This seemed like an impossible dream, because it would take many hours each week for this to be accomplished. However, in an answer to prayer, the Lord provided a wonderful young man named Jeff, who was training to be a doctor and who had been a teaching assistant for Sharon's Anatomy and Physiology professor, to volunteer to do just that. With Jeff's superb tutoring, and with the Lord's help, Sharon not only passed this most difficult course, but she actually made an "A" in it! And she also made "A's" in her other courses, once again earning a 4.0 grade point average for the semester! How thankful we all were for the wonderful way in which the Lord had answered prayer for Sharon during that hard semester, in a way that was "exceedingly abundantly above all that we could ask or think."

Having access to Jeff's individual instruction made the material not only accessible, but most importantly understandable! He truly was a 'godsend' and an answer to prayer!

As Sharon worked on her assignments during that fall semester of 2001, she was encouraged as she realized that her ability to study and retain information had improved, and that she required less time to write papers and to prepare for tests than she had needed just a year before. In fact, it took her only four hours to write a very eloquent and well-written paper describing her philosophy of recreation leadership, even though that was a subject that required much thought and organization. And she found that, for the first time since her accident, she was actually able to postpone studying for her exams until the day before her tests, and to successfully cram for her finals. Though she realized that this method of studying was probably not the best, it was a wonderful evidence of the fact that her brain was continuing to heal—more than four years after her accident!

When Sharon studied the brain and the cranial nerves in her Anatomy and Physiology class, she gained a new appreciation for the tremendous miracle that the Lord had done to preserve her life, heal her brain, and make it possible for her to once again live independently as a normal adult. This understanding was reinforced by a conversation she had with a woman who was an emergency medical technician. After hearing Sharon describe the extent of her injuries, the lady shook her head in amazement. "Sharon, did you know that brain stem injuries, such as you had, are almost always fatal?" she asked. "Do you realize what a miracle it is that you and I are sitting here having this conversation?" And Sharon realized anew that it was, indeed, an amazing miracle.

I've since had many other similar conversations with numerous medical personnel. I've been reminded over and over that there is a reason I am still here – my work here is not finished yet!

The year 2001 was a wonderful year for Sharon. Her successful summer of working as a camp counselor, her ability to excel in the challenging courses that she took during that fall semester, the honors that she had received the previous spring, the new friends that she had made, and her renewed realization of the fact that the Lord had miraculously healed her, and that He was personally involved in her life and was meeting her needs--all these things combined to greatly encourage her and to give her new hope for her future. She finally began to believe that she would be able to have a good and fulfilling life, in spite of her accident and its lingering effects. As she said, when she shared her story with a church youth group activity which she was involved in leading, "Now I'm excited to see what the Lord is going to do in my life in the future!"

The spring semester of 2002 was a busy one for Sharon, as she did her practicum in therapeutic recreation. This involved spending many hours each week at the Greeley Senior Center—interacting with the seniors there and supervising their activities, as well as learning more about some of the practical, financial aspects of her future profession, such as making budgets and writing grants. Her other course, Administration of Leisure Delivery Systems also involved many hands-on projects, as well as a comprehensive paper detailing her own personal philosophy of therapeutic recreation, which would guide her in her professional career. At the end of the semester, she was once again rewarded with outstanding grades for her hard work. And she also received the wonderful news that she would be able to graduate in May 2003— a year earlier than she had expected—although she would still have to do her internship during the summer of 2003.

How exciting to learn that I would be graduating a year earlier and to receive validation that I was doing well not only in my coursework in the classroom, but also practically as I interacted successfully with my clientele during my practicum!

Although Sharon did well in school, she continued to struggle with the physical and emotional results of her injury. Twice more, in January and in May, the neurologist injected Botox into Sharon's spastic leg and foot muscles, and both times, the treatment had absolutely no effect, which was a tremendous discouragement to Sharon. However, in spite of the fact that she continued to limp slightly when walking, Sharon thoroughly enjoyed skiing! When she was on skis, she didn't feel disabled, and not only did her previous skiing ability fully return to her, but she also progressed to the point where she was an even better skier than she had been before her accident. Before her injury, she had been an intermediate level skier, but she was now able to ski on advanced intermediate ski runs! And she enthusiastically took every opportunity to enjoy this sport—the one athletic activity in which she could still participate as completely and skillfully as she had done before her injury.

How liberating it was to fly down the ski slopes! This was the one arena where disability did not exist for me! I felt equal to others skiing and was not self-conscious about the way I walked or performed, as I skillfully cut through the powder turning from side to side, with the icy wind numbing my face.

With the fifth anniversary of her accident approaching on July 12, 2002, Sharon began to feel that she had never taken time to adequately grieve all that she had lost as a result of it. She also felt that her injury had greatly damaged her self-concept and her ability to set limits and to say "no" to others to keep them from taking advantage of her. So she began seeking counsel from Pam, a psychotherapist who herself had suffered a severe traumatic brain injury at age 17, and who specialized in working with people who were dealing with the issues of grief and loss surrounding their injuries, so that she could use her experience to help others. With Pam's help, Sharon began working through these deep feelings of loss, grief, and inadequacy, and learning how to cope with the situation in which she found herself, so that she would be able to accept her limitations, compensate for them as effectively as possible, and move ahead with her life.

I cannot adequately describe the profound impact that Pam had on my life in guiding me as I grieved the many losses I had experienced as a result of my brain injury! She provided a patient, listening ear and a safe place for me to explore these overwhelming emotions. One source of incredible grief was the loss of my relationship with Ernie and my fear that I would never find anyone with whom I could build a life. She always encouraged me that I was doing the "hard work" and I suppose that was true – it did take courage to actually feel these strong feelings and to explore what this meant for me going forward. I truly feel this is a necessary part of the journey in recovering from brain injury – exploring deep emotions and learning to navigate their tumultuous maze. It is hard work, but vital!

Sharon also found opportunities to encourage others who had suffered traumatic brain injuries (TBI) similar to hers. One of these people was Sammi, a 14-year-old girl who lived near us, and who had suffered a severe traumatic brain injury due to a fall from a horse. Although Sammi had made a truly miraculous recovery physically, she was encountering some of the same struggles that Sharon had faced after her accident. Sammi's friends began to distance themselves from her. She also found that doing her schoolwork had become a huge challenge since the accident, and that her teachers didn't seem to understand her difficulties. Because of these problems, she was experiencing severe depression. When Sharon heard of her need, she identified with what Sammi was feeling and she began mentoring Sammi via e-mail. This was a tremendous encouragement to Sammi, and enabled her to survive a very difficult period of her recovery.

Sharon was a great comfort to Sammi because she knew that Sharon understood what she was feeling. She was also a wonderful role model to her because she had experienced the same difficulties and had come through them successfully.

I found tremendous satisfaction in the opportunity to encourage Sammi by being able to identify with her feelings and struggles. It was one of the first times I had truly been able to use my experiences to help someone going through a similar ordeal.

In addition to this, Sharon proved to be a tremendous comfort to Bev and Rocky, some dear friends of ours, after their 15-year-old son, Denver, was involved in a horrendous multiple roll-over car accident and received a brain injury similar to Sharon's. Although Denver was still hospitalized and in a coma at this time, seeing her gave tremendous hope to his parents at a very discouraging time in his recovery, because they knew that she had experienced "brain shearing," just as their son had. To see her smiling face and know that she was once again able to function normally and to live independently was a balm for their aching hearts! And after Denver woke up from his coma, Sharon's picture board symbols played a role in designing a means for Denver to communicate until he was once again able to speak.

Sharon had a wonderful chance to share the perspective of someone who has an acquired disability when she was invited to be a member of a panel that spoke during Disability Awareness Week at the University of Northern Colorado where she was a student. The panelists were each asked to describe a day in their lives and to tell how their disability had affected their everyday lives. They were also asked two additional questions—what, if anything, they had gained as a result of their disability, and what was the most important thing that they would like to communicate to the audience. In response to the first question, Sharon said, "I've gained empathy for others because of my disability." And she answered the second question by stating, "I'd like everyone to know that I have not always been disabled, and I would like each of you to think carefully about how you treat people with disabilities, and realize that at any moment you could become one of us!"

I thoroughly enjoyed being a member of this panel and viewed it as my opportunity to educate a wide variety of people at the same time. The feedback from the panel attendees' surveys conveyed that my objective had been met, abundantly!

The summer of 2002, five years after her accident, found Sharon once again working at the Rocky Mountain Village Easter Seals Camp, using the unique empathy and understanding that she had developed as a result of her experiences to reach out to others who were struggling and to make a difference in their lives.

Getting the chance to serve as a camp counselor again at the Rocky Mountain Village Easter Seals camp was tremendously rewarding and I experienced a joyous reunion with many of the same counselors I had worked with my first summer there!

Chapter 15

The fall semester of 2002 was an extremely busy and challenging one for Sharon. In order to be able to graduate in the spring of 2003, she had to take three very difficult courses—Clinical Aspects of Therapeutic Recreation, Programs in Recreation, and Research and Development in Recreation. The classes involved doing many complicated projects—writing a research paper about a specific disability, doing a case study on an individual patient, designing a therapeutic recreation program, and designing, conducting, and analyzing a survey to determine the effectiveness of a program. Once again, her work proved that her intellectual and writing abilities had remained intact, as her papers were well-written and were very knowledgeable and professional. Her hard work was rewarded with an "A" in the Clinical Aspects of Recreation course, and with "B's" in the other two classes.

This semester proved to be a very challenging one indeed so I was grateful for the B's. Although I would have preferred A's, I had learned early on in my return to college that I had to adjust my expectations regarding grades now that my abilities had changed.

With the fifth anniversary of the accident past, Sharon was pleasantly surprised to find that she was still continuing to heal both physically and cognitively. Although her voice was still soft and husky, it continued to gradually grow better in volume and quality, and her vision suddenly made such an improvement that she found that she needed a weaker prescription for her contact lenses. As she studied, she found that some of her visual learning abilities were beginning to return. Although this was encouraging, it was also a bit confusing to her, because she had become accustomed to studying by listening to her professors' lectures and to her textbooks on tape. Now, she was uncertain as to how many of these accommodation strategies she still needed to use and how much she could once again rely on her visual learning abilities.

This was an encouraging, yet perplexing discovery as I had previously learned a "new way to learn," that now appeared to need some revising.

However, the most surprising development of that fall occurred when Sharon returned to the neurologist for another round of Botox shots to see if they could relieve the spasticity in her leg, foot, and toe muscles and enable her to walk better. Although this treatment had failed repeatedly to help her in the past, Sharon and the doctor agreed to give it one more try. This time, the doctor performed a sophisticated test to determine whether or not the medication was being injected into the correct muscle, and to everyone's amazement, they discovered that all of the previous shots that Sharon had received had been injected into the wrong place! They found that Sharon had an anatomical variation in the muscles of her leg, and that the muscle that is usually found to the left of the Achilles tendon was to the right of that tendon in Sharon's leg, and also that the muscle that is behind that tendon was much deeper inside Sharon's leg than it is in most people.

When the doctor discovered her mistake and placed the injection in the correct muscles, Sharon's spasticity was greatly reduced and her walking improved. She was able to walk much faster and more evenly, so that she was hardly limping at all. Although the doctor cautioned her that the effects of the treatment might wear off within three to six months, and she might have to return for additional shots, it was still encouraging that she was finally experiencing some improvement in her ability to walk as a result of the injections.

As 2002 drew to a close, we looked back and thanked the Lord for sparing Sharon's life several times during that year when she had faced some potentially dangerous situations. Twice she had been involved in skiing accidents that could have caused her serious injury or death. Once, as she was getting off the ski lift, the ski lift chair suddenly hit her and knocked her to the ground, causing her to hit her head. And another time, she lost control as she was skiing, somersaulted down a steep hill, and landed upside down on her head. However, both times she was wearing a helmet, as she always does when skiing, and when she fell down the hill, she landed in soft snow, rather than on a hard surface. Also, on the day after the fifth anniversary of the accident, while we were visiting Sharon, we were all involved in another accident when a deer ran across the road and our car hit it. Although Sharon was sitting in the front seat of the car, she was not injured at all. We were once again reminded that "safety is of the Lord" and that our lives are in His Hands, and that we had to commit Sharon to Him, because only He can keep her safe.

While Sharon was home during Christmas break, we had a special treat as we had the opportunity to meet with Kim and Krickitt Carpenter, a young couple who live in Farmington, New Mexico. In 1993, they were involved in a terrible car accident, leaving Kim with serious injuries and Krickitt with a severe traumatic brain injury (TBI), which left her unable to remember meeting and marrying Kim. Over the next several years, Kim courted her a second time and she learned to know and love him once again. He then proposed to her and they had another wedding ceremony. Their story is internationally known, and they have written a book,

The Vow, which tells about their experiences. They presented Sharon with an autographed copy of their book. "Sharon," they wrote, "We hope you enjoy the book and find it inspiring. The Lord has truly blessed us, and we pray He bestows many blessings on you as well. Always remember that you are a blessing to many as a result of God's wonderful work. Keep striving for success and keep your eyes fixed on the Lord! All the best, Kim and Krickitt. Philippians 4:13. 'I can do all things through Christ Who strengthens me.'" Sharon greatly enjoyed fellowshipping with someone else who had undergone the same trauma that she had experienced and who could truly understand what she had gone through. But best of all were their encouraging words to her. "Sharon," they told her, "we would never have guessed that you have suffered a traumatic brain injury unless you had told us. You have made a truly remarkable recovery during the past five years, and you will continue to heal. Krickitt is still improving, even though it has been nine years since her accident. You have an amazingly wonderful positive attitude, and you will help many people!"

How amazing it was to meet someone else who had sustained a severe traumatic brain injury, just as I had, and who was living a "normal" life now! Their encouraging words stayed with me and continued to encourage me long after!

The spring semester of 2003, Sharon's last semester in college, proved to be an eventful and encouraging one for her. Even though it had now been more than five years since her accident, her brain continued to heal and she experienced additional recovery physically, emotionally, and cognitively. In late February, she received another round of Botox shots, which once again helped to relax the spasticity in her calf, foot, and toe muscles. This time, however, she followed the treatment by going to physical therapy, in order to take full advantage of this improvement. Susie, the physical therapist who had treated Sharon previously, was amazed at how much progress she had made in the two years since she had last seen her. This time, during therapy, Susie was able to give her some very practical pointers that improved her walking. One tip that helped her greatly was Susie's reminder to take the same size steps with each foot. When Sharon began doing this, her gait became much more even, and her limp disappeared almost completely

Not only did Sharon's walking improve—her skiing ability did too. During spring break, she and Joe began skiing "expert" ski runs, and she found that since she could walk better, she could also ski better! And then, in May, Sharon proudly informed us, "Mom and Dad, I can run again!" Tears of joy filled our eyes as she proceeded to demonstrate her ability by running back and forth on the sidewalk in front of her apartment, with even strides, at a good pace.

Oh, to be able to run again! It still felt a bit awkward and clumsy, but to be able to move at a faster pace was so normalizing. This gave me hope for continued improvement now that it had been almost six years since my injury.

However, the most encouraging development of that spring came when Sharon went to a voice specialist named Fran. Her slow progress in regaining her voice had continued to be the thing that discouraged Sharon most about her recovery. After seeing numerous specialists, she had almost given up hope that anyone could help her, but she decided to give voice therapy one more chance. Fran scoped Sharon's vocal cords and found out that they were still not completely meeting at the back. This allowed air to escape between them and caused Sharon's soft, breathy voice. However, Fran suggested that Sharon try to talk at a higher pitch. To Sharon's amazement, when she followed Fran's advice, the volume of her voice increased, and the quality of her voice improved greatly. To her delight, she found that not only her speaking voice, but also her ability to sing, had gotten better.

Sharon did well with the two courses that she took that final semester—Techniques of Recreation Therapy and Management and Issues in Recreation Therapy, and she made A's in both of them. She was pleasantly surprised to find out that she no long needed to listen to her textbooks on tape or tape her professors' lectures. And she also found that she was regaining the ability to cram for tests and to put off doing assignments until the last minute! This confirmed the fact that her visual learning ability and her other cognitive processes were indeed returning to normal as her brain continued to heal.

In February, Sharon was honored by being inducted into the Golden Key International Honor Society, and I had the joy of being present for that happy occasion. How amazing it was to realize that this was the second honor society that she had been invited to join since her accident. Soon after Sharon became a member of this group, she was chosen to be their Publications Editor, and she participated in a weekend officers' retreat. As she interacted with the others in attendance, she suddenly realized that she was feeling more like her old self—the "Sharon" she had been before her brain injury. She was finally beginning to feel confident again in her ability to contribute something meaningful to the discussions in which she was involved. And to her joyful surprise, her new friends didn't even seem to notice that she had a disability.

As the Publications Editor, I had to write an article as an entry into the Golden Key magazine for potential publication. I drafted an article summarizing the retreat experience and highlighted the bonding that took place among the attendees over the course of the weekend. Although my entry was not selected for publication, it definitely was a confidence-building exercise to be selected as an officer for my chapter of the Golden Key Honor Society.

That spring, Sharon once again had an opportunity to speak during Disability Awareness Week as a member of a panel discussion. As she shared her story and her unique perspective concerning disabilities, she realized that she thoroughly enjoyed speaking in front of people. When she mentioned this experience to her counselor, Pam remarked, "Sharon, I think that you have the ability to be a great motivational speaker and writer!" She then invited Sharon to attend a Brain Injury Association retreat, as a representative of the Statewide Independent Living Council, the council to which Sharon had been appointed by Colorado Governor Bill Owens.

Saturday, May 10, 2003 was a day of great rejoicing for our family, as Sharon graduated with a 3.66 grade point average, and with honors, from the University of Northern Colorado, and received a Bachelor of Science degree in Therapeutic Recreation! How we praised and thanked God through tears of joy as we watched Sharon walk up to receive her diploma! It was a day of celebrating the many miracles that God had done for Sharon—a marvelous day that would never have been possible without God's gracious intervention in Sharon's life, as He did the impossible!

*I could not believe I had **finally** graduated! The satisfaction in my achievement and realization that all of my hard work had finally paid off was absolutely unbelievable!*

However, Sharon's graduation was also extremely memorable for another reason. The spring 2003 commencement proved to be the most unusual one ever held at the University of Northern Colorado. The night before the ceremony, several inches of heavy wet snow fell in Greeley, collapsing the canopy under which the dignitaries were to sit, and making it impossible for the graduation to be held outdoors, as had been planned. Early on the morning of Sharon's graduation day, we received a tearful phone call from her. "Mom," she sobbed into the phone. "They cancelled my graduation!"

"They can't do that!" I exclaimed in disbelief, but it was true! The University of Northern Colorado had indeed cancelled the graduation, due to the weather. A few minutes later, we received another call from Sharon, informing us that the graduation would be held in the gymnasium, with only the graduates present, because there would be no room for any guests. However, the university soon changed this plan, no doubt due to the protests of irate parents, and announced that family and friends would be allowed to come into the building until it was filled to capacity.

We hurried over to the gym and found a seat on the bottom row of the bleachers. As the graduates arrived, they were directed to stand in the middle of the basketball court, since there was no seating for them in the stands. After they had all assembled there, they were instructed to be seated—on the floor, because no chairs had been provided for them (as all of the chairs were in the football field covered with snow). It was an unforgettable and incongruous sight—to see an entire class of college graduates in their caps and gowns sitting cross-legged on the floor like kindergartners. But we had a ringside seat, right next to where Sharon was sitting, instead of being high up in the bleachers where we would barely be able to see her. And nothing could quench our joy at the great miracle that took place that wonderful day.

To say that my graduation was memorable would be a monumental understatement, but the reasons for this were unbelievable even to those who experienced it! About a week prior to graduation I had received a letter from the university informing me that the graduation ceremony would be held outside "rain or shine" and instructed me to plan accordingly. **They** *did not plan on snow, even though it had been predicted on the weather for at least a week before the ceremony was scheduled to occur. So when, a few weeks after the graduation debacle, I received a letter from UNC informing me that the problem was that they did not have a contingency plan (REALLY?!?) and the letter went on to promise me that they would never allow this to occur again.in the future, I can assure you that I was not relieved to know that no other graduates would not have to suffer this same demeaning treatment I had experienced! They even included a VHS video of the ceremony that was (I suspect) a copy of a parents' taping of the graduation but it accurately captured the mayhem that ensued, as you could not really make out anything that was going on, but only heard background noise. It was obvious to me that they did not have a contingency plan and were therefore unprepared.to the point that all of the graduates had to sit on the gymnasium floor in full regalia because all of the chairs were in the football field covered with snow! I was perturbed to say the least!*

However, although Sharon had "marched" with her class on May 10th, her education was not yet completed. She still had to do 12 credit hours of internship in therapeutic recreation. On May 19th, she began this part of her training at the King Adult Day Enrichment Program (KADEP) in Denver, a day program for adults with neurological illnesses and disorders such as Multiple Sclerosis, strokes, and brain injuries. For the next seventeen weeks, she worked there full-time, gaining invaluable practical experience that would prepare her for her future career. During this time, she was also required to do several major papers and projects, since the internship was a course done for college credit.

*Though I was immensely blessed to have been granted an internship at KADEP, as the application process was quite competitive, and the training I received there was top notch, another challenge soon presented itself. I had to commute an hour each direction from Greeley to Denver and back again every day. The cumulative fatigue began to take its toll on me. My advisor at UNC began to express concern that I was wearing myself out with all the driving. I had to acknowledge that she was right, so I began brainstorming with another professor about possible solutions to my predicament. She suggested the possibility of extending my internship in an attempt to relieve some of the pressure on me. This would allow extra time for me to complete major projects and to maximize the time I was spending down there. My internship was slated to last 15 weeks, but with the extension I completed a total of 17 weeks at KADEP. I was pleased to find out that I would actually be helping **them** out by providing coverage during the interim between semesters – so it was truly a win-win scenario!*

While serving as an intern at KADEP, Sharon was responsible for leading three recreational classes. One was humor therapy— "Laughter is the Best Medicine", and the other two involved doing crafts—"Knotty Macramé", which focused on macramé projects, and "Mayflower Crafts", which included various handcrafts from pioneer days. She also co-led 3 other groups—"Bowling", "Backyard Barbecue", and "Friday Afternoon Club", which featured a variety of activities, and she helped with hydotherapy and with other types of exercise. In addition to this, she also learned much about the medical aspects of therapeutic recreation, such as assessing and evaluating clients, making care plans, working one-on-one with clients, and writing clinical notes. By the end of her internship, she had received very practical, well-rounded training in the field of therapeutic recreation.

Although the summer of 2003 was filled with wonderful learning opportunities for Sharon, it was also a very challenging time for her. When she first began her training, she felt overwhelmed by the demands of the job. As she sat in staff meetings and listened to professionals discussing the typical characteristics of people who had suffered brain injuries, she sometimes wondered if she would really be able to function adequately in this field. Another issue that she struggled with was whether or not she should disclose to her co-workers and clients that <u>she</u> had suffered a brain injury.

However, she soon learned that her coworkers had already been informed of this fact by her supervisor. Unfortunately, some of the staff at KADEP, including Sharon's boss, had trouble believing that she would be able to perform her responsibilities because of her disability, so she found that she had to work extra hard to prove that she could do the job. Fortunately, there were other staff members who encouraged Sharon because they saw her great potential and believed in her ability. By the end of the summer, the entire staff, including her boss, was convinced of Sharon's unusual gifts as a Therapeutic Recreation Specialist. Her supervisor wrote a glowing letter of recommendation for Sharon, ending with the words, "Thank you for giving me this chance to 'brag on' Sharon!" She also recommended that Sharon receive an "A" for her internship course, although for some unknown reason, her professor only gave her a "B", to Sharon's great disappointment. In spite of this, Sharon found great satisfaction in knowing that she had done her job well, and she realized that she actually deserved an "A", even though she had not received one.

How immensely rewarding and tremendously satisfying to be able to successfully complete my 17 week internship! I received top-notch training and experience while I was at KADEP, and I learned that I had chosen a career in a field that would be fulfilling to me—because I had the opportunity to use my own life experiences as well as the gift of understanding to help my clients achieve their maximum potential.

Throughout the summer, several of Sharon's clients asked her if she had a brain injury, as they observed the slight hesitation in her gait and the softness of her voice. She was honest with them about her disability, and she became a source of great encouragement for these clients, as they realized that she truly understood what they were going through. One patient had a weakened left side and was in a wheelchair, due to a stroke. Other staff members had tried to convince her to use a walker, but she had refused. When Sharon suggested that she should attempt to walk with a walker, the lady finally agreed to try, since she knew that Sharon had experienced a similar disability and overcome it. By the time the summer was over, this lady was using her walker most of the time, and was hardly using the wheelchair at all. Sharon was discovering that the empathy that she had gained as a result of her accident and all its aftermath was the greatest asset that she could bring to her career in therapeutic recreation.

Another challenge that Sharon faced was speaking loudly enough to be heard by the groups that she was leading. Although her voice had greatly improved, it was still difficult for her to make herself heard when she was speaking to a large group or to someone who was hard of hearing. This problem was solved by a wonderful device called the ChatterVox, which was provided for her by the Department of Vocational Rehabilitation. It consisted of a small headset, which contained a microphone, and an amplifier that she wore around her waist. This amplified her voice enough so that she could easily be heard by her clients. However, by the end of the summer, her voice had become louder and of much better quality, so that she found that she did not need her voice amplifier as frequently.

The ChatterVox was an amazing device that enabled me to effectively lead my groups during my internship without having to consciously think about trying to project my voice. This allowed me to reserve my mental energies for concentrating on what I was trying to communicate rather than on the act of communicating itself—very liberating!

One of Sharon's clients, a young man in his twenties, suffered from an unidentified neurological disorder, which caused him to have a very whispery voice. He was extremely interested in getting a system similar to Sharon's ChatterVox. However, he died suddenly during the summer, and Sharon experienced for the first time the difficult experience of losing a client to death.

This was not to be my last experience with losing a client to death during the time I worked with him or her. It never got any easier even though I knew death was an inevitable part of life. Each time I encountered the death of a young client in particular, I was overwhelmed at the seeming injustice, and I felt that they were "robbed" of life all too soon!

As Sharon began leading her activity groups, she was surprised to find that her clients were much more severely disabled, both physically and mentally, than she had expected that they would be. In her handcraft groups, there were several people who had the use of only one hand, and one who was blind. And many of the clients in her laughter therapy group had cognitive impairments that made it difficult for them to grasp the humor that Sharon was trying to present. However, as the summer progressed, she learned how to simplify and adapt what she was doing and how to help her clients learn to use the abilities that they <u>did</u> have to accomplish their projects.

One highlight of Sharon's summer occurred when she invited Josh Blue, a friend she had worked with at the Rocky Mountain Village Easter Seals Camp, who had Cerebral Palsy and who had become a comedian to perform at KADEP. All of the clients greatly benefited from his example of finding humor in life despite his disability. Another memorable experience was her opportunity to go on an overnight camping trip in the mountains with some of her clients.

Josh offered to come perform his comedy routine for my Laughter is the Best Medicine humor therapy group, but once my supervisor learned of his proposed performance, she suggested we open it up to all the clients at KADEP. His routine was thoroughly enjoyed by everyone in attendance, as each client readily identified with his struggles and was encouraged by his humorous approach to life! Laughter truly is the best medicine! ☺

In the midst of this busy and fulfilling summer, the sixth anniversary of Sharon's accident, July 12th, 2003, came and went. Once again, we rejoiced in God's miraculous healing of Sharon and her continued recovery, but now our joy was multiplied as we saw how the Lord was using her experiences to enable her to be a blessing to others who had undergone similar traumas. "Mom," she said to me, "I <u>love</u> this job, and I love my clients." And Sharon's clients loved her too. As her internship drew to a close, they hated to see her go. One of them begged the director of KADEP to hire her, and two others offered to write letters of recommendation for her. Unfortunately, however, there was no position open there at that time, so Sharon had to look elsewhere for a job.

I would have loved to have been able to be hired on at KADEP and how unbelievable it was to be offered letters of recommendations by my clients, but that was not where I was meant to be, so I began my job search in earnest upon completion of my internship.

By the time that Sharon finished her internship, on September 12, 2003, she felt that she had gained the experience and abilities that she needed to be a competent Therapeutic Recreation Specialist. One day she remarked to me, "Mom, KADEP was the very best possible place for me to do my internship. I've received wonderful training there, and I feel confident now that I'm well prepared for working in the field of therapeutic recreation." How my heart rejoiced to see Sharon so happy and at peace as she got ready to begin her chosen career!

Part 6—A New Life

Chapter 16

As Sharon was completing the final days of her internship, she began looking for employment. The first job opportunity that she investigated had already been filled, but that facility forwarded her resume to another branch of their company. Several days later, she was pleasantly surprised to receive a call from them requesting an interview, and the following week, during her second interview, they hired her immediately.

On September 19, 2003, Sharon turned in her final papers and projects, thus officially completing her college education, and on September 22, 2003, she began her new job as a Recreation Assistant at Applewood Living Center in Longmont, Colorado! There, she led a wide variety of recreation activities for more than 100 residents, ranging in age from 33-104. She also took them out into the community for various activities, which involved her driving the Center's bus after securely fastening the residents' wheelchairs so that they would be safe during these outings.

Driving the facility bus with capacity for eight ambulatory passengers and four passengers in wheelchairs was a daunting task at best, if for no other reason than the sheer size of the vehicle. On one occasion, I took about nine residents on a "country drive" and accidentally made a wrong turn onto a highway which took us into downtown Boulder during rush hour! I soon suspected that I had made a wrong turn, but this suspicion was confirmed when I heard a voice from the back of the van inquire, "Sharon, do you know where you are going?" I guardedly answered, "No, do you know where we are going?" Fortunately, there was another resident on this outing who had lived for many years in Boulder prior to moving to Applewood, and he was able to help me navigate the congested streets and highways, ultimately guiding us safely back to Applewood!

In addition to this, she also worked one-on-one with residents who were at risk for isolation—those who had withdrawn from interaction with others. She sought to interest them once again in socializing with other people and participating in recreational activities. One of these clients, Ethel, was a 95 year-old woman who was totally blind and almost completely deaf. Even though Sharon had a soft voice, this lady learned to listen for Sharon's voice and was able to understand her, and she responded to Sharon's efforts to encourage her although she had rejected the attempts of many other staff members. As she expressed to Sharon one day, "I know that you understand!"

"Yes, I do," Sharon responded. Once again, Sharon's experiences in dealing with her own disability proved to be her greatest asset in encouraging and ministering to others with similar struggles.

I truly looked forward to my one-on-one time with Ethel each week as I made each of us ice cream sundaes and we were able to spend time just visiting as we shared this sweet treat! She would express her frustration with the "kids" as she called the CNAs who roughly handled her without properly identifying themselves or explaining what they were trying to do, but merely "threw her around" without much care or consideration. She required assistance with sitting and standing, and as I observed the impatience of staff members towards her, my heart went out to her as I could readily identify with her feelings of being mistreated because of my own experiences. Early on during my one-on-one intervention with her, I shared my story with her and this created an immediate bond between us since she knew someone else understood how she was feeling.

I recall one day while I was interacting with Ethel, who had been an RN in her professional career. I observed a nurse enter her room with medication to administer. He did not announce himself or tell her the medications he wanted her to take, but simply thrust them at her in a little paper cup. She, being blind and mostly deaf, understandably became upset and yelled at him. Following this incident, I attempted to talk with the nurse in the hallway, explaining that I felt he would have more success with this particular resident, in addition to other residents, if he would announce himself as well as communicate the medications he was administering. He didn't respond, but just grunted and conveyed that he did not have time for such pleasantries.

Another client that Sharon was able to help was Jose, a Hispanic man who had suffered a stroke and was unable to speak. Recalling how her picture and spelling boards had helped her during the time when she could not talk, she helped develop a communication book for him so that he could make his needs known. It was written in Spanish, and included an English translation for those who did not speak Spanish.

I shared a special connection with Jose also as I too, had been unable to communicate verbally for a time. We soon joked with each other easily as I worked with him and became familiar him and his needs.

In March 2004, I had the wonderful privilege of accompanying Sharon to Applewood one day. It was such a joy to observe how she worked with the residents. She interacted with each one just as a loving granddaughter would treat a beloved grandparent. It was obvious that she enjoyed working there, that she loved the residents, and that they loved her.

Although I did truly enjoy providing services in an attempt to increase the quality of life of the residents at Applewood, it was disheartening to witness these men and women, each of whom had led productive lives prior to moving to Applewood, being warehoused and treated like an annoyance or irritation rather than the worthwhile, respected individuals they were.

My Recreation Director, Brenda, was outstanding and always put the needs of the residents first, as well as conveyed respect for them by encouraging us to address each of them with appropriate titles such as Mr. or Mrs. when speaking to them. She would routinely schedule manicures for the ladies during the recreation programming activities so that the ladies would get a chance to be "pampered", and they thoroughly enjoyed this as evidenced by their fighting over the time slots to get their nails done! We also offered Bingo as a regular activity for the residents, and did their competitive streaks ever come out during this activity, as they competed to win quarters – what fun!

May 2004 proved to be a time of significant accomplishment and honor for Sharon. On May 5, 2004, she took the national certification examination to become certified in her field and passed this test, thus earning the title of Certified Therapeutic Recreation Specialist. She was now Sharon Mehesy, CTRS! With this milestone, her long years of preparation and training were over at last, and she was officially qualified to serve in her chosen vocation.

What an immense relief to have taken and passed the exam designating me as a Certified Therapeutic Recreation Specialist (CTRS)! Knowing that all of my hard work and dedication had finally paid off, I was well-prepared to enter my new career.

On the very same day that Sharon passed her certification exam, she received word of another honor. About a month earlier, she had entered a poem in the Celebrate Life! Overcoming Suicide Art & Poetry contest. Now she was informed that she had won first place, which included the publishing of her poem on the Internet, as well as a cash prize. Her poem was especially poignant because it reflected her own journey from depression to hope as a result of a change in her perspective.

PERSPECTIVE

Depression seductively beckons to me—
Feigning to offer comfort from the pain,
But once I have sampled her 'comfort',
It is too late—No comfort is felt—
The iron doors slam shut behind me,
Forever imprisoning me in this cell

Yet Hope calls to me through the open window
Hope reassures me, "It is not too late! Turn your eyes back
To the Peace that was once yours when we shared this room
You are still in the same room,
The only thing that has changed is your perspective."

My eyes are opened, for the first time it seems,
And I see the life rope
Hope hoists me up to help me stand
I bask in the warm sunshine of freedom that Hope has shone on me

On May 21st, Sharon was honored by receiving the Hope Award, which is given annually by the Colorado Neurological Institute to individuals whose lives exemplify triumph over seemingly insurmountable obstacles, and whose stories would give hope to others who are struggling against great difficulties. As part of the banquet at which she received her award, a video was shown which included Sharon telling about her experiences, and a booklet was distributed which featured Sharon's picture and story.

It was truly an honor to receive these awards! I have always enjoyed writing poetry and to have this pastime not only validated but also rewarded was simply amazing! Having passed my certification exam, being chosen for first place in the poetry contest, and then being selected as a recipient for the Hope Award, I felt that my life was finally beginning!

After Sharon had received her certification in therapeutic recreation, it soon became apparent that she needed to seek a different job. Although she enjoyed working at Applewood, her position there did not offer the opportunity for her to fully utilize her skills as a CTRS. She had been trained to assess clients, to establish goals for them, to develop programs to meet those objectives, and then to evaluate whether or not the goals had been met. Since her job at Applewood was that of a recreation assistant, her main responsibility was to implement plans which had been designed by others.

Ever since my accident, it had always been my desire to be the resource I didn't have when I attempted to reintegrate into my community upon discharge from the hospital. I exited the hospital with a different set of abilities and no clue how to "get back into life." I desperately longed to help others bridge the gap between hospitalization and community life. I knew first-hand how underserved this area was, and I desired to provide a smooth transition for people who found themselves needing this type of assistance.

Also, she was not interested in working permanently as a caregiver for residents in an institution. Instead, Sharon desired to use her unique experiences and skills to help people with disabilities become more involved in their communities by enabling them to participate in a variety of recreational activities. Therefore, she decided to look for employment that would allow her to use her training and pursue her career goals more effectively, as well as provide the continuing education that she would need when the time came for her to renew her CTRS credential.

By the beginning of June, 2004, Sharon had found a position that appeared to satisfy all of these criteria. On June 7th, she began working with Round & Round (R & R), an agency that specialized in making it possible for people with developmental disabilities to participate in a wide variety of recreational activities. She was thrilled to have found a job that seemed to fit so perfectly with her abilities and goals and that would enable her to reach out to many other people with disabilities and share with them the invaluable lessons which she herself had learned at so great a cost.

When I was hired at R & R, I truly felt I had found my "dream job" as they proclaimed that they provided community-based recreation and leisure services for people with developmental disabilities. How exciting! Although I did not specifically have a desire to work with people who had developmental disabilities, I felt that I would be able to gain valuable job experience that would take me to the next level, as I was still relatively fresh out of college.

As the seventh anniversary of Sharon's accident approached on July 12, 2004, it became apparent that she had entered a new phase of her journey toward healing. The multitude of treatments and therapies that had helped Sharon in her recovery had finally come to an end, due to the realization that there was nothing to be gained by any further medical intervention. Between the fall of 2003 and the spring of 2004, Sharon received three more series of injections to help reduce the spasticity in the muscles of her left leg and foot. Although these shots had worked in the past, the Botox ceased to be effective, so it was discontinued, and the doctor could offer no other options to replace this treatment.

However, even though Sharon continued to experience some tightness in these muscles, her walking improved, in response to a simple discovery that she made by herself. One day she suddenly realized that the reason that she was still limping was because she had formed bad habits during the time when she was unable to walk correctly. When she began consciously concentrating on how she was walking, she found that she was able to walk much more rapidly and more evenly, and that her limp became almost imperceptible. As she continued doing this, she was able to relearn correct walking habits that gradually became more automatic.

Also, although there were no medical treatments that could improve Sharon's voice quality and volume, as time went by, her voice also gradually improved. Sharon had now entered the period of healing that would only be accomplished by the continued touch of God's Hand over time.

However, the most wonderful areas of Sharon's healing at this time were the emotional and spiritual aspects. In the months approaching the seventh anniversary of her injury, she began to look at that milestone in a new light. Now, instead of continuing to mourn over what she had lost, she began rejoicing in all that God had done for her. She began praising Him for the many miracles that had made possible the new life that He had given her and being thankful for the exciting opportunities that He was opening up before her. She had grieved her losses, and was ready to move on and begin a new chapter in her life. This was evidenced by the fact that she began referring to July 12th as her "re-birthday" and viewing it as a time for celebration, not as the heartbreaking anniversary of a terrible tragedy. She had truly learned the truth that God had given her "beauty for ashes, the oil of joy for mourning, and the garment of praise for the spirit of heaviness", so that she would be "a tree of righteousness, the planting of the Lord, that He might be glorified."

I felt relieved to have been given the gift of a "perspective shift" regarding the anniversary of my accident – to now focus on what I had to be thankful for, rather than what I had lost and to recount the blessings in my life rather than the losses. I can't say exactly what caused the shift to occur, but was I ever grateful for it! Life is much easier to navigate when you are looking at where you are going rather than where you have been!

Although Sharon enjoyed her new job with R & R, the summer of 2004 was an extremely busy and exhausting time for her. In addition to helping people with severe disabilities to participate in various recreational activities in the community on the weekdays, she also worked many weekends taking those with less severe disabilities to sporting events, plays, and dances. In August, in order to be closer to her job, Sharon moved to Longmont, Colorado, where she found an apartment which was both beautiful and affordable.

Fortunately, in the fall, her schedule changed for the better as she was given greater responsibility and more opportunity to use her therapeutic recreation training. As coordinator of a weekly activity called "Friday Night Out", which was designed for higher-functioning clients, she was responsible for planning and leading activities for a group of up to thirty-five individuals and for supervising the other nine staff members who worked with them. Sharon was also asked to fill in for the director of R & R's internship program while she was on maternity leave. During this time, Sharon wrote a top-notch internship manual, which put into writing, for the first time, all of the requirements for students doing an internship in therapeutic recreation at R & R. Later that fall, when Sharon was evaluated for the first time by her supervisor, she received a glowing commendation for her outstanding work.

While I appreciated being given greater responsibility with regard to planning activities as well as filling in for the internship supervisor, I was challenged by the fact that I was given an "office day" with no office and I was expected to author an internship manual with nothing to go on, as the internship supervisor had been, up to this point, supervising interns from "what was in her head."

On September 16th, however, an event took place that could easily have ended Sharon's career as a recreation therapist, or could have even taken her life. She was involved in another car accident! As she was attempting to pass a bus which had stopped to pick up passengers, she was hit on the driver's side of her little car by a much-larger Jeep, which was traveling at a speed of forty-five or fifty miles per hour. The force of the impact pushed her car forward and caused it to go in front of the bus and jump the curb. Miraculously, even though her car was demolished, Sharon received only minor injuries—a bump on the head behind her left ear, and some sore muscles in her neck, left shoulder, and back. How we praised the Lord for protecting Sharon and sparing her life once again. Of course this accident also left Sharon without transportation, but amazingly enough, by the very next day, the Lord had provided another car for Sharon which was newer and in better condition than the one that she had lost. How we thanked Him for His abundant provision for Sharon's needs.

I was reminded anew of how much I had to be thankful for as I looked at my totaled car and realized how close I had come to being seriously injured or killed! Fortunately the Jeep hit the frame of my car just behind the fender, but if it had hit my car just a foot further back, I would probably have no legs!

As the new year of 2005 dawned, Sharon found herself increasingly busy. The number of people in the "Friday Night Out" program had grown to the point that it was necessary to divide it into two groups, thus making it necessary for Sharon to plan and supervise two of these activities each week. She was also assigned to assess a group of eleven clients and design individualized therapeutic recreation plans for them. In addition to this, she was given the responsibility of collaborating with other recreation therapists to make the entire recreation program at R & R more therapeutic. All of these responsibilities were added to her daily schedule of taking clients out into the community for various activities.

As if all of this would not be challenging enough, again all of these duties were to be performed without the luxury of an office! On my scheduled "office day" I would have to vie for a computer, so I would begin using someone else's computer—only to be asked to give it up as soon as they arrived, and then I would have to go in search of another computer that I could briefly use! So I was in a state of continual flux—constantly saving my work, only to be kicked off a computer once again to go in search of another one I could borrow temporarily.

However, although Sharon did an outstanding job with these new challenges, she found that the attitude of her superiors toward her had undergone a dramatic change. By this time, the internship supervisor who had been on maternity leave had returned to work. Since she was also in charge of the therapeutic recreation program at R & R, she now became Sharon's boss. Unfortunately, she began giving Sharon rigid and unrealistic time frames for completing her various responsibilities and also specifying exactly how much time was allotted for doing each task. In addition to this, Sharon was scheduled to work shifts which often lasted until one or two o'clock in the morning, and then required to be back at work again by eight o'clock on the same morning. When Sharon was unable to meet these impossible demands, her boss reported to her own supervisors that Sharon was incapable of doing an adequate job as a recreation therapist.

Therefore, in February 2005, as a result of this unfavorable report, Sharon was demoted, and all of her therapeutic recreation responsibilities were taken away from her. From that time on, Sharon no longer had any opportunities to perform the specialized duties for which she had been trained as a recreation therapist. She was only allowed to provide physical care and supervision for individual clients during recreation activities which had been planned by others—a rather menial job which could be performed by anyone who had only a high school education. Suddenly, Sharon's "dream job" had turned into a nightmare!

I cannot adequately explain how it felt to be given responsibility and to have confidence shown in me, only to have this responsibility and confidence suddenly stripped away – re-categorizing me as a simple "worker bee." I was in utter disbelief, and returning to work under these conditions was demoralizing at best.

Although Sharon enjoyed working individually with her clients and she endeavored to provide them with the best care possible, she became increasingly frustrated with the disrespectful treatment which she was receiving from her supervisors at R & R and with the lack of opportunity to use her skills as a Certified Therapeutic Recreation Specialist. By the spring of 2005, she realized that if she wanted to utilize her training and abilities, she needed to find a different job, and she began actively looking for one. Throughout the next year, she applied for a variety of positions in the field of therapeutic recreation, but although she was often called for interviews, she was never hired by any of these organizations.

The co-workers who were my friends at R & R all felt the same way as I did about the dismal working conditions. I referred to us as the "core rebel group," because while we provided excellent care to our clients, we all strongly disagreed with the management at R & R. Slowly, one by one, my friends disappeared as they left in search of other employment. I did not feel that I had the luxury to quit without having another job lined up, though I would have been extremely relieved to be able to simply walk away from R & R. I felt I had to apply for alternate employment on the down low – without anyone in a supervisory role knowing about it, because I feared that if they found out, they might concoct a reason to fire me. So I would apply for jobs secretly and when I managed to secure an interview, I discreetly found coverage for my shifts and arranged to attend the interview. Stressful was the name of the game during this period of my life!

During this time, however, Sharon had an opportunity to receive additional training which proved invaluable in understanding the work situation in which she found herself. In the spring of 2006, she attended a training session on bullying, and she recognized that she had been a target of workplace bullying. To her astonishment, she learned that the motivation for this type of bullying is the bully's jealousy of people who are more competent than she is, and that the bully's goal is to discredit these people so that she can feel better about herself! As Sharon considered these new revelations, she suddenly realized that what she had experienced during the previous year of working at R & R did not reflect adversely on her abilities at all. Instead, it demonstrated that she was extremely skilled in her field, since bullies only attack people who are competent.

As I learned more about bullying, I began to realize that rather than being targeted because of my incompetence, as I had been led to believe, it was actually because of my competence! It was like a huge back-handed compliment!

During this miserable year, Sharon continued to seek ways to improve her clients' quality of life. Since she herself had once been unable to speak, she realized that one of their greatest needs was to have a means of communicating with others. Therefore, she proposed to her employer that she should work on developing communication systems for those participants who were unable to speak. However, although her supervisor grudgingly allowed her to do so, she was never given adequate time to perform this crucial task.

Although Sharon did an outstanding job with client care, in April 2006, she was falsely accused of causing physical harm to a client. This was the last straw for Sharon, and she realized that even though she had not yet found another job, she could no longer continue to work at R & R. Also, the extreme stress and lack of adequate rest caused by her hostile work environment during the past year had taken their toll on Sharon and had brought her to the point of both physical and emotional exhaustion. Because she was physically exhausted to the point of being ill, she went to see the doctor, and he immediately put her on medical leave for the entire month of May. During this time off, she gave notice to her employer that she would not be returning to work, and that she would be resigning at the end of May.

This was the most devastating blow, because up until this point, I could always reassure myself that although I was being attacked on every other front, I knew I was providing excellent care for my clients. Although the word "negligent" was never used, it was implied very strongly but with no specifics, which I later learned was a very common tactic with bullying. Bullies make vague accusations which contain only a shred of truth in order to make their claims seem believable, but there is actually nothing of substance in them.

I was unemployed for the entire summer of 2006, but I desperately needed this time to recover from the severe emotional and mental abuse that I had suffered. I continued to apply for, and even interview for various jobs. However, although I was consistently in the top three interviewees, I was unable to secure any position. This turned out to be a blessing in disguise, as I had been mentally and emotionally battered for over a year, so I needed time to completely rebuild myself. I had zero self-esteem and no confidence in my abilities. During this time, various friends would ask me, "What do you do with all your time?" Invariably I would respond with, "I am taking care of myself – I am eating, sleeping and exercising!"

Because of the extreme stress and the hostile working conditions I had experienced during the previous year, these were all facets of my life that I had neglected, so it was welcome indeed for me to have the opportunity to care for myself again! Because of my inability to attend to my physical needs, I began experiencing various physical problems related to my brain injury. One of these was a recurrence of my double vision so I had to have a prism installed in my glasses to correct it. My body also began to shut down due to the extreme fatigue, which resulted in my falling twice – breaking the big toe on my left foot in one instance. I also began to experience odd physical sensations, which a neurologist later diagnosed as complex-partial seizures. I would suddenly feel a sensation of warmth begin to spread up my body from my stomach into my head and I would feel the pressure build. Then I would feel slightly light-headed and feel like I might pass out. I would also have a strong metallic taste in my mouth and I would then have a lingering headache. I began taking Dilantin to control these episodes, but the side effects of this medication were so dreadful that I felt extremely drugged and was in a mental fog much of the time. Consequently, this made it difficult for me to focus, concentrate and perform the most basic tasks. All of the above, combined with the fact that these episodes occurred so infrequently, caused me to decide to discontinue taking this medication.

As Sharon contemplated what direction to take in her ongoing search for employment, she continued to feel a very strong desire to use her own experiences to help other people who had suffered brain injury. Therefore, she developed a proposal describing a program and a position that would enable her to do this. She created a position called "Traumatic Brain Injury Resources Specialist", which would involve her being a mentor, role model, and advocate for people with brain injuries. It would also include her retraining them in social skills, cognition, daily living activities, and household responsibilities, and her helping them to achieve independent living in the areas of housing, transportation, education, employment, and recreation. She called her program "Snowflakes", because each individual is so unique, so precious, and so fragile, and each brain injury has such different effects on the person who experiences it. It was a wonderful proposal, which would fulfill a tremendous need. The only problem was that, as far as Sharon knew, such a program did not exist, and there were no funds to create it.

The concept of Snowflakes captured what would be my ideal job, one for which I knew I was uniquely equipped and to which I could bring my individual experiences to enhance the program. The only problem now was locating an agency that would "sponsor" or fund this vital service, which to my knowledge did not yet exist.

Chapter 17

Throughout the summer of 2006, Sharon continued her job search. Then, in July, when she came home for a visit, she decided to check on employment opportunities in Durango, Colorado, which is about one hour's drive from our house. She found there was an opening for an Independent Living Coordinator at People Helping People (PHP). This position involved helping people with a wide variety of disabilities to live as independently as possible in their community. She immediately applied for this job, was called for an interview in August, and was hired to begin working in her new position in September.

For the first month, she commuted to work from our house, but by the beginning of October, she had found housing in Durango. Her new home was a beautiful and unusually affordable trailer just outside the city limits of Durango. As she began learning what her responsibilities were, she was thrilled to discover that they encompassed everything that she had envisioned in her proposal for a Traumatic Brain Injury Resources Specialist in her Snowflakes Program. Although she was working with people with various disabilities, she soon found herself working with a good number of individuals who had sustained brain injuries and leading a brain injury support group. She loved her new job, because she felt that she was finally able to use all of the experiences she had been through to help others and to make a difference in their lives.

I was overjoyed to secure this position as Independent Living Coordinator at PHP! I was in a position that actually valued my experiences with disability and saw them as an asset – what a contrast to my last job! I was able to utilize my personal experiences on a daily basis to encourage my clients to not give up and to keep moving forward – how tremendously rewarding!

Sharon felt that she had come "full circle", because she herself had once been a client at PHP, when she had previously lived in Durango following her accident, and her new home was located on the very same highway where her injury had occurred. As Sharon said to me one day, "Mom, even if I could, I wouldn't change having the accident, because if it had never happened, I wouldn't be the person I am now, and I wouldn't be able to do the job I'm doing."

As I contemplated trying to integrate the "pre-injury Sharon" with the "post-injury Sharon" I composed the following poem that depicts the marriage of my two selves. It is such a foreign concept for people who have not experienced such a life-altering event to understand the idea of having two selves. However, following my severe Traumatic Brain Injury (TBI), this image seems to ring true because I now feel as though I have lived two separate lives.

INTEGRATION

How do I integrate   the two that are different
But the same   in part?
How do I determine   which parts stay
& which go?   Is it possible
To bring the   two together
To form the sum which
Is greater than
The two individual
Parts?

Yes, it is possible!
The possibilities are endless—
The compassion from before
Enhanced by the understanding
Dearly bought by this experience
Have prepared me for greater
Things than I could have ever
Imagined!

July 12, 2007, the tenth anniversary of the accident—the day that Sharon now called her "tenth re-birthday"—was a wonderful day of celebration for our family! We praised the Lord together for sparing Sharon's life, for miraculously healing her, and for leading her into a profession in which she was able to minister to others by using the things which she learned during the very difficult experiences of those ten years. Sharon's perspective of the miraculous unfolding of her new life was vividly portrayed in a poem which she had written several months earlier.

I wrote the following poem to convey the idea of emerging from a TBI rather than recovering, as recovery implies returning to the pre-injury state. Following a TBI, one emerges as a new person as they begin to live the new life entrusted to them.

EMERGENCE

Rising out of the ashes
A Phoenix emerges
Slowly, bit by bit...
Not the old, yet not completely new
Traces of the former
Enhanced by this all-consuming transformation
Arise and step boldly forth
Beautiful, fragile, spectacular masterpiece!

Working as the Independent Living Coordinator was tremendously rewarding as I soon realized my dream to be the resource I didn't have in Durango after my accident! Because I had lived in Durango after my injury, I had first-hand knowledge of the services available in the community and had benefited greatly from many of them as well. I had also been a client at PHP and had identified a need that was not being met by PHP at that time. I craved the mutual understanding that came from being with other TBI survivors because the average person, in my experience, did not understand what we went through in an effort to function "normally" on a daily basis. So with the help of another TBI survivor, I started the Brain Injury Support Group at PHP.

Once I started working at PHP, I revived and began facilitating this Brain Injury (BI) Support Group that I had helped to start back in 1998 shortly after my accident. The BI group met once a month when I first began facilitating it, but the group members soon expressed a desire to meet more frequently, as the monthly meeting was not adequately meeting their needs. I approached the director of PHP and proposed that the group meet twice a month, with the first meeting being an afternoon meeting and the second meeting taking place in the evening to accommodate clients who were working during the day.

I also developed and began leading a support group for women with all types of disabilities in which we were exploring the healing powers of laughter. I called the group the Munch Bunch and we began meeting every Friday at noon. We encouraged each woman to bring a brown bag lunch and come join in the laughter. I would find humorous stories and jokes to read. At times we would even share our most embarrassing moments and other humorous stories—all resulting in hearty, healing belly laughs!

A truly amazing thing happened when I began receiving referrals from Dr. Ed, the neuropsychologist I had seen after my accident for counseling and testing. I realized he and I had transitioned from a patient/therapist relationship to being colleagues – unreal! He would refer a client to me and then call to let me know who was coming and what their needs were. He even came as a guest speaker for the BI support group once and so a mutually beneficial relationship continued for many years.

I quickly became known throughout the community as "the person" to refer clients with brain injury to! I routinely delivered presentations about brain injury to other agencies in town that worked with BI survivors such as Alternative Horizons, an agency that provides services to survivors of domestic violence. I would provide trainings to their advocates who may not have been familiar with the effects of BI and I would make them aware of the signs to look for when working with their clientele. I was even contacted by agencies from out of town to assist them with organizing and promoting presentations about BI before they arrived. I helped to put together a focus group to discuss how to better serve people with brain injuries in the community and as a result of this meeting, I helped set up and began facilitating the 4 Corners CIRCLE Group that later became known as the 4 Corners Brain Injury Professionals Networking Group (BIPN). When the Durango Herald ran an article about this group's formation, the number of new clients with TBI that I received increased exponentially!

One of the most rewarding and fulfilling aspects of my job was the opportunity I had to help various clients with TBI identify their previously undiagnosed brain injuries. There were many times when I'd be meeting with a client to enroll them in the Independent Living Program. They would describe their disability and express confusion and bewilderment at their symptoms. Invariably, I would suspect a brain injury, as indicated by their symptoms (i.e. headaches from an unknown cause, difficulty concentrating or paying attention, memory problems, inability to screen out background noise and/or extreme sensitivity to outside stimuli) in conjunction with a previously unconnected accident. I would always preface my suspicions with the caveat, "I'm not a doctor, but the symptoms you are describing and the accident you experienced seem indicative of a TBI to me. I would strongly encourage you to get checked out by your doctor as soon as possible." A challenge which often presented itself was that many of my clients had sustained Mild Traumatic Brain Injuries (MTBIs), for which there is often no objective evidence through a CT scan or an MRI indicating a brain bleed. Each time I encountered a situation like this, I was reminded anew that I was blessed, because my TBI had been so severe that there was no denying its existence. This was yet another example of one of those "cleverly disguised blessings" – you know blessings in disguise! ☺

In the day-to-day operations at PHP, I met with clients individually to enroll them in the Independent Living Program, evaluate their specific needs and then refer them to the appropriate services available in the community. I also assisted them with completing applications for these services and would accompany them to appointments to serve as an advocate to ensure they would receive the services they were entitled to.

*I had assembled a special intake packet that I used specifically with clients who had brain injury (BI) that included education materials about BI and its effects. I taught that after BI, a person has very limited reserves and is much more prone to fatigue, so consequently must pace themselves. I shared that after a BI, the slate is essentially wiped clean so now they must "**think** about thinking, **think** about focusing and **think** about paying attention," all of which takes a tremendous amount of energy! I handed out a pie chart that depicted a person's "energy pie" before and after brain injury and highlighted the fact that a person's reserves are extremely limited following a brain injury, primarily because of the extra effort required to do the most basic tasks.*

251

When I shared this information with my clients, they each breathed a sigh of relief as they received validation that what they were experiencing was quite natural and to be expected following BI. I taught them strategies to "protect" their limited reserves by implementing structure and routine to do activities which over time would become more or less automatic. This practice, in and of itself, protects the limited cognitive reserve because less thought is required to perform each action. I also cautioned TBI survivors to protect their limited emotional energy reserves by surrounding themselves with positive, supportive people. I warned that after BI, people tend to become "emotional chameleons" who take on the emotions of the people around them. And I encouraged them to be mindful of their physical exertion, because fatigue is cumulative following BI and they could not recover from physical activities after only a good night's sleep. I instructed them to" pace themselves" when involved in any activity, whether cognitive, emotional or physical, because this would enable them to be able to perform at their best for a longer period of time. The following are examples of the energy pie charts I handed out to my clients:

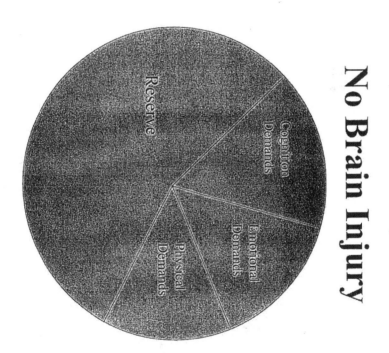

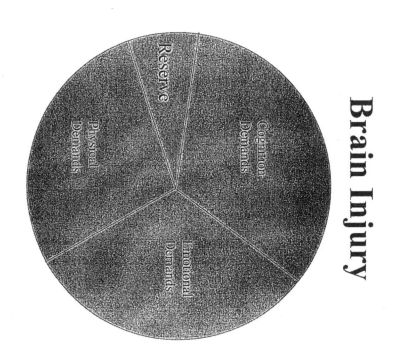

Brain Injury

I explained that after BI, it is as though the internal framework is gone. So now an external framework must be constructed in order to provide support while learning these new skills that will enable them to navigate this uncharted territory. I encouraged BI survivors to be kind to themselves as they learned to adjust their expectations to match their new abilities.

I would also often write and submit individual grant applications requesting financial assistance to help my clients purchase hearing aids, dentures and even on one occasion orthopedic shoes. Because my job duties were never clearly delineated, I did my best to help anyone who walked through the door with any need under the sun, whether I had any prior experience with the issue at hand or not!

On any given day, I was asked to be a doctor, lawyer, nurse, therapist, or a mother. I took on many roles and wore many hats in my position at PHP. I never knew what the day would bring, so I always had to be prepared for anything. I always used to say that at least I was never bored, but some days, I would have given anything for a little boredom. Many days I worked late into the evening as I did my best to keep up with the ever expanding documentation monster, as well as to contain the mushrooming pile on my desk. Because I had been taught in my classes in college, "If it isn't written down, it didn't happen," I worked tirelessly to document all of my client interactions, which could easily get away from me, because on most days I would deal with an average of six to eight clients. When I started at PHP, I inherited a caseload of around 70 clients. By the time my employment ended there, my caseload had ballooned to over 200!

I was already working beyond full capacity, but in spite of this fact, new and ever expanding responsibilities were continually being added to my work load. I was constantly asking God to give me the strength and wisdom to be able to perform my job, because I knew I would never be able to do it on my own. God would send me special gifts of encouragement in the form of appreciative clients or commendations on a job well done—coming just at the perfect time when I needed it most!

I was keenly aware that I was working in the job God had uniquely equipped me for through my life experiences with TBI and disability. Although I loved my job and truly felt I was making a difference in my clients' lives, working full-time was the only thing I had time and energy for. It took all I had and then some. I knew I was abundantly blessed to be able to work full-time, as most TBI survivors I knew were only able to work part-time, but one of the most debilitating and longest lasting effects of Traumatic Brain Injury (TBI) was the bone-crushing, mind-numbing, all-consuming, overwhelming fatigue, and I was no exception to experiencing this effect. Whenever I would describe fatigue to the average person, inevitably they would hear" tired." I know, I know, you are probably thinking, "Everyone is tired, so what's the big deal?!?" No, I'm talking about total mind-body shutdown exhaustion here, not just the "I over-did it on my bike and need to take a nap" kind of "tired" thing. This is complicated further by the fact that the effects of fatigue are cumulative, so once a TBI survivor gets fatigued from too much cognitive exertion, for example, they cannot recoup from it with a good night's sleep. Add to this the fact that most TBI survivors also experience sleep disturbances, and you end up with a recipe for disaster – a multitude of zombies walking around – the lights are on, albeit dimly, but nobody's home!

In an attempt to understand more fully the fatigue monster I battled on a daily basis, I wrote a poem, as I often did, in an effort to process difficult emotions, entitled simply "Fatigue". This poem vividly conveys the daily struggle I engaged in while attempting to balance my never-ending responsibilities between work and daily life.

FATIGUE

Fatigue, you are an ever-present, unwelcome intruder
You suck the life out of every moment
And the color out of every situation
How can you be so cruel & malicious?
You have robbed me of fluid movement & ease of speech
In exchange for an iron weight around my neck
Oh to be relieved of the burden
To fly once again, unhindered & unencumbered –
To be free
This is what I long for!

While I was able to work full-time, it took so much out of me that this was the only thing I was able to do. I would work all week, sleep all day Saturday, try to catch up on a few chores and errands on Sunday and before I knew it, Monday had rolled around again and another week had begun! The cycle of madness created an atmosphere that caused me to feel overwhelmed and defeated most of the time. This scenario left me feeling much like Sisyphus – endlessly rolling the bolder up the hill, and then having it roll back down to the bottom, only to futilely begin the process once again.

Chapter 18

Outside of work, there was nothing left of me to be able to have a life. I desperately longed to find a partner I could build a life with, but given my lack of expendable energy, I had no idea how or where I would ever meet someone – let alone have the energy to begin a relationship with him once I found him!

Fortunately, I met my knight in shining armor in my driveway! Brian was my neighbor, and although we had lived only about 100 feet apart – with him living at the top of the hill and me at the bottom of the hill, for a little over three years, we had never met. Due to the fact that he worked nights and I worked days, our paths never crossed, until one snowy afternoon in January 2010. As I attempted to drive up the driveway after work that day, I got stuck. He helped push my car out of the snow and as we walked back up the hill, Rosie, our landlord's wife, excitedly encouraged us to get to know each other following my car's extraction. She eagerly said, "I need to go check on my mom, but you two talk..." and so began an exciting journey that continues today!

Brian was an amazing support to me during this time, as he routinely devised strategies that would enable me to function in the midst of the mayhem. With no set boundaries for meeting with clients, my appointments tended to be unlimited and could easily fill hours. This consequently took its toll on me, so he suggested that I limit my appointment times to 30 minutes. And because I was having trouble turning my brain off once I got home in the evenings, he suggested that I put an "Open/Closed" sign on my office door, changing it to "Open" when I arrived at work each morning and then turning it to "Closed" when I left in the evenings. These ideas helped immensely, as the reduced appointment times allowed me the time and space I needed to combat the ever-expanding documentation monster, and the "Open/Closed" sign provided a tool for me to utilize when anxieties about my clients arose after work. I could simply acknowledge the anxiety, recognizing there was nothing I could do about it at that moment, while saying to myself, "I'm sorry, we are closed right now, but will reopen at 8:30 tomorrow morning. We can deal with your concern at that time."

As if my work life wasn't challenging enough, a nightmarish construction project began right outside my door at home. The Colorado Department of Transportation (CDOT) initiated construction of a frontage road to intersect with Highway 160. This project began in February and continued through November in 2011. The crews would begin working at 7:00 AM and would not finish until 6:00 PM on weekdays. Before long, they expanded to working at night and even on the weekends! My home had now been converted to Construction Central 24/7 and no longer provided the sanctuary that allowed me the peace and quiet I needed to recoup from each day's grueling demands. I attempted to speak with the foreman of the project in an effort to convey the challenges I dealt with on a daily basis in optimal conditions—let alone attempting to function amidst the chaos caused by the noise and lights of a construction site. However I was only met with skepticism and disbelief.

*The true confusion began one morning in mid-May when I turned left onto the highway out of my driveway, as I had done for the previous four and a half years, but returned home at the end of a long day to find a concrete barrier sealing off my former driveway! The concrete barrier eventually ended at a little unmarked path which ultimately led to my house. After a few weeks went by with this arrangement in place, I returned home to find a "Road Closed" sign at that entrance, directing me to proceed to County Road 232. Again, this arrangement lasted for a few weeks until I returned home after work one evening to find yet another "Road Closed" sign at the entrance to County Road 232. As I stopped on the highway with my blinker on in an attempt to turn into my most recent "driveway," a construction worker motioned me to continue on down the road and instructed me to go down to County Road 232. I exclaimed in exasperation, "I thought this **was** County Road 232!?!" As irritated drivers zoomed by with horns blaring, he explained, "The next road is County Road 232 too." The road was a loop, and so I toured an entire neighborhood before I was finally able to get back to my house.*

*So the name of the game was "Musical Driveways", with no advance warning or notice to the residents. Accompanying this game was "Musical Mailboxes", as the construction workers would continually relocate our mailboxes to accommodate their construction project, again, with no communication with the residents. All told, I believe they moved our mailboxes three times. However the most comical time was when they moved the mailboxes after placing the notice that they were relocating the mailboxes **in** the mailboxes! I was only able to discover their newest new location after calling Rosie, my landlord's wife, who told me they had been moved to County Road 232, about half a* *mile from my house, and she sadly told me with resignation that this was most likely where they would stay.*

There seemed to be no escape from excessive noise and outside stimuli, as I was continually bombarded with the noise and lights from the construction site that had occupied my home. At the same time I began having to share an office at work with my co-worker. Whereas before, if the background noise of the office got to be too loud and distracting for me, I could just close my office door and have the uninterrupted, quiet space required for me to be able to perform my job effectively, I now no longer had that luxury. My clients who had brain injuries often commented that they did not know how I did it, because there was no way they would be able to function in this extremely overstimulating and distracting environment. The inability to screen out background noise and stimulation is a common effect following BI, and I had always considered myself fortunate because I had never experienced this symptom. However, because of the constant assault on my senses between the continual construction at my home and the new shared office space at work, I began to develop an acute sensitivity to these stimuli. I started to experience what my doctor diagnosed as "migraine variants." I would start having a headache that quickly began to include a burning sensation inside my skull just behind my eyes, which I described as "feeling as though my head was going to spontaneously combust!" He told me that if Maxalt, the medication he prescribed helped, this would prove it was a migraine. When I took it, the heat inside my head instantly began to dissipate along with the pain – praise God for the wonder of modern medicine!

My work environment was untenable at best, while my living situation was beyond unbearable. Each morning, I would prepare to go to work amidst the cacophony of back-up alarms, backhoes, excavators and the noise associated with of all other types of construction equipment. Once I had maneuvered my way out of my driveway, which no longer existed, onto the highway, I would go to work to face whatever challenges lay in wait for me, only to return home so that I could begin it all again the next day! I was definitely "burning the candle at both ends," as they say, and I could see no way out of my current situation.

Add to this mix the fact that I had just begun a new relationship with Brian who worked long hours as a mechanic, often late into the evenings. Because we wanted to spend time together, I would stay up late to see him, even though I was already greatly sleep-deprived due to the construction nightmare at and around my home, combined with my stressful job. I was walking a very narrow tightrope—in danger of falling at any moment.

*I worked intensively with people who had Traumatic Brain Injuries (TBIs) while working at PHP, and I was very effective as I had the understanding only a fellow TBI survivor could offer. I understood the daily challenges from a personal perspective rather than purely from an academic standpoint of having merely studied about BI in books. Now don't get me wrong—we **need** the academic perspective, especially when dealing with the medical aspects of BI and seeking treatment, but we as survivors **crave** the understanding only provided by experience. The main problem with this scenario was the fact that although I knew how to support survivors of TBI and how to teach compensatory strategies that many survivors were not even yet aware they needed, I acted as if everything I was communicating applied to my clients only and not to me. I was much better at "preaching" than "practicing," especially when I routinely instructed my clients, "You can't take care of anyone else unless you take care of yourself first!" Oh if only I had heeded my own advice and followed my own suggestions, I might have been able to avoid the coming calamity.*

In the fall of 2012, after 15 years of pushing myself to perform and function as a "normal" person, I ultimately had an emotional and mental breakdown, resulting in a lengthy period of illness and depression, during which time my brain was unable to function properly. This was shocking especially that far post-injury and after having been able to work for nine years in three pretty demanding jobs, not to mention returning to college and earning a degree. Of course all of this most likely contributed to my breakdown, because I never took the time to take care of myself,

*but simply kept pushing myself to improve. None of us ever
expected anything of this nature to happen, given that I had only
continued to get better ever since my injury on July 12, 1997.
However the combination of chronic sleep deprivation, the extreme
stress from my job(s), and the overstimulation from the noise and
lights of the construction project right outside my door in 2011
was a recipe for disaster!*

*On September 27, 2012, I experienced another medication reaction
while I was working at PHP. I had to go to the ER and after
extensive testing revealed no discernible cause, I was instructed to
go home and rest. The chronic sleep deprivation and extreme
stress that I had been under, combined with the medication
reaction, caused me to have another episode similar to the one I
had experienced in 1998. I had racing thoughts, was unable to
sleep and had to be hospitalized again. Because of the significant
symptoms I was still experiencing, I had to take more time off from
work.*

*By the beginning of 2013, I realized that I was still unable to
return to work. Because I had exhausted all of my sick and
vacation days by this point, I had a decision to make. I chose to go
and clean out my desk, removing all of my personal belongings, on
New Year's Day when the office was closed. I wrote and submitted
my letter of resignation on January 10th with an effective date of
February 11, 2013, thus giving a month's notice. Because I needed
to have some sort of income, my mom helped me apply for Social
Security Disability Insurance (SSDI) on January 8th. Since I had
helped many clients apply for SSDI benefits while working at PHP,
I knew this would be a **very lengthy** process and not a quick
solution to my need for an income, by any stretch of the
imagination.*

*Because I knew the SSDI process could take years (**literally!**), in
March I decided to pursue other means of income by applying for
Unemployment Insurance Compensation (UIC). This required me
to apply for three jobs per week to be eligible to receive UIC. I was
called for several job interviews, but when I "bombed" the
interviews, I realized that I still had not recovered to the point that*

I was able to work. This realization caused me to spiral even further down into the deep dark depression that had come to occupy my days. (I later learned that depression was a common side effect of the medication I had been taking, as well as causing a person to feel emotionally flat – thus reinforcing the fact, as well as my own experience, that after BI, people are more sensitive to the effects of medication.)

I had been emotionally "flat" for the first half of 2013, so when I discontinued my medication and my emotions began returning in June, I described them as "delicious" and "intoxicating," which I felt was only natural because I had been without emotion for such a long period of time. In May, I had received a denial letter from the Social Security Administration (SSA), denying my application for SSDI benefits. I figured that this did not matter because I felt I would soon be back to work, so I began looking for a job in earnest. Because I was feeling so much better by this point, I wrote the following poem.

A NEW DAY DAWNING

*Morning has finally come
The long dark night is drawing to a close
Rays of sunshine suddenly burst thru the dark clouds
Revealing clear blue sky!
Hope has rescued me once again
I bask in the warm sunshine of freedom
As I revel in her warm embrace!*

Unfortunately, during this time, I also felt immense pressure to secure a paid position, since my SSDI application had been denied and I had to have a means of income. The stress from actively searching for a job, combined with the fact that I actually was not yet fully recovered from my breakdown, caused me to have another episode during which I had to be hospitalized again for a longer period of time.

Since I was still unable to work after I was discharged from the hospital, I chose to appeal my SSDI denial. However, after two *appeals, I received my third and final denial to my SSDI application in February 2016. In spite of this, God truly provided for my needs in a variety of other ways. My sister Carol had graciously been paying my rent for the first five months in 2014, but was unable to continue beyond the month of May. I began stressing and worrying about how I would pay my rent and even considered trying to find another place to live. Toward the end of April, I received a call informing me that I had been awarded a State Housing Voucher that would be effective May 1st and that would allow me to continue living in the trailer I had lived in for the previous eight years! I saw the deliberate Hand of God through His provision at just the right moment! Also, He had provided Aid to the Needy Disabled (AND), which is a temporary cash assistance program for people who have applied for SSA benefits and are waiting to receive a decision on their application. This income, with frugal management, when combined with other types of assistance programs, enabled me to cover my basic living expenses. Because I had helped numerous clients at PHP apply for and secure assistance through various programs such as Food Stamps, Medicaid, and the Low Income Energy Assistance Program (LEAP), I was very familiar with the resources available to low income individuals in Durango. I soon found myself applying for and receiving assistance from many of the same services I had helped my clients apply for – quite humbling to say the least!*

Although being without a job was extremely challenging for me as I sought to find purpose and meaning in my life, I realized that I had been given a rare opportunity to work on several major projects. It had long since been my dream to publish a small book of poetry and I found that during this time, I was finally able to compile my poetry into a book which I called <u>Seasons – a book of poetry reflecting on the Seasons of life</u>. I had also desired for quite some time to work on writing this book with my mom about my accident, TBI, and subsequent recovery, but I never would have had the time or energy to devote to this process if I had been working full-time. I also became involved in a local writers' group which provided me with resources I had previously been unaware of and also gave me the opportunity to brainstorm with other *writers. After numerous discussions with my mom, she suggested that I could view this period as a "Time of Preparation" for the next chapter of my life. I wrote the following poem to convey this sentiment.*

A TIME OF PREPARATION

Beauty from the ashes of lost dreams
Mosaics from shattered dreams
New dreams I never could have imagined possible!
Patience during this Time of Preparation
Waiting & trusting while not knowing
History has proven – no need to be afraid
Trust & obey always moving forward

And still, I found myself always looking at my friends and people I had gone to college with who were working in fulfilling careers, and I always fell short by comparison as I was still unemployed. But because I had been raised to believe God was intimately involved in every aspect of my life, I had to believe God still had a plan for me. So in an effort to capture this idea, I wrote the following poem entitled simply My Path.

MY PATH

Constantly comparing to accomplishments of others
Never measuring up
Should have so much more to show
Always lacking
Yet I have this sense,
"That is not your Path"
Straining to move forward
Seeking purpose, meaning, fulfillment
Keep listening for that still small voice saying,
"This is the way; walk in it."
That is my Path

I never would have been able to make it through the three years after my breakdown without the unending dedication of my loving boyfriend Brian and the ongoing support of my devoted family and friends! Of course, I truly never would have made it through without the healing touch of my Lord and Savior and His unbelievable promise to bring "beauty from ashes!" I'd like to conclude with my life verse:

Jeremiah 29:11
"For I know the plans I have for you," declares the Lord, "plans to prosper you and not to harm you, plans to give you hope and a future."

To contact the authors

Sharon may be reached at smehesy8807@gmail.com and you can contact Eberly at eberlymehesy@gmail.com

32878353R00156

Made in the USA
Middletown, DE
21 June 2016